THE GREATEST STORM

Daniel Defoe, engraving by Michiel van der Gucht after painting by Jeremiah Taverner. *(© National Portrait Gallery, London)*

THE GREATEST STORM

Britain's Night of DESTRUCTION

NOVEMBER 1703

MARTIN BRAYNE

SUTTON PUBLISHING

This book was first published in 2002 by
Sutton Publishing Limited · Phoenix Mill
Thrupp · Stroud · Gloucestershire · GL5 2BU

This paperback edition first published in 2003

British Library Cataloguing in Publication Data
A catalogue record for this book is available from the British Library.

ISBN 0 7509 3516 2

Typeset in 10/12pt Goudy.
Typesetting and origination by
Sutton Publishing Limited.
Printed and bound in Great Britain by
J.H. Haynes & Co. Ltd, Sparkford.

CONTENTS

THE

STORM:

OR, A

COLLECTION

Of the moſt Remarkable

CASUALTIES

AND

DISASTERS

Which happen'd in the Late

Dreadful TEMPEST,

BOTH BY

SEA and LAND.

The Lord hath his way in the Whirlwind, and in the Storm, and the Clouds are the duſt of his Feet. Nah. I. 3.

LONDON:

Printed for *G. Sawbridge* in *Little Britain*, and Sold by *J. Nutt* near *Stationers-Hall*. M DCC IV.

Title-page of Daniel Defoe's *The Storm*.
(By permission of the British Library: Ref. 1136.i.1)

List of Illustrations

DEFOE'S TERM	BEAUFORT NUMBER	STANDARD NAMES	EVIDENCE - SEA	EVIDENCE - LAND	SPEED - KNOTS
Stark calm	0	Calm		Smoke rises vertically	Less than 1
Calm weather	1	Light air	Just gives steerage way	Wind direction shown by smoke not by vanes	1 - 3
Little wind	2	Light breeze	Speed of man-of-war under full sail in smooth water	Wind felt on face	4 - 6
	3	Gentle breeze		Leaves and small twigs in constant motion	7 - 10
Fine breeze	4	Moderate breeze		Raises dust, leaves and loose paper. Small branches moved	11 - 16
Small gale	5	Fresh breeze	Ships can just carry all sails	Small trees in leaf begin to sway	17 - 21
Fresh gale	6	Strong breeze	Ships can just carry topsail	Large branches in motion	22 - 27
Topsail gale	7	Moderate gale	Reefed topsail	Whole trees in motion. Difficulty in walking against wind	28 - 33
Blows fresh	8	Fresh gale	Double-reefed topsail gale	Breaks off twigs. Generally impedes progress	34 - 40
Hard gale of wind	9	Strong gale	Closer reefed topsail	Slight damage to buildings (roof slates, chimney pots)	41 - 47
Fret of wind	10	Whole gale	Ships can barely carry reefed lower mainsail	Trees uprooted. Considerable damage to buildings	48 - 55
Storm	11	Storm	Reduces ships to storm stay-sails	Widespread damage	56 - 63
Tempest	12	Hurricane	No canvas could withstand		Over 63

Table1: Classifying Wind Force

PREFACE

The British Isles are not, generally speaking, subject to extremes of weather: our floods, heat waves, droughts and storms, inconvenient and expensive as they occasionally are, rarely threaten life and hardly compare with those of less equable environments. Occasionally, however, an event occurs which, as long as those who lived through it survive, sticks in the popular mind. Many still living remember the great snowfalls of February 1947, the long, dry summer of 1976 and the fearsome storm of 16 October 1987. Yet the weather, once it has slipped into history, has rarely excited much interest. We might know of the bad weather that delayed Duke William's invasion in 1066 and of that which so nearly wrecked D-day in 1944. We may well be aware that the Irish Potato Famine, or rather the fungus which ruined the crop, was caused by an exceptionally cold, wet summer. More fortunate, we have often been taught to believe, was the so-called 'protestant wind', every variation of which in November 1688 favoured William of Orange and the Glorious Revolution. Of the Great Storm of 26/27 November 1703, although we may have read of it following that of '87 – often described as 'the worst since 1703' – most people will dimly recall a catastrophe involving a lighthouse, but little more.

Such, at least, was my case until I came across it in reading G.M. Trevelyan's history (raised to the status of literature), *England under Queen Anne*. In a passage as striking as his great set piece battle scenes, of Blenheim and Ramillies, Trevelyan summarises the significance of a storm 'without rival in the recorded history of our island'. It is an inspirational passage which itself has entered literature. In her 1997 novel *Fugitive Pieces* the fine Canadian novelist and poet Anne Michaels has her narrator say:

> I began to research my second book, on weather and war . . . The book took its title, *No Mortal Foe*, from a phrase of

> Trevelyan's. He is referring to the hurricane that destroyed the British naval force during the war with France. Trevelyan is correct in his identification of the real enemy: a hurricane at sea means spray crossing the deck at one hundred miles an hour, a screaming wind that prevents you from breathing, seeing or standing.

By the time I read these words I was myself, metaphorically speaking, in the teeth of the Storm, amazed that nobody had written of it at length since Daniel Defoe in 1704 and still more surprised that his early masterpiece had not become a classic.

Meteorologists have done their best, given a very limited amount of quantitative data, to explain what happened. For a science that relies heavily on detailed statistical modelling to predict what it is likely to happen, interest in what happened 300 years ago and may not recur for another 300 is, understandably, not compelling. Nevertheless, in recent years, stimulated by the work of the late Professor H.H. Lamb, greater attention is now given to climatic fluctuations and to periods of exceptional meteorological activity such as occurred between 1690 and 1710. The Great Storm took place at a time of unusual extremes in north-west Europe.

It is not difficult to understand why historians have not been attracted to the Storm. In the event no great diplomatic or military consequences can be ascribed to it, it caused no social revolution and sparked no major economic crisis. It was a natural phenomenon which came and went, killed a lot of people, and caused a great deal of temporary disruption but was of no lasting significance. Trevelyan himself saw the Storm in just this light. By 16 December, little more than a fortnight after this massive attack upon the nation, 'England was herself again'.

The Storm was, however, of immense significance to those who lived through it and were old enough to remember it. For millions of English and Welsh men and women, still alive in the reign of George II, this was the great experience they had all shared. And to the overwhelming majority of them it was not simply a storm of terrifying intensity and destructiveness. It was, quite literally, an Act of God: a blow deliberately delivered by an all-powerful, omniscient deity as a warning and in anger. Some had the kind of unquestioning faith which survives among the religious 'right' in America to this day. Following the attack upon the World Trade Centre, conservative evangelicals were quick to point out that an angry God had allowed the terrorists to succeed – 'The abortionists have got to bear some burden for this,' said the Revd Jerry Falwell, 'because God will not be mocked.' There were, however, enormous differences; Queen Anne's English men and women, although they would have understood Falwell's language, were far from being a uniform population of former-day Southern Baptists. Their opinions, not least on last Sunday's sermon, varied greatly and, although there were many obstacles in the path, they were struggling towards toleration. The orthodox view, however, was that God intervened directly in the affairs of Man. This was the belief, variously interpreted, of Isaac Newton, Archbishop Tenison and the Astronomer Royal, John Flamsteed, just as it was of countless illiterate labourers and milkmaids. It was a God-fearing population, many of whom knew no books other than the Bible and Bunyan. Was a greater proportion of the population ever again at church than on Wednesday 19 January, following the Storm, the fast day set aside for asking God's forgiveness and blessing? Like the Storm itself this day was an event of mass participation and it confirmed the significance of the disaster in a solemn and memorable way.

The Storm was by no means seen as a freak, inexplicable event; it posed all kinds of questions, scientific and technical as well as religious. Where did it come from? Why was this low building unroofed and that higher one not? Why did this ship remain at anchor when that was blown on the sands? How far inland was the salt spray carried and what effect would it have upon the land? Many of these questions are raised in the work of Daniel Defoe, himself a brilliant, articulate and imaginative writer but also a man who, thanks to his journalistic invention, provides us with all kinds of experiences of the Storm, related by all manner of people.

To Trevelyan and, especially, Defoe, I am much indebted. That their genius has not rubbed off was neither their fault nor my good fortune, but it is to be hoped that what follows will, at least, reawaken interest in an event which stimulated the one and inspired the other.

I owe a debt of gratitude to many others: to my oldest friend Brian Morley for his wisdom and encouragement; to Roy Creamer and Geoff Molyneux with whom, since far off days at university, I have talked history and explored many miles of the footpaths and byways of England and Wales. Fellow members of the Parson Woodforde Society have searched their local records for me and I would particularly mention the late Jim Holmes of Great Yarmouth, Cynthia Brown of Woodbridge in Suffolk and Phyllis Stanley and Clifford and Yvonne Bird of Norfolk. Agreeable as is living in the Peak District, it is not the ideal place from which to study events which almost exclusively took place south of the Trent and I am tremendously grateful to Ann and David Williams and David and Susan Case for providing me with hospitality on my visits to Bracknell and East Kent respectively. I am indebted to David Smith for assisting my Kentish research.

A number of people whom I have not had the good fortune to meet have nevertheless been immensely helpful and I want especially to mention Beryl Alexander of West Horsley, Dr Colin Clark of Bruton, Margaret Lawrence of East Peckham, Peter Meadows, Keeper of the Ely Dean and Chapter Archives, and Anne Crawford his opposite number at Wells, Jackie Morton of Birdingbury, David Perkins of the East Kent Archaeological Unit, Stephen Porter of the National Monument Record, the Revd John Stevinson of Winchcombe and Dr A. Wyatt of Christchurch.

Peter Alderson, Roy and Pat Creamer, John Sharp and Jim Thornely have all been good enough to read and comment upon parts of the work-in-progress, and Helen Roberts helped with translations from the Latin. I am hugely grateful to Christopher Feeney of Sutton Publishing for his enthusiasm for the idea and to Elizabeth Stone and Martin Latham for their help with its execution.

It would be impossible to list the staffs of libraries, record offices and museums across the south of England whose politeness, patience and professionalism have been exemplary. I must, however, mention two small museums, Saffron Walden, where

Vicky Turner was most considerate, and Ramsgate Maritime Museum, a Mecca for all interested in the Storm, where the help of the curator, David Hunt, has been invaluable. It was a particular pleasure to work in the Guildhall, National Maritime Museum and National Meteorological Libraries.

Best of all has been the loving support of Ann and the amused tolerance of Adam and Oliver. This is for them, with love.

Chinley, August 2003

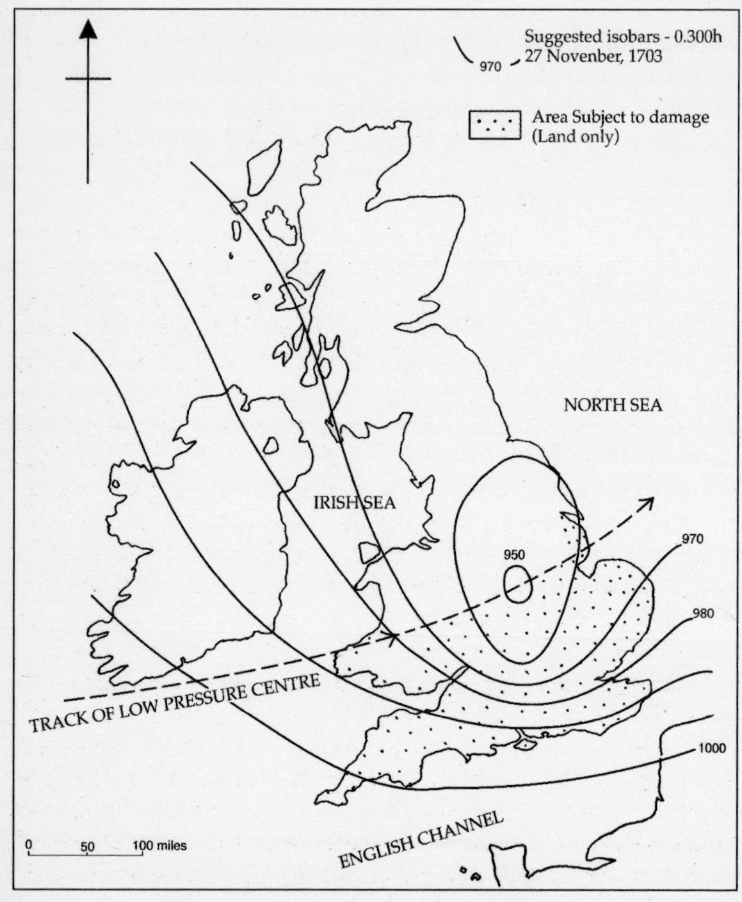

Figure 1: The Passage of the Great Storm

1

Dies Irae

At some point in the pitch black of the November night, the painted glass bulged, exploded and crashed to the nave floor, skimming and splintering. Through the gaping hole in the Great West Window shrieked a destructive stream of air. The creaking of ancient timbers and the thunderous falling of stonework filled the church with a massive, pandemonic fugue. As the storm raged on, more glass was torn from the mullions and tracery so that by daylight, with a gale-force wind still howling, one of the finest works of English medieval art lay in ruins. But all had gone unheard in the greater roar; an unearthly and terrifying sound that covered the south of England from Land's End to the North Foreland. The new day was 27 November 1703. The worst storm experienced in historical times in England was playing itself out at Fairford in Gloucestershire.

Once the wind had begun to die down, chimneys ceased to crash through roofs, tiles stopped flying through the air, thatch and haystacks no longer filled the sky with wind-borne straw, and the vicar ventured out to examine the damaged fabric of his church. His home, a large house on the south side of what is now London Road (then Vicarage Street), was a couple of hundred yards from the church. As he picked his way across the debris-strewn Market Place, passing the inns which provided the small Cotswold town with much of its prosperity, parishioners, like Job's comforters, may well have led him to expect the worst. In common with the 600–700 members of his flock, Edward Shipman, must have been both relieved to be alive and amazed by the degree of devastation. His church of St Mary the Virgin, having resisted the ugly iconoclasm of the civil wars half a century before, its marvellous painted-glass windows lime-washed over, still stood. But its glory was in ruins, a blasted wreck of late medieval magnificence.

Unlike most English parish churches, the exterior of St Mary's is all of a piece, having been rebuilt in the Late Perpendicular style in the last decade of the fifteenth century: 'John Tame began the fair new Church at Fairforde and Edward Tame finishid it'. So symmetrical was the building that Shipman, who had been vicar for seventeen years and had known the church all his life, would immediately have noticed that part of the battlemented wall above the porch was missing and that on the roof the wind had rolled up the sheets of lead like scrolls of paper. Only when he got to the west end of the church, however, would the real loss become apparent: the sickening sight of the Great Window, 25 ft high, and 15 ft across, smashed through so that little remained above the transom, and the windows on either side, especially that to the south, were likewise blown in, wrecked.

This must have been a grim spectacle all too clearly brought into focus when he entered the church. As the smithereens of glass crunched beneath his feet, the familiar scene, which had inspired him, his father before him and the parishioners of Fairford for so long, was revealed in ruins. Shipman perfectly understood, none better, the true nature of the loss. A few weeks later, by which time he would have known that this was no freak storm which had singled out his little corner of Christendom alone, he wrote a letter describing the damage:

> It is the fineness of our church which magnifies our present loss, for in the whole it is a large and noble structure, within and without of ashlar, curiously wrought and consisting of a stately roof in the middle and two aisles running a considerable length from one end of it to the other, makes a very beautiful figure. . . . It is also adorned with 28 admired and celebrated windows. . . . Now that part of it which most of all felt the fury of the winds was a large middle west window . . . it represents the general Judgement. . . . The upper part of this window, just above the place where our Saviour's picture is drawn sitting on a rainbow and the earth his footstool is entirely ruined. . . .

In reconstructing in his mind's eye the windows through which the light of day was once so gloriously filtered, Shipman would have had no prompts such as assist today in the repair of damaged works of art, no architects' drawings or photographs. Nor would he have needed them. The Great Window with its circles of angels and martyrs, red, blue and polychrome, concentric about the figure of Our Lord, was the incontrovertible fact of his spiritual life, the reification of his faith, his link in a world of frail and transitory lives, with the eternal. At the height of the Storm his thoughts may well have turned to a particular detail of this portrayal of the Doom: at the focal point of the great central window, the earth, Christ's footstool, was depicted with towers and palaces crumbling. In the clamour and violence of that night the God-fearing majority of the age must have believed that they were witnessing just such a scene; that this was the wrath of God levelling man's feeble works with the dust.

Many must have been the inhabitants of Fairford who, as they cowered in their houses, believed the Last Day to be upon them and every louder blast of wind the Final Trumpet. As their houses were rocked and buffeted and the noise increased to levels previously unheard and tiles and slates flew across the streets and lanes, many would have fallen to prayer and imaginations would have conjured up thoughts of the church windows so instrumental in teaching them the fundamental stories of their faith. The minds of many would surely have concentrated on that part of the Great Window below the central transom that featured in brilliant colour and startling detail the consequences for the dead, rising from their graves, of eternal judgement. The central figure was of St Michael, clad in gold armour and weighing the souls of the judged in the balance. To his right, the dominant colours were white, yellow and gold portraying the entrance of the blessed into Paradise. To his left, reds and purples showed the descent of the damned into Hell and the torments that await them. Did any old widow woman, thought to have nagged her husband to an early grave and suspected by the local gossips of witchcraft, tottering on the edge of dementia, believe that, like the crone in the window, a devil was pushing her in a wheelbarrow into the Inferno? Certainly many, in that more literal age, must have expected the opening up of the earth and the dread spectacle of the flaming pit.

Even sophisticated minds must have been troubled. The young vicar of St Keverne on the frequently windswept Lizard peninsula in Cornwall and one of the first parishes to receive the full impact of the Storm as it drove in from the west, described the event with a mixture of scientific accuracy and religious credulity typical of the educated classes of the day; standing, as it were, trembling, at the door of the Enlightenment. According to his account, the Storm arrived from the north-west between eight and nine o'clock in the evening. By ten it had veered from west to south-west and back to west again and between eleven and midnight blew in such a manner that 'the Country hereabout thought the great day of Judgement was coming'. That this was the anger of the God of the Old Testament few across England could have doubted. Richard Chapman, the vicar of Cheshunt could hardly have been surprised. The previous May he had published a tract entitled, *The Necessity of Repentence asserted: to avert those judgements which the present war and unseasonableness of the weather at present seem to threaten this nation with.*

By the following morning, back at Fairford, although a great deal of physical damage had been wrought, Shipman's parishioners appear to have escaped remarkably lightly. Far from enduring the miseries and confusion of Hell, nobody had been killed or even significantly injured. The poor, living in cottages shorn of their thatch, probably suffered the most, as always tends to be the case when natural calamity strikes. Although chimneys had collapsed and tiles had been stripped from the roofs of houses, Shipman believed that to dwell upon the fate of the poor cottagers 'would be frivolous as well as vexatious'.

The Storm, however, had not quite finished with Fairford, for at two o'clock on the Saturday afternoon, 'without any previous warning a sudden flash of lightning, with a short but violent clap of thunder, immediately following it, like the discharge of ordnance, fell upon a new and strong-built house in the middle of the town, and at the same time disjointed two chimneys, melted some of the lead of an upper window and struck the mistress of the house into a swoon . . .'.

In Fairford, as across southern England, it was the upstanding features of the landscape, churches, chimneys, windmills and trees, which had proved, together with the ill-built hovels of the poor, most vulnerable to the onslaught. In most small market towns and villages the church was the only building of significance. Thirty years earlier, Count Lorenzo Magalotti was travelling about England with the Grand Duke of Tuscany. His description of Axminster in Devon, could have served for any number of similar settlements: 'a collection of two hundred houses, many of which are made with mud and thatched with straw. It contains nothing considerable except the parish church . . .'. Because of their significance in the lives of the population, their architectural pre-eminence within most communities and the literacy of the clergy, the damage suffered by churches and church buildings tends to be best recorded.

Church spires were toppled across the south-east of England, possibly because gusts there reached the highest levels or maybe because design standards were lower than in the generally more stormy south-west where stumpy, wind-resistant towers tend to be the norm. The tall spires of Kent and Sussex, arguably the counties worst-affected in the kingdom by the Storm, seem to have been particularly vulnerable, especially where they stood on relatively high land such as at Brenchley and nearby Great or East Peckham. One Thomas Figg, writing of the spire at Brenchley, where he was curate, claims that it was the highest in Kent, 'at least 10 rods [165 ft] some say 12 [198 ft]', before being levelled to the ground by the Storm. There it became 'the sport and pastime of Boys and Girls who to future Ages, tho' perhaps incredibly, yet can boast they leaped over such a Steeple'.

Although churches in Kent and Sussex may have been worst hit, spires were damaged across the country from Cardiff to Maldon in Essex. One of them was at Stowmarket in Suffolk where a 77-ft spire had been taken down in 1674 and replaced with one far more ambitious. Samuel Farr, the vicar at the time of the Storm, described this new structure as involving 'the Addition of 10 Loads of new Timber, 21 thousand and 8 hundred weight of Lead' so as to form a spire 100 ft high with 'a Gallery at the height of 40 ft all open wherein hung a Clock-Bell of between 2 and 3 hundred weight'. Although the spire stood 'but 8 Yards above the Roof' such was the force of the wind that it crashed down into the nave so that 'a third part of the Pews are broken all in pieces'. Farr's estimate was that 'It will cost 400 pounds to make all good'.

Although towers were better able to withstand the violence of the Storm than spires, they were by no means immune to the assault. In the West Country, Somerset appears to have suffered most. The tower at Compton Bishop, at the foot of the Mendip Hills facing across the flat expanse of the still unreclaimed marshlands of the Brue and Ax Rivers, was described as 'much shatter'd', while at St Mary's, Batcombe, 'all the battlements of the church on that side of the tower next to the wind were blown in'.

As at Fairford, the windward-facing west end of churches tended to experience most damage. St Michael's, Beccles, in Suffolk stands on a spur of higher ground overlooking the low-lying Waveney Valley and is visible for miles around. The tower stands a little apart from the main body of the church at the west end of which the Great Window was blown in, just one casualty in a town which was 'exceedingly shatter'd' by the Storm. A large stone window at the west end of the church at Fareham in Hampshire was 'broken down'. In Oxford, the church of St Peter-in-the-East was badly damaged by several sheets of lead, 'judged near 6000 lb weight', which were torn from the roof of Sir Joseph Williamson's new building at The Queen's College and hurled across Queen's Lane through the west window of the church breaking a great iron bar. The lead made such a deafening noise as it fell that those who heard it thought the church's tower had collapsed. By contrast, 'a fine painted Glass Window' in Lord Salisbury's chapel at Hatfield House in Hertfordshire was broken 'tho' it looked towards the East'. This and the ruined north transept window of Bristol cathedral were, perhaps, exceptional.

Cambridge probably suffered rather more than did Oxford. St Mary's, the University Church, was 'much shattered' and, according to the anonymous author of *A Wonderful History of All the Storms, Hurricanes, Earthquakes etc.*, published in 1704, a fall of masonry 'battered in pieces a curious Organ lately set up and purchased at £1500'. Worse, the architectural masterpiece of Cambridge, King's College Chapel, was badly damaged. Many of its pinnacles were blown down and 'the fine Windows with the Old and New Testament histories drawn on the glass, in a very strange manner much broken and defaced'.

In the course of this narrative the truth of the old saw about an ill wind will often be demonstrated. Stonemasons were obviously much sought after following the Storm but few could have benefited more than the nation's plumbers, literally those skilled in the working of lead. The roofs of many of the better buildings were covered with lead, available relatively cheaply from the mines and furnaces of Derbyshire. An excellent material for keeping out the wet, lead has the disadvantage that it lacks rigidity so that if a roof has a steep pitch the lead sheet will sag or 'creep'. The consequence was that roof design had changed as the medieval period had progressed: the pitch was gradually reduced and eaves were replaced by lead box gutters concealed behind a battlemented parapet. For the most part this was a practical and entirely adequate design but, in the event of exceptionally high wind speeds, lead sheets lying almost flat on a roof would have been torn up relatively easily, especially if the protecting parapet had already collapsed. While during the normal range of wind conditions in the British Isles, the weight of the lead was such as to keep it in place, storm-force winds could get beneath the sheets and lift them from the roof. Differential air pressure on either side of the roof may well have helped to literally suck the lead into the air. Generally, however, in such conditions the aerodynamic forces exerted by the wind are most important. Such forces tend to be directed inward on the windward facing wall – hence the vulnerability of west windows – and outwards on the roof, leeward wall and side walls of a building. If the sheets of lead on the roof were well secured along their upper edges, the effect of exceptionally strong winds was often to roll them up 'like so much paper', to use the words of Mr Shipman of Fairford. Similar imagery was used to describe what happened at Northampton where 'Many sheets of lead on that Church [All Saints'] and also St Giles's and St Sepulchre's roled up like a Scroll'. Elsewhere a similar effect was compared to a bale cloth. Thus at Monmouth, 'The lead of the roof of the great church [St Mary's] tho' on the side from the wind was roll'd up like a roll of Cloth' and at St

Philip's, Bristol, the wind 'ripped off the lead . . . and wrapped it up like folded cloth'. From Leamington Hastings in Warwickshire came this graphic account:

> Between Eight and Nine the 27th I went up to the Church where I found the middle Isle clearly stript of the Lead from one end to the other and a great many of the sheets lying on the east End upon the Church, roll'd up like a piece of Cloth. I found on the ground 6 sheets of lead 50 hundred weight, all joyn'd together, not the least parted but as they lay upon the Isle, which 6 sheets were so carried in the Air 50 yards and may have been carried further but for a tree.

There was a similar occurrence at Berkeley in Gloucestershire:

> 26 sheets of lead hanging all together were blown off from the middle Isle of our Church and were carried over the North Isle and into the Church yard 10 yards distant . . . the Plummer told me the sheets weighed Three hundred and a half.

Likewise there was a report from Ewell in Surrey where:

> the Lead from the flat roof of Mr Williams's house was rolled up by the wind and blown from the top of the house clear over a brick wall near 10 feet high without damaging either the House or the wall, the Lead was carried near 6 Rod from the House.

The scene conjured up by these descriptions of airborne sheets of lead is astonishing. Because the highest wind speeds were reached before daybreak over most parts of the country affected by the Storm, no eyewitness descriptions of flying lead appear to have survived but some years later, in 1739, central Scotland was hit by a devastating hurricane and the *Caledonian Mercury* carried this account by a man who described what he saw as he clung for dear life to the railings about the Equestrian Statue in Parliament-close, Edinburgh. He saw part of the lead from one of the buildings about the close and, 'weighing about 1200 weight . . . tore up, and carried to an incredible Height above the Edifice, where it hovered above half a Minute, waving like a Blanket, and then came down gently and with ease, till within 20 Foot of the Ground'.

In the days following the Great Storm plumbers must have surveyed a great variety of damage and been presented with all kinds of work. At Christchurch in Hampshire the roof of the priory church was uncovered and 12 sheets of lead 'rouled up together'. At Middleton Stoney in north Oxfordshire, the leads of the church were rolled up and 'the stone battlements of the Tower were blown upon the leads'. Although the general pattern appears to have been either for the lead sheets to have been rolled up or lifted clean off the roof, in some cases, as at Ewell, even rolled-up sheets of lead were blown off the roof. There is evidence too of less severe treatment, thus at Brighton the church leads were simply described as 'turned up' and at Tewkesbury Abbey they were 'strangely ruffled'.

Churches were further damaged by falling masonry. Although collapsing spires would have caused most devastation, the fall of ornamental battlements and pinnacles also gave rise to much destruction. Bristol was hard hit in all manner of ways during the Storm and, of the churches, St Stephen's and the cathedral were worst affected. Three of the elaborately buttressed and pierced pinnacles of St Stephen's collapsed and 'beat down the greater part of the church', taking the clock with them and breaking the brass eagle and candlestick. The cathedral battlements suffered also as did two of the windows, although the damage does appear to have been far less than that experienced by the great cathedrals of Gloucester ('the beautiful Cathedral Church of Gloucester suffer'd much') and Ely ('the loss which the church and college sustained being by computation £2000'). From Bristol comes a touchingly Victorianised vignette of events about the cathedral on the night of the Storm. In his *Annals of Bristol in the Eighteenth Century*, published in 1887, John Latimer quotes from the memoirs of one James Stewart who recalled that his father, who was usher to the boys of the Gaunt's Hospital School, was called from his bed 'to attend the Children to the Chapter House in the Cloisters were they remained and sang psalms all the night.' Latimer adds to Stewart's account that 'a part of the Cloisters was blown down during this strange nocturnal concert and the great north transept window of the Cathedral was demolished no doubt to the increased terror of the quavering little vocalists.'

The churches of Northampton were also badly damaged. All Saints', in the Market Place, had been rebuilt in the Renaissance style following a fire which had devastated the town in 1675. The new church had been opened in 1680 thanks, in part, to a gift of 1,000 tons of timber from the royal forests of Whittlebury and Salcey. In 1701 an imposing portico had been added beneath the shelter of which, in future years, the peasant-poet John Clare was to spend many contemplative hours. During the Storm not only were the roof leads rolled up, as we have seen, but the church's weathercock, although 'placed on a mighty spindle of Iron was bowed together and made useless'. A similar indignity was inflicted upon the church weather-vane at Swansea in South Wales where 'the tail of the Weathercock which stood in the middle of the tower was blown off and found in a Court near 400 yards distant from the tower'.

Widespread as was the damage to church property, from Fairford's irreplaceable windows to Swansea's broken weathervane, the clergy, with one very eminent exception, appear to have escaped unscathed. The story of Bishop Kidder of Bath and Wells deserves detailed attention not only for what it tells us of the Storm but also for what it tells us of the England upon which the Storm broke. Richard Kidder was seventy in 1703. He was a controversial figure in a Church in which controversy was endemic, although his unpopularity in his diocese was very largely due to the fact that he had replaced, in unusual circumstances, the much admired, to some saintly, figure of Bishop Ken.

Thomas Ken is best known today for his *Morning and Evening Hymns*, which include such famous lines as 'Awake my soul, and with the sun' and 'Praise God from whom all blessings flow'. He is rightly described as one of the fathers of modern hymnology. In his lifetime he was probably most famous for his refusal to accept William of Orange as the legitimate king. When, as a consequence of the Glorious Revolution of 1688, William and Mary replaced James II on the throne of England, a significant number of the clergy, including five bishops of whom Ken was one, refused to swear allegiance to the new monarchs on the grounds that to do so would be a breach of the oath they had already sworn to James. These non-jurors clung to two of the fundamental doctrines of what was to become known as High Church policy. They believed in the hereditary right of kings and in non-resistance: the doctrine that whatever wrongs a monarch inflicted upon his people, it was a greater wrong to oppose his hereditary, God-given right to rule. As the historian G.M. Trevelyan colourfully has it: 'Men who turned purple with rage when the Dissenters asked them for Toleration . . . knew so little of their own high temper that they vowed that if Nero were hereditary king of England, they would let him take their lands, their tithes, their laws, their very lives without raising a hand against him.' Rather more fairly perhaps, believing that kings ruled by Divine Right, they had been appalled by the act of regicide earlier in the century and were determined that it should not happen again. In Ken's case this did not mean that he was servile to the wishes of the king. Famously, in 1683 when Charles II visited Winchester, Ken's prebendal house in the Cathedral close was chosen as a suitable residence for the King's mistress, Nell Gwynne. Ken objected, arguing that 'a woman of ill-repute ought not to be endured in the house of a clergyman'. He won his point and alternative accommodation for the former orange vendor was found. To his credit, Charles admired Ken's obstinate piety and when, in the following year, the bishopric of Bath and Wells fell vacant, the King asked for 'the good little man that refused his lodgings to poor Nell'.

The bishops chosen by William to replace the non-jurors tended towards latitudinarianism, that is to say towards toleration and an avoidance of doctrinal extremes. In the eighteenth century latitudinarians were to dominate the bench. In the seventeeth century, by contrast, what was perceived as doctrinal uncertainty aroused the gravest suspicions and Ken, not, admittedly, the most neutral of critics, described Kidder who superseded him as 'a latitudinarian traditor', a 'hireling' and 'a stranger ravaging his flock'. It would, however, be unjust to dismiss Kidder as a prototype for that celebrated clergyman who would maintain:

Unto my dying day, Sir,
That whatsoever King shall reign
I will be Vicar of Bray, Sir!

At the time of Ken's deprivation Kidder was Dean of Peterborough and he was offered the see of Bath and Wells following the intervention of the great preacher Archbishop Tillotson. He was initially unwilling to accept the mitre and later regretted that he had done so for 'though he could not say that he had acted against his conscience, he did not consult his ease'. He was consecrated at Wells on 30 August 1691 and quickly became, in the eyes of High Churchmen, one of the most reviled priests of the Church of England. Nor has he been very generously treated subsequently. In 1924 when the wife of the then Dean of Bath and Wells introduced Kidder's autobiography, she did so with the scarcely sympathetic words: 'Bishop Kidder, if not an attractive character . . .'.

But Kidder was by no means a mere time-server. Indeed, to the modern liberal mind he is in some respects a more accessible character than his 'saintly' predecessor. In January 1696 a Jacobite plot, aimed at the assassination of William and the restoration of James II, was discovered. Some of the conspirators, men of little social significance, were rounded-up, tried and executed. Some months later Sir John Fenwick, a man of far higher social rank, was also arrested. The law required that nobody could be convicted of treason unless upon the evidence of at least two witnesses and Fenwick succeeded in having one of the two witnesses against him smuggled out of the country. Frustrated, the government brought in a bill of attainder. This was a medieval device which in effect bypassed the judicial system and condemned the accused to death. It was the last time it was ever used. Kidder was approached to go to the House of Lords to vote for the attainder. The Bishop responded that he first wished to know the merits of the case, upon which, he was asked 'Don't you know whose bread you are eating?' and is said to have replied, 'I eat no man's bread but poor Dr Ken's.'

How true this story is it is impossible to say but of the nature of Richard Kidder's end there can be no doubt. On the evening the

Great Storm struck, the Bishop and his wife, Elizabeth, were at home – that is to say at the Bishop's Palace in Wells. When, probably during the previous year, Celia Fiennes, author of *The Journeys*, passed that way she was unimpressed: 'the Bishop's Pallace is in a park moated round, nothing worth noticing in it'. Subsequent generations, with a greater appreciation of medieval building than the thoroughly modern Miss Fiennes, have agreed in finding the fourteenth century hall and chapel of the Palace especially beautiful.

Accounts of the Kidders' fate differ as to the detail but the essential facts are clear enough: at the height of the Storm a chimney stack collapsed through the Palace roof into the couple's bedroom, killing them both. According to one account, from Somerset, the late Bishop and his Lady were killed 'by the Fall of two Chimney Stacks, which fell upon the Roof and drove it in upon my Lord's Bed, forced it quite through the next Floor down into the Hall and buried them both in the Rubbish: and 'tis supposed my Lord was getting up for he was found some Distance from my Lady who was found in her Bed; but my Lord had his Morning Gown on . . .'. Another version of the event comes from Oxford and, despite the claim that 'This account is Authentick', appears to have undergone some elaboration en route from the West Country: 'He [the Bishop] perceiv'd the fall before it came, and accordingly jump't out of Bed, and made towards the Door, where he was found with his Brains dash'd out; his Lady perceiving it wownd all of the bed Cloaths about her, and in that manner was found smothered in Bed.'

On hearing the news from Wells, Ken, who had been staying with his nephew, Izaak Walton junior, at Poulshot in Wiltshire during the Storm, pointed out that he had himself narrowly escaped a similar fate. In a letter to his friend Bishop Lloyd of Norwich and dated 27 November, he wrote:

> I return you my thanks for both yours. I have no news to return, but that last night there was here the most violent wind that ever I knew; the house shaked all the night; we all rose and called the family to prayers, and by the goodness of God we were safe amidst the Storm . . .

In a later letter to Lloyd, Ken elaborates on the event:

> I think I omitted to tell you the full of my deliverance in the late Storm, for the house being searched the day following, the workmen found that the beam which supported the roof over my head was shaken out to that degree that it had but half an inch hold, so that it was a wonder it could hold together; for which signal and particular preservation God's holy name be ever praised!

At that time Ken was obviously still unaware of the fate of the Kidders, for in a further letter to Lloyd he wrote

> . . . I then did not know what happened at Wells, which was much shattered, and that part of the palace where Bishop Kidder and his wife lay, was blown down in the night, and they were both killed and buried in the ruins, and dug out towards morning. It happened on the very day of the Cloth fair, when all the country were spectators of the deplorable calamity . . .

Ironically, his *Evening Hymn* contains the lines:

> Teach me to live that I may dread
> The Grave as little as my bed.

Bishop Kidder and his lady were just two of approximately 8,000 of the subjects of Queen Anne who perished in the Storm.

2

THE BIRTH OF 'THE STORM'

Mem^{d} that on ye 27th November 1703 was y^{e}
greatest hurricane and storme that ever was known
in England; many churches and houses were extreamly
shattered and thousands of trees blown down;
thirteen or more of her Majestyes men of war
were cast away and above two thousand
seamen perished in them. N.B. the Storme
came no further north than Yarmouth.
(Parish register, St Oswald, Durham, 1703)

The storm that blew across southern Britain on the night of 26/27 November 1703 was the most terrifying and catastrophic that this island has known. So much so that the rector of St Oswald's, Durham, well to the north of the area worst affected, saw fit to record it in the parish register, while thirty years after the event commemorative 'Great Storm' sermons were still being preached in London and in the 1760s accounts of the disaster continued to be published. Yet, despite the fact that thousands lost their lives and the properties of tens of thousands were damaged or destroyed, the Great Storm has faded from the popular imagination in a way in which those other great calamities of the Late Stuart period, the Plague and the Great Fire of London, have not. By the nineteenth century, when Thackeray came to write an historical novel set in the period, the event can go unmentioned: *Henry Esmond* is not so much *Hamlet* without the Prince as *The Tempest* without the Storm.

Insofar as the Great Storm is still remembered, it is for two widely separate and otherwise unconnected consequences, the demolition and almost total obliteration of the first Eddystone lighthouse and the destruction in the Downs, off the Kent coast, of a significant part of the Royal Navy at an especially perilous time, when England was at war with France. The most notable exception to this national state of amnesia is G. M. Trevelyan's *England under Queen Anne*, in which considerable attention is given to the Storm, which is there described as 'the sudden, brief and unprovoked intervention of a neutral power' which very nearly broke England's naval supremacy, for the losses at sea were, in many respects, more devastating than those on land. It may be argued, of course, that our awareness of the two earlier disasters is a tribute to the literary skills of Defoe and Pepys. The definitive account of the Great Storm was published eight months after it took place but has never been separately republished since 1706. It came from the hand of an obscure writer, pamphleteer and religious controversialist, none other than the author of *A Journal of the Plague Year* and *Robinson Crusoe*, Daniel Defoe.

We do not know for certain where Defoe spent the night of the Great Storm other than that it was in 'a well-built house on the skirts of the city' [of London]. The probability is that he was staying at the house of his wife's mother and her second husband at Newington Green. He does not seem to have had a house of his own for the simple reason that he was bankrupt, having been released only a couple of weeks earlier from the secure, if uncomfortable confines of Newgate prison.

On the eve of the Storm, Defoe, already forty-three, had achieved some recent notoriety but was still many years from the time when he was to write the books which were to ensure his immortality. Because our knowledge of the events of 26/27 November is heavily dependent upon one of Defoe's least known works, *The Storm: or a Collection of the most Remarkable Casualties and Disasters which happened in the late Dreadful Tempest both by Sea and Land*, it is helpful to know something of the man through whose mental apparatus so much of our evidence is filtered.

Defoe's England – he was born in 1660, the year of the restoration of the monarchy – was one periodically convulsed by the aftershocks of the civil wars of mid-century. The divisions opened up by those events remained, even if few were prepared to risk the renewal of warfare. Of the two broad-based coalitions that emerged on the political stage, the Tories, updating the old Cavalier sentiments, had a particular horror of the act of regicide. This led many of them, as we have seen in the case of Thomas Ken, to support the doctrine of non-resistance. Tory support was strongest in the Church and amongst the squirearchy. Their opponents, the Whigs, were committed to parliamentary government and limiting the power of the monarchy. They feared moves to re-establish royal supremacy and the Catholic religion of Charles II and his brother James II. Whig support came from some of the great aristocratic families, who resented regal power, the urban middle-class and, often the same thing, Nonconformists – or Dissenters – who were excluded from political power and whose civil rights were constrained.

The high-handedness and overt Catholicism of James II in particular had threatened the peace. Monmouth's rebellion of 1685, which sought to overthrow James, was bloody and unsuccessful but the Glorious Revolution, which came three years later, and replaced the Catholic king with the Protestant William of Orange and his Stuart wife Mary, was, at least in England, both bloodless and triumphant. Revolution brought with it the threat, or promise, of counter-revolution: Jacobite, Catholic, absolutist. The age was thus one of plots and counter-plots, spies and *agents provocateurs*, political intrigue and religious controversy. As we shall see, Defoe was deeply, dangerously involved.

By 1703 both Mary and William had died and had been succeeded by Mary's sister Anne, who, although a daughter of James II and strongly sympathetic towards the Tories, was a staunch supporter of the Church of England. In 1700, however, the last of her many children, the little Duke of Gloucester, died and although the Act of Settlement of the following year had sought to preserve 'the peace and happiness of this kingdom and the security of the Protestant Religion', many still feared succession by the Jacobite candidate, James II's Catholic son, the future 'Old Pretender'. War with France – and French support for the 15-year old who regarded himself as James III of England – although producing a degree of national solidarity, did little to stifle religious and political feuding.

The year 1703 had, in a metaphorical sense, already been a tempestuous one for Daniel Defoe. He had stood in the pillory on three successive days and had been imprisoned in Newgate with no certainty of release, being by no means a stranger to trouble. The son of a London merchant, born into a Nonconformist household and educated at dissenting academies, he would have been conscious from an early age of the punitively oppressive restrictions placed upon Dissenters, while being, at the same time, aware of the contribution being made to rising national wealth and confidence by the class into which he had been born. These are the considerations which, together with an almost fatal tendency to flirt with danger, had persuaded him, as a young man in June 1685, to ride into the West Country and join the Duke of Monmouth's ill-starred rebellion. The only direct evidence we have that Defoe took part in the rebellion comes in the form of a royal pardon granted on 31 May 1687. He never makes any reference to participation in the uprising in any of his published works, although in two of his novels, *The Memoirs of a Cavalier* and *Colonel Jack*, he vividly describes the experiences of a fugitive after battle. A recent biographer of Defoe, Richard West, sums up this formative, not to say traumatic, experience:

> The defeat at Sedgemoor, the frantic escape and then two years spent in dread of arrest and appearing before Judge Jeffreys would have tested the courage of any man, and undoubtedly left their mark on Defoe. His experience gave him the lifelong sense of being a lone fugitive in search of a hiding place.

Secretiveness then became second nature to Defoe. It was a characteristic which both aided and was reinforced by certain aspects of his working life.

Unsurprisingly, for one of his background, Defoe was involved in a number of business enterprises. His father, James Foe – Daniel's prefixed 'De' being typical of his efforts to re-create himself – had been a tallow-chandler, member of the Butchers' Company and freeman of the City of London. Fortunately for posterity, but not either for his peace of mind or physical comfort, Daniel was not a successful businessman. Setting himself up, doubtless with his father's help, as a hosiery merchant in 1681, by 1684 he appears to have been doing sufficiently well to persuade a wealthy City cooper to give him the hand of his daughter, Mary Tuffley, together with the very substantial dowry of £3,700. Within eight years, however, not only had Defoe involved himself in the disastrous Monmouth rebellion, he had, thanks to a combination of misfortune and misjudgement in a series of speculative ventures, lost his wife's dowry, been declared bankrupt and found his way to the Fleet prison.

By the beginning of 1693 Defoe was once again at liberty but, in addition to the dowry, he had lost his hosiery business which was, however, quite inadequate to repay a debt estimated to be an enormous £17,000, so that his future earnings were already spoken for. Fortunately for Defoe and his growing family, he was not without useful connections, which enabled him to obtain two minor public offices, one connected with the collection of duty on glass and the other as manager of the royal lottery. More importantly, he was able to develop some land of his father's near the Thames at Tilbury into a brick and pantile manufacturing business. In a letter written to Robert Harley in 1703, about eighteen months after William died, Defoe says of the Tilbury brickworks that 'all of the late King's bounty to me was expended there'. The Tilbury works, some 27 miles downstream of London Bridge, would have been ideal for supplying the capital by water and evidence still exists that in 1697 Defoe was paid £20 for brick used in the building of Wren's Greenwich Naval Hospital. During the construction of the London, Tilbury and Southend Railway in 1860, Defoe's tile factory was discovered and the pantiles described as:

> . . . of excellent manufacture, and still retain a fire red colour, close texture and are quite sonorous. Neither the Dutch nor any other tiles could have driven them out of the market, and the maker would be able, from proximity to London and

facilities for conveyance, either to undersell the foreign dealer or to realise a proportionately larger profit.

Despite the apparent success of this business, however, he continued to be dogged by creditors and sought to supplement his income through the hazardous occupations of writer and spy.

What exactly persuaded William to grant Defoe a 'bounty' is uncertain. Some time in the late 1690s Daniel made his first visit to Scotland, possibly to sound out opinion on a subject close to William's heart, the union of England and Scotland. It was a project which was to come to fruition in the following reign when, to that end, Defoe was once more to cross the border in the service of his sovereign. Certainly he was involved in pamphleteering in support of the king, although his most significant work in this regard was almost certainly produced after the bounty had been granted. As the century drew to a close the enthusiasm with which William had been greeted in 1688 had begun to wane. Many Tories had been reconciled, albeit uneasily, to the change of dynasty for as long as Mary was alive: as the daughter of James II she gave an acceptable degree of legitimacy to the dual monarchy. Once Mary had died – of smallpox in 1694 – the allegiance of many Tories came under increasing strain. Nor were the Whigs indiscriminate in their support of William, whose Whig ministers felt that real power lay not so much with them as with his kitchen cabinet of Dutch advisors. Public opinion compelled William to return his 7,000 Dutch Guards to Holland, while what Trevelyan calls 'the anti-monarchical spirit of the age' persuaded Parliament to refuse the renewal of the Licensing Act, thereby establishing the freedom of an increasingly critical press. It was by writing in support of William against the scurrilous attacks of a xenophobic opposition that Defoe first achieved notoriety.

In August 1700 John Tutchin, a Whig and fellow Sedgemoor veteran, published an attack upon the cronyism of William and his compatriots in a poem entitled 'The Foreigners'. Defoe always firm in his defence of William – and very probably in his pay – responded with the verse satire 'The True-Born Englishman', describing an essentially hybrid creature in whom xenophobia was nonsense because:

The Romans first with Julius Caesar came,
Including all the nations of that name,
Gauls, Greeks and Lombards; and by computation
Auxiliaries and slaves of ev'ry nation.
With Hengist, Saxons; Danes with Sweno came
In search of plunder not in search of fame.
Scots, Picts and Irish from the Hibernian shore,
And conqu'ring William brought the Normans o'er.

The dregs of armies, they of all mankind;
Blended with Britons who before were here,
Of whom the Welsh have blessed the character.
From this amphibious ill-born mob began
That vain, ill-natured thing an Englishman . . .

so ill-natured as to bite the hand of King William, that had saved him:

William the Great Successor of Nassau
Their prayer heard and their oppression saw;
He saw and saved them; God and him they praised,
To this their thanks, to that their trophies raised.
But glutted with their own facilities
They soon their new deliverer despise . . .
But English gratitude is ever such
To hate the hand that does oblige too much.

In his lifetime 'The True-Born Englishman' was always to be the work for which Daniel Defoe was best known. He had tapped into that trait of self-mockery which, sometimes gentle, often less so, was to become a characteristic of English satirical writing.

The clash between Defoe and Tutchin is a reminder of the fact that politics at the turn of the eighteenth century were a good deal more convoluted, the alliances and factional splits more complex, than a straightforward divide between Whig (Low Church and for the Protestant Succession) and Tory (High Church and Jacobite) would suggest.

One reason why William had fallen from popularity with many

Dissenters was the Act of Toleration of 1689, which was seen as a poor reward for their efforts in the cause of a Calvinist king. While it granted Protestant Nonconformists, who subscribed to the 39 Articles, the right to worship in meeting houses licensed by the bishop and thus ended the 'Great Persecution', it was seen by many as grudgingly granting little more than their minimum needs. The Test Act of 1673, which demanded that all who held civil or military office under the Crown take the sacraments of the Church of England, remained on the statute book. Many Dissenters consequently evaded the issue by taking Communion once a year in the parish church; the practice of occasional conformity.

By March 1702 William had died and was succeeded by his wife's sister, Anne whose sympathies were with the High Church party so that the Tories in the Commons were encouraged to believe that they could reverse those of William's policies which favoured the Dissenters and those traditional enemies of the Tory backwoods squires, the merchants of the City. Ironically, Defoe had played into their hands. Four years before he had produced a pamphlet entitled *An Enquiry into the Occasional Conformity of Dissenters, In Cases of Preferment* in which he denounced those fellow-Dissenters, such as the Lord Mayor of London, Sir Humphrey Edwin, who, in Defoe's view, compromised their consciences by, in Sir Humphrey's case, attending St Paul's on a Sunday morning and Pinner Hill Conventicle in the afternoon. The High Church party, led by the rabble-rousing Dr Henry Sacheverell, seized upon the ammunition supplied by Defoe to castigate the Dissenters and demand an end to occasional conformity.

The Occasional Conformity Bill, debated in Parliament during the winter of 1702/3, sought to impose fines on holders of public office, local and national, who having taken the sacrament in church later appeared in chapel. It also incorporated a measure typical of the worst type of police-state: it awarded the whole of the fine to the informer. Although the Bill passed through the Tory-dominated Commons, it was held up in the Lords and was eventually lost; but by this time Defoe had dealt himself a self-inflicted wound of life-threatening savagery.

Having alienated himself from many Dissenters with *An Enquiry into Occasional Conformity*, he now proceeded to inflame the advocates of the Bill. As the political temperature rose, Defoe rejoined the fray with an anonymous but devastating attack upon the so-called High-fliers, *The Shortest Way with Dissenters*. Whether this was intended as a hoax or a brilliant, deadpan satire is still the subject of debate but Defoe took the arguments of those who favoured the prosecution of the Bill to their logical conclusion: the shortest way with Dissenters was to get rid of them entirely. Less than twenty years earlier the revocation of the Edict of Nantes had had just such an effect upon the Huguenot population of France.

The Tories initially greeted the pamphlet with glee but when they discovered it was to all intents and purposes a hoax their delight rapidly turned to rage. Even Defoe's future patron and friend, the moderate Tory Robert Harley, was incensed; anything that threatened the unity of the nation, as war once again broke out with France, was unwelcome to the Ministry of which he was a key member. The author was soon identified and a warrant was issued for Defoe's arrest and for five months he was in hiding before he was eventually detained in the house of a Spitalfields' weaver on 21 May 1703, £50 having been offered to 'whomsoever shall discover' him. An advertisement to this effect in the *London Gazette* provides us with one of the best descriptions we have of Daniel Defoe:

> He is a middle siz'd spare man, about forty years old, of a brown complexion, and dark brown-coloured hair, but wears a wig; a hooked nose, a sharp chin, grey eyes and a large mole near his mouth.

He was interrogated by the Secretary of State for the Southern Department, Daniel Finch, Earl of Nottingham – 'Dismal Daniel' to Defoe – who wanted to know, amongst other things, about the secret work he had done for King William. The prisoner was not willing to cooperate and was turned over to an essentially vindictive justice system.

Defoe's trial took place at the Old Bailey on 7 July 1703. The City aldermen who sat as judges included a number who had been mercilessly lampooned by the defendant. In the hope, perhaps, of avoiding prison, which would ruin his successful brick-making business, and on the advice of his counsel, he pleaded guilty to the charge of seditious libel. Only the severity of the sentence remained in doubt. Even though the judges stopped short of whipping, the sentence must have unnerved even so brave a man as Defoe. He was to stand in the pillory for three successive days, was fined 200 marks (about £130) and was to remain in prison for an indefinite period of time.

Although the pillory superficially resembles the game, much favoured today by the organisers of school summer fairs, in which the 'victim', usually the headteacher, puts his head through a hole in a board in order to be bombarded with wet sponges, it was, in fact, no joke. A well-aimed stone could blind the miscreant and William Fuller, another Dissenting pamphleteer who had stood in the pillory just a few months before Defoe, claimed that the sheer quantity of filth flung had almost stifled him and that at one stage his body was so battered that he 'fell down and hung by the neck'. This was the treatment that Defoe was condemned to endure for three consecutive days at different locations in London, at the Royal Exchange, Cheapside and at Temple Bar, before being returned to the appalling squalor of Newgate indefinitely. Such, at least, appears to have been the expectation of the judges.

In fact, Defoe's appearance in the pillory, which took place over the last three days of July 1703, seems to have been something of a personal triumph. Typically, he had taken the risk of exacerbating his vulnerability by circulating a *Hymn to the Pillory* which suggested that it was the judges rather than the prisoner who should be facing the rough justice of the London mob. In the event he seems to have been treated as something of a hero; being the target of nothing more harmful than flowers. Whether he was protected by an organised body of Dissenters keen to preserve their most devastating, if occasionally unreliable, weapon in the pamphleteering wars; whether bribes purchased the goodwill of the crowd, as the Tories alleged; or whether he was simply the recipient of a groundswell of popular support because he had humiliated the high and mighty, we shall probably never know.

After the pillory Defoe was returned to Newgate where he

would remain until the fine imposed upon him was paid off. Given his bankrupt state this did not appear imminent, or even likely to happen at all. Early in November, however, he was released following intervention on his behalf by the rising star of the Tory party, Robert Harley. Harley appears to have recognised the power of Defoe's pen for he wrote to Sidney Godolphin, the Lord Treasurer – and nearest thing there then was to prime minister – suggesting that 'if his [Defoe's] fine be satisfied without any other knowledge but that it is the Queen's bounty to him and grace, he may do service and this may engage him better than after rewards and keep him more under the power of obligation'. Godolphin spoke to the Queen and was able to write to Harley saying, 'it may be done when you will and how you will'. By 9 November it had been done and Defoe, 'a mortified stranger', wrote to Harley full of gratitude.

Had Defoe resisted the temptation to embroil himself in the dangerous game of religious controversy he would have avoided the pillory, Newgate and further financial problems. He would have kept his tile and brick-making business at Tilbury and would have been on the point of making a great deal of money, possibly enough to shake off his creditors for good. The Great Storm was about to hit London, toppling chimneys like ninepins, ripping away roofs and filling the streets with shattered tiles, the price of which would rise from 21*s* per thousand to £6 for plain tiles and from 50*s* per thousand for pantiles to £10. He would not have needed to compile *The Storm*.

Daniel Defoe was nothing if not versatile, however, and on 2 December, just five days after the Storm had devastated the capital, the following notice appeared in the *London Gazette*:

> To preserve the Remembrance of the late Dreadful Tempest, an exact and faithful Collection is preparing of the most remarkable Disasters which happened on that Occasion, with the places where and Persons concern'd, whether at Sea or on Shore. For the perfecting so good a Work 'tis humbly recommended by the Author to all Gentlemen of the Clergy, or others, who have made any Observation of this Calamity, that they would transmit as distinct an Account as possible, of what

> they observed, to the Undertakers, directed to John Nutt, near Stationers Hall, London. All Gentlemen that are pleased to send any such Accounts, are desired to write no Particulars but that they are well satisfied to be true, and to set their Names to the Observations they send, which the Undertakers of this Work promise shall be faithfully recorded, and the favour publickly acknowledged.

Edward Shipman of Fairford was one of many who responded to Defoe's appeal.

3

Dark is His Path

The Great Storm took place at a time when the English Enlightenment was dawning: astrology was rapidly developing into astronomy, alchemy was being transmuted into chemistry and meteorology was emerging from the world of folklore into that of science. The Scientific Revolution was well underway. Robert Boyle who, among much else, had invented the first practical anemometer and gave to Torricelli's apparatus for measuring atmospheric pressure the name 'barometer', had been dead for over a decade. In the year of the Storm itself Robert Hooke, a founder member of the Royal Society, died as did another early member, Samuel Pepys, while Isaac Newton was for the first time elected President and was about to publish his *Opticks*.

Among the tiny but remarkable scientific élite the importance of precise mathematical observation was already accepted. Writing in 1700, Dr John Arbuthnot – later the recipient of Pope's famous *Epistle* and of Dr Johnson's encomium 'the most universal genius' – averred that 'The advantages which accrue to the mind by mathematical studies consist chiefly . . . first, in accustoming it to attention; secondly, in giving it a habit of close and demonstrative reasoning; thirdly, in freeing it from prejudice, credulity and superstition.' The greatest paradigm shift in the history of scientific thought was under way and although the repercussions, in terms of man's perception of his relationship to his environment, were of a disturbingly profound nature, growing scientific confidence was supported by a steady flow of precisely measured data.

The importance of scientific instruments capable of accurate measurement and of tables of such measurements were gradually being recognised. In 1693 Edmund Halley, using demographic data from Germany, *The Breslau Table of Mortality*, had created the actuarial basis for life insurance; some years before he had produced a map of ocean trade winds and in 1701, using his own observations, he produced a map showing magnetic variation in the Atlantic Ocean. In 1703 Halley was appointed Savilian Professor of Mathematics at Oxford. The buccaneering navigator William Dampier was making important contributions to the mapping of the Pacific and to knowledge of ocean currents, and in 1699 had published a *Discourse on Winds*. On a humbler geographical scale, a growing number of men, scattered across the country were beginning to compile meteorological statistics, men such as the Reverend Thomas Robinson of Ousby in Cumberland who in 1698 provided the first account of the helm wind which blows down from Cross Fell into the Eden valley. An important figure in the present story, because he is the source of reliable meteorological data relating to the passage of the Storm, was Richard Towneley of Towneley Hall, Burnley, in Lancashire.

The Towneleys, Richard and his uncle Christopher before him, were at the centre of an important group of northern scientists and mathematicians. Contrary to the stereotypical view which sees Reason as strongly allied with Protestantism, the Towneleys were also devout Catholics and committed Jacobites. Richard had himself been deeply implicated in anti-Williamite plots in the 1690s; his father, Charles, was killed fighting for the Royalist cause at Marston Moor and his grandson, Francis, who joined the Young Pretender in '45, was captured at Carlisle and hung, drawn and quartered in London.

The Towneley Group were as provincial as they were inventive; few had attended university, and a number of their important ideas did not filter through to the wider world until long after their authors were dead. Typical was the case of the astronomer and instrument maker William Gascoigne, another Catholic and Civil War victim, whose micrometer, when fitted to a telescope, allowed for the accurate measurement of stellar magnitude. This was 'discovered' when John Flamsteed, the future

Astronomer Royal, visited Towneley in 1671. Richard himself played a key part in one of the outstanding developments of this remarkable era in the history of science. He had for a number of years been taking barometric readings; down local mines, on nearby Pendle Hill and on Beacon Hill above Halifax, home of the physician and naturalist Henry Power. In 1661 Power was responsible for introducing Richard, then in his early thirties, to Robert Boyle. It was at that meeting that Towneley made a remark about his investigations into atmospheric pressure that suggested to Boyle a line of enquiry which was to lead, in the following year, to the formulation of his famous Law. Greatly to his credit, in writing up his findings, Boyle was generous in acknowledging the part that Towneley had played.

Richard Towneley's meteorological interests were not confined to measuring atmospheric pressure. He invented his own rain-gauge and kept a record of his measurements from 1677 to 1704, three years before his death. When Ralph Thoresby, the Leeds antiquarian, visited the 'famous mathematician and eminent virtuoso' at Burnley in 1697 he saw and admired the rain-gauge and considered the idea of keeping a similar record himself but in the end decided that he lacked the patience! The instrument involved a funnel on the roof of the Hall from which a pipe descended 9 yds vertically before turning in through a window and decanting the water into a collecting vessel. It is today generally accepted that the instrument under-recorded the actual precipitation but Towneley's figures nevertheless constitute the first continuous rainfall record known to survive.

This change from dependence on superstition to reliance on science rarely took the form of sudden revelation. Since the time of Francis Bacon early in the seventeenth century, most educated men had more or less happily accepted a set of beliefs which, in variable proportions, involved an incongruous mixture of rationality and credulity. Samuel Pepys was withering in his contempt for those who saw the hand of God at work when Charles II's coronation celebrations ended with a tremendous thunderstorm, some seeing it as a blessing others as a portent of evil. Such auguries were all 'foolery' as far as Pepys was concerned but this did not prevent him from wearing a hare's foot as a charm against the colic.

Calamities, both natural and man-made, were often regarded as warnings from on high. Among those guilty of 'foolery' in Pepys's view was the Presbyterian clergyman Richard Baxter who was reminded of the earthquake said to have been experienced during Charles I's coronation. Others, no doubt, were reminded of the dreadful storm of 30 August 1658 when the Devil was said to have 'taken Bond' for the soul of Cromwell who died three days later. Across Europe, 'Windy Tuesday', 18 February 1662, was associated with the death of the Queen of Bohemia. In 1666, Thomas Hobbes, the founder of modern philosophical empiricism, who saw man as machine and nothing more, was condemned in Parliament for provoking the wrath of God and hence being personally responsible for both the Plague and the Great Fire.

Attitudes were, however, changing dramatically. By the end of 1714 the last woman to be executed for witchcraft in England had died (in 1712) as had the last monarch to attempt to cure scrofula by the royal touch and a far more enlightened Parliament had passed the Longitude Act, allowing for the award of a huge prize to anyone devising a 'Practicable and Useful' means of establishing meridional location. Arbuthnot's 'Prejudice, credulity and superstition' were giving way to scientifically-established fact, sound theory, repeatable experimentation and their practical benefits.

The development of science, however, was rarely regarded as a challenge to the existence of a divinely inspired order. Although some among the intellectual élite came close to denying God, they were very much in the minority. Of the leading scientists of the day, a number, such as Flamsteed, were ordained ministers of the church and most believed that scientific observation supported rather than contradicted revealed religion. Newton believed that 'There exists an infinite and omnipresent spirit in which matter is moved according to mathematical laws' and his champion Samuel Clarke expressed a similar idea in the following terms:

> There is no such thing as what men commonly call the course of nature. It is nothing else but the will of God producing certain effects in a continued, regular, constant and uniform manner.

Although some among this élite were undoubtedly sceptical in matters of religion, the commonly held view can probably be represented by the words of another clergyman and fellow of the Royal Society who made an important contribution to the study of the Storm by, like Towneley, recording atmospheric pressure during its passage. His name was William Derham, vicar of Upminster in Essex, and his belief was that 'Man was made as 'twere on purpose to observe, and survey, and set forth the Glory of the infinite Creator, manifested in his Works.'

The great majority of the population at large, of course, while they shared Derham's reverence for the Creator and all his works, lacked his rationalising instinct; but there was also a growing class which, although not themselves members of the tiny scientific community, did possess a degree of scientific awareness and understanding of the emerging methodology of science. Daniel Defoe, who had received a relatively liberal education at dissenting academies and was, in many respects, a practically-minded man, belonged to this group. In writing *The Storm* he found himself 'bound in Duty to Science in general, to pay a just Debt to Philosophical study' in which he was, he confessed, 'a meer Junior and hardly any more than an Admirer'.

However, although he quoted Francis Bacon's experiment to create a wind in a closed room – 'in the Case involving his Feathers' – he could not believe that the 'Influence of the Sun upon vaporous matter' was sufficient to account for the winds. For Defoe, God's wonders were performed at His direction through the still largely mysterious workings of natural phenomena, an attitude encapsulated in the words, from the Book of Nahum, which he chose for the title-page of *The Storm*:

The Lord hath his way in the Whirlwind and in the Storm, and the clouds are the dust of his feet.

While his first chapter is concerned with 'the Natural Causes and Origins of Winds', Defoe's conclusion is that, 'there seems to be more of God in the whole Appearance, than in any other part of Operating Nature'. How closely God intervened in 'operating Nature' varied:

> . . . for we never enquire after God in those Works of Nature which depending upon the Course of Things are plain and demonstrative; but where we find Nature defective in her Discovery, where we see Effects but cannot read their Causes; there 'tis most just, and Nature herself seems to direct us to it, to end the rational Enquiry, and resolve it into Speculation: Nature plainly refers us beyond her Self, to the Mighty Hand of Infinite Power, the Author of Nature, and the Original of all Causes.

Although the ancients explained winds in terms of 'a System of Exhalation; Dilation, and Extension' they came to no generally accepted, 'plain and demonstrative' conclusions, suggesting to Defoe the hand of God. Indeed, scriptural authority seems to confirm as much for 'He holds the Wind in his Hand':

> as if he should mean that other things are left to Common Discoveries of Natural Inquiry but this is a thing he holds in his own Hand, and has concealed it from the most Diligent and Piercing Understanding; This in further confirmed by the Words of our Saviour, 'The Wind blows where it listeth, and thou hearest the Sound thereof, but knowest not where it cometh' 'tis plainly expressed to signify that the Causes of the Wind are not equally discover'd by Natural Inquiry as the rest of Nature is.

The image of a vast white-locked patriarch with hair streaming and cheeks inflated was clearly not far from his mind as he considered the causes of the Storm but this did not prevent Defoe from examining the natural processes which might have offered some explanation of its development. He suggests, for example, that the Storm may have begun as a West Indian hurricane as it came from the west – and a few days before an 'unusual Tempest' was reported on the coasts of Florida and Virginia – this despite the fact that the idea of travelling pressure systems would not be formulated, by George Hadley, for another three decades. This was not, however, an original idea. Following 'Windy Tuesday',18 February 1662, Dr Robert Plot of Oxford, a future professor of chemistry at the university, quoted 'an able seaman of Bristol' who had expressed the opinion that 'this was the fag-end of a Hurricane which began in New England about three hours before'. Defoe's suggestion that the Storm had taken some days to cross the Atlantic was, however, far more realistic. Furthermore, he included a table showing 'the Height of the Mercury in the Barometer' as recorded by Richard Towneley at Towneley Hall in Lancashire as well as by William Derham in Essex, together with a letter written by Derham, addressed to the Royal Society describing the Storm and comparing it with others that he had known.

Derham's letter begins with a lengthy account of the weather during the preceding part of the year 'particularly as to wet and warmth, because I am of opinion that these had a great influence on the late Storm'. After speculating on the causes of the thunder and lightning which accompanied the Storm at Upminster, Derham describes in some detail the weather of Thursday 25 November – high wind in the afternoon with rain and hail which 'did some Damage'. He goes on:

> The next Morning, which was Friday, Novem. 26. the Wind was SSW and high all Day and so continued until I was in bed and asleep. Almost 12 that Night, the Storm awaken'd me, which gradually increased till near that Morning; and from then till near 7 it continued in the greatest excess: and then began slowly to abate, and the Mercury to rise swiftly. The barometer I found at 12h½ p.m. [on the 26th] at 28.72 where it continued until about 6 the next Morning, or 6¼ and then hastily rose; so that it was gotten to [28.] 82 about 8 of the clock . . . How the Wind set during the Storm I cannot positively say, it being excessively dark all the while, and my Vane blown down also, when I could have seen: But my information from Millers and others that were forced to venture abroad; and by my own guess, I imagine it to have blown about SW by S or nearer to the S at the beginning, and to veer about towards the W towards the end of the Storm as far as WSW.
>
> The degree of the Wind's strength being not measurable (that I know of, though talked of) but by guess, I thus determine with respect to other Storms. On February 7 1698/9 that did much damage. This I number 10 degrees; the Wind

then WNW . . . Another remarkable Storm was Feb. 3 1701/2 at which time was the greatest descent of the barometer ever known: This I number 9 degrees. But this last of November, I number at least 15 degrees.

Derham, himself a fellow of the Royal Society, was clearly well aware of the importance of measuring the characteristics of the Storm and, in the absence of more accurate data, devised his own method of quantifying the relative strength of storm winds. He obviously regarded the Storm, at '15 degrees', as an altogether more significant occurrence than the kind of annual events with which he compared it.

The probability is that many other records in addition to those of Derham and Towneley were forwarded to the Royal Society but, regrettably, at some future date in the eighteenth century the custodian of the meteorological records decided that they had no future use and destroyed them! Fortunately, Derham's account is preserved both in the *Philosophical Transactions of the Royal Society* and in Daniel Defoe's book.

Defoe also tried to place the Storm into some kind of context by supplying for his readers a 12-point 'table of degrees', consisting of what he called the 'bald terms used by sailors' to describe wind strength. It is a forerunner of Beaufort's table of wind force devised in 1806 and eventually adopted by the Admiralty in 1838 for use in 'the Log Books of all Her Majesty's Ships and Vessels of War'. Table 1 (p. viii) compares Defoe's 'bald terms' with Beaufort's more sophisticated but not dissimilar classification.

But while Defoe sought in this way to describe the Storm in scientific terms and even endeavoured to explain its origins, as a West Indian hurricane, he clearly found any explanation which relegated the significance of God's direct involvement – 'the mighty hand of infinite power' – unsatisfactory. Doubtless, Defoe the bankrupt was trying to appeal to as wide a readership as his, admittedly, not very flexible principles would allow. In appealing to both the unashamedly God-fearing and the more scientifically-minded he was probably reflecting a dichotomy which co-existed, for the most part harmoniously, in his and many men's minds. The result is, nevertheless, a first-class piece of journalism, a worthy attempt to organise accounts of the event from a wide variety of sources. The fact that many of the contributors are acknowledged by name increases our faith both in their stories and in Defoe's rendition of them, the great majority being quoted verbatim. Not all writers, however, have been convinced of Defoe's dependability.

What might be called the doubting tendency can be represented by the views expressed in Sir John Martin-Leake's biography of Admiral Sir John Leake whose ship, the *Prince George*, was one of the few to ride out the Storm in the Downs. Here it says of the 'eyewitness' letters that they 'may be genuine and authentic' but it is arguable that the author of *A Journal of the Plague Year* may very well have invented them together with the picturesque and convincing detail they contain'. Such scepticism is understandable. Not for nothing has Defoe been called the 'Great Fabricator'.

It is, of course, true to say that while *A Journal of the Plague Year* purports to be a memoir of the dreadful visitation of 1665 by 'H. F', 'a citizen who continued all the while in London', it was entirely of Defoe's own invention. What is more, although he almost certainly spent the plague year in London, he was only four or five at the time so deceit was certainly involved in presenting the *Journal* as that of an adult contemporary. Nevertheless, it is today commonly recognised that the device only adds to the authority of a work which many regard as his masterpiece and few dispute is the definitive account of the contagion, unsurpassed in its realism.

The Storm is quite different. It is an earlier, less mature work and one in which he relied far less upon imaginative re-creation. It must be remembered that it was published within eight months of the event and that by far the greater part of the population of London and the rest of southern England would have vividly remembered what had taken place. To fictionalise, especially in so acerbic a cultural environment, would have invited the literary equivalent of the pillory.

This is not to say that *The Storm* is to be relied on absolutely. It is journalism and its bankrupt author was doubtless more concerned with getting his work into print than double checking the facts. Mistakes do occur – Mr Shipman of Fairford, for example, appears as 'Shipton' and, occasionally, passages are inexplicably vague, as when he refers to '______, a town in Norfolk'. It seems likely too that, for dramatic effect, he may have sought to enhance the quality of some of his contributors prose, but the notion that they are his own inventions would be difficult to sustain. In later pamphlets he did create fictional, necessarily unnamed, 'insiders' in order to strengthen a case, for example in defending Harley against the charge of treason. *The Storm*, however, was neither a legal defence nor a polemic but reportage which, in the view of Defoe's recent biographer, the journalist Richard West, 'puts to shame all modern accounts of disaster, whether in books, newspapers, radio or television'. Furthermore, we know that the appeal for eyewitnesses was genuine – it is reported in the *London Gazette* – and most of the contributors were prominent in their local communities. The American Defoe scholar Laura Ann Curtis is surely right, therefore, to conclude that:

> Although he was a very efficient editor and secret censor, he would not have done a great deal of revising in *The Storm*, because many of the correspondents must have been waiting eagerly for publication of the book in which their own letters would appear in print, and heavy-handed redaction would have caused a storm of a very different nature from the one described in the book.

Defoe could not, however, resist the temptation to use the Storm in his propaganda war against his High Church opponents and the City aldermen who had sentenced him to the ignominy of the pillory. This fortunately, was in another and altogether inferior work, a long poem entitled 'An Essay on the Late Storm' published together with a rather self-pitying 'Elegy on the Author of the True-Born Englishman'. Its couplets creak along almost as plaintively as an ill-built house in the Storm itself:

> Soon as I heard the horrid Blast,
> And understood how long 'twould last,
> Viewed all the fury of the Element
> Consider well by whom 'twas sent
> And *unto whom* for Punishment:

Not, of course, he and his fellow Dissenters or their Low Church sympathisers. In a clear analogy with the so-called 'Protestant Wind' which had carried his hero William of Orange's Dutch fleet down the Channel to Torbay in 1688 while keeping King James's navy trapped in the Thames, Defoe turned on his religious opponents:

> They say this 'twas a High Church Storm
> Sent out the Nation to Reform,
> But th' Emblem left the Moral in the Lurch'
> For't blew the Steeple down upon the Church.
> From whence we now inform the People
> The danger of the Church is from the Steeple.

Defoe was by no means alone. Both High and Low Church parties used the Storm as a stick for beating their enemy, ignoring the fact that the Low Countries, Denmark and north Germany were affected quite as badly as England.

In selecting letters for inclusion in *The Storm* Defoe certainly allowed his own prejudices to influence the editorial process. A 'Gentleman from Somerton' wrote asserting that the Bishop of Bath and Wells had once sworn that he would rather have his brains knocked out than harbour the, presumably High Church, views of his inferior clergy. This gentleman saw the Bishop's death as the Judgement of God upon him but Defoe, who certainly would not have agreed, refused to publish the letter on the grounds that its writer had not given his name, an omission which did not prevent him from including letters from other unnamed hands.

Many shared the more general opinion of a different writer who expressed the view that 'So remarkable and signal a judgement of God on this Nation (as lately befell in the dreadful Tempest on Saturday morning, Nov. 27th last) no History, either foreign or domestic can parallel . . . This greater calamity appears as a Goliah to those of lesser and dwarfish disasters that have happen'd in former times in England.' Less sophisticated souls than those actively engaged in the national sport of sectarian point-scoring doubtless regarded the Storm as yet another, more terrifying, act of an omnipotent and vengeful God. Typical must have been the townsfolk of Basingstoke where:

> Most of the people were in great Fear and Consternation; insomuch, that they thought the world had been at an end.

4

On the Wings of the Storm

Modern interpretations of the meteorology of the Storm begin with a rather mixed collection of data. Far more information is available than for what had hitherto very probably been the worst storm in historic times in southern England, that of January 1362. On the other hand, the great eighteenth-century clerical vogue for recording the weather had yet to come into fashion and the remarkable Victorian developments in meteorology were far in the future. The astonishingly fertile mind of Christopher Wren nevertheless presaged many of these developments. In 1662, long before making his reputation as the nation's favourite architect, in an address to the Royal Society, he suggested that:

> I might seem to promise too much, should I say, an Engine may be fram'd, which if you visit your Chamber but one half Hour of the day, shall tell you how many Changes of Wind have been in our absence . . . Neither shall the Thermometer need a constant Observance, for after the same Method may that be made to be its own Register . . .

Had Wren concentrated his mind on meteorology such apparatus may very well have seen the light of day; as it was another two centuries had to elapse before these ideas were converted into such practical equipment as William Henry Dines's pressure-tube anemograph, registering by means of a pen trace on a revolving drum, a continuous record of the pressure, and hence the speed, of the wind.

So what information is available to enable the modern meteorologist to determine exactly what was taking place in the atmosphere above southern Britain on the night of 26/27 November 1703? Firstly, as we have seen, there is the wealth of descriptive material collected by Daniel Defoe, together with the scattered references in contemporary diaries, memoirs and letters. While many of these accounts bear witness to the unusual strength and destructiveness of the wind and to the geographical distribution of the places worst affected, mention of wind direction, rain, thunder and lightning is rare. As we know, Defoe provides a table of the atmospheric pressure as recorded by Richard Towneley in Lancashire and William Derham in Essex. Helpful pressure data is also available from the Paris Observatory, established in 1667. There was no standardised method of taking such recordings, however, so it is necessary to adjust the raw figures to take into account factors such as height above sea level and temperature. Nor can we be absolutely sure how different observers calibrated their thermometers or where they were positioned (often indoors in an unheated north-facing room). Defoe himself apparently had access to a barometer but although he did not make any precise observations he did provide an excuse for his negligence:

> . . . about 10 o'clock [on the evening of the 26th] our barometers informed us that the night would be very tempestuous; the mercury sunk lower than ever I had observed it on any occasion whatsoever, which made me suppose the tube had been handled by the children.

By great good fortune the three locations for which readings are extant – Paris, Upminster and Burnley – fall along a south-east/north-west line which lies across the path of the north-easterly moving Storm.

In addition to these barometric readings, further evidence comes from the weather reports recorded in the logs of ships of the Royal and merchant navies and of the Dutch and Danish navies. Many of these survive and they are full of information which is, on the one hand, reliable and precise and, on the other, powerfully expressive of the uniqueness of the occasion. Thus from the *Newark* off the Isle of Wight, the log for 27 November reads:

> At 4 yesterday afternoon veered out our long service it blowing a hard gale at West. At 12 at night the wind at WSW blowing a great storm. At 3 this morning our ship drove . . . In my opinion it was the greatest storm that ever I saw in England.

The preference of English admirals at the beginning of the eighteenth century was to spend the winter in England. Indeed in some areas, most notably in the Mediterranean, they had no option for although by the end of the war they were in possession of both Gibraltar and Port Mahon, in 1703 they had no such base. Consequently, the first weeks of November saw ships converging on home waters from various points of the compass, from the West Indies, Virginia, the Mediterranean and Russia. By the third week of November the ports and harbours were already crowded with shipping that had either arrived home or was seeking shelter from a succession of storms. French privateers had wrought heavy losses amongst merchant shipping, which required convoying by the Royal Navy. The homeward-bound Jamaica fleet was reported safely arrived at Spithead on 16 November and the following day Sir Cloudesley Shovell, who had been conducting a not particularly damaging campaign against the French in the Mediterranean, arrived back in the Downs with an ill-victualled and half-starved fleet. Last to arrive was a fleet of Virginia traders convoyed by the *Guernsey* and the *Oxford* which did not cross the Grand Banks of Newfoundland until the 14th. Some impression of just how stormy the North Atlantic was that winter is given in a letter, dated the following 6 February, from the governor of Barbados, addressed to the Council of Trade and Plantations:

> The *Dreadnought* which sailed from England in September last arrived here on the 1st inst: she had bin all that time at sea, bin separated from her fleet and suffer'd much damage at sea by the violent storms and bad weather. Colonel Seymour, the governor of Maryland and his family on board.
>
> Signed: Bevill Granville

Even prior to the arrival of the Great Storm, November 1703 had been exceptionally stormy with a number of deep depressions, together with their associated 'daughter' or wave depressions, chasing one another across the Atlantic. How exceptional this was can be seen by looking at the modern definition of a 'gale'. A day which experiences gale is one in which a wind speed in excess of 34 knots, measured at the standard height of 10 metres above the ground, occurs over any period of 10 consecutive minutes. Between 1941–70 the annual average varied from 0.1 days/yr at Kew to 51.8 at Lerwick in the Shetland Isles. On an average day in January, the stormiest month, the odds against a gale vary from 900:1 at Kew to a little over 3:1 at Lerwick. During such gales sudden gusts can see the wind speed rise to in excess of 80 knots, causing severe damage.

We do not, of course, have accurate measures of wind speed to prove that November 1703 was unusual, but the non-quantitative evidence is overwhelming. For day after day the logs of ships in the Atlantic and in British waters contain, under the heading 'Remarkable Observations & Accidents' comments such as 'blowing exceeding hard from the SW', 'blowing extreme hard' and 'a mighty tempest of wind'. On 18 November 'a very great storm' was reported at Milford Haven while off Flamborough Head it was 'blowing prodigious hard'. The only moderately calm days experienced during the passage of the Virginia fleet were 17 and 24 November. As each gale system passed over, pulling air into its anti-clockwise circulation, the wind veered from S to W to NW. Thus the Dutch vessel *Schieland*, south of the Scillies on the morning of Saturday 20 November reported winds from the South-West but by the early afternoon, off the Wolf Rock, they had veered round to North-West. The sudden change of wind direction suggests the passage of the cold front and the even more rapid frontal shifts which can be deduced from the log of HMS *Antelope* at Portsmouth, with accompanying squalls and heavy showers, suggest the centre of the depression was over south central England. On the southern side of such depressions wind direction and the track of the migrating low would tend to coincide to give a strong westerly component which would have been continually reinforcing wave energy so that great seas were running up the Channel.

Nor where conditions much quieter in the North Sea. At 2 o'clock on the morning of 19 November 'it blew a mear [i.e. absolute] storm' off Grimsby; the height of the gale coming some 8 hours later. The following day another Dutch ship, the *Callenburgh*, entering the North Sea from the Skaggerak met a strong south-westerly wind which eased off as what is presumed to be a depression moved away to the north-east and a small ridge of high extended from the continent. This tended to be the pattern for the next couple of days; small but deep lows heralded by strong southerly winds veering sharply westwards with the passage of fronts and their accompanying heavy, squally showers. Geographical variations in the weather were often sharp and even dramatic. The *Callenburgh*, making little headway on her return to Holland, was by the 22nd still in the northern North Sea in calm conditions between depressions but further south things were very different and by night-time the passage of a further depression appears to have brought disaster as the 60-gun HMS *York* at anchor off the Suffolk coast was driven by what the *London Gazette* called 'stress of Weather' on to the sands of the Shipwash. There she went to pieces, remarkably losing only four of her complement of 235. This was the harbinger of far worse to come for the Royal Navy.

By the evening of Tuesday the 23rd strengthening winds in southern England indicated the imminent arrival of another deep depression which, by the following morning, was probably centred over Ireland. A sudden veering of the wind from S by E to WSW recorded in the log of the *Antelope* at Portsmouth suggests the passage of a particularly distinctive front. A series of wave depressions appear to have developed along this front, moving rapidly northwards from the Bay of Biscay over the British Isles pulling in gale force winds across the Channel coast. In London structural damage was already being caused and Daniel Defoe, who noted that 'the nearer it came to the fatal 26th of November, the Tempestuousness of the wind increased', was fortunate to escape the collapse of a house.

By the 25th both Towneley and Derham must have observed that their barometers had begun to dip ominously, while in the Channel Lieutenant William Houlding aboard HMS *Hampton*

Court noted in his journal the wind blowing hard, as it shifted from W by S to SW by W, squally weather and 'a great sea'. Heavy bursts of rain and hail and occasional flashes of lightning were experienced all along the Channel coast while rapidly drawn curtains of cloud would suddenly shut out all visibility to give what the sailors called 'thick weather', cutting out all 'observation' and demanding that they rely upon 'judgement' alone to fix their position. 'Excessive hard gales and rain' were reported on the coast of Cornwall and, at Plymouth, all thought of sending out a boat to relieve the Eddystone lighthouse keeper had to be abandoned.

Things were still bad in the North Sea too. A Newcastle collier, the *John and Mary*, one of very many plying the sea-coal trade with the capital, having been attempting to reach the Thames for almost a week but being continually blown northwards, was by the Wednesday evening (25th) and 'with much Difficulty and Danger' off the north Norfolk coast. There 'it blew so hard . . . that we could not keep the Sea nor fetch the Roads of Yarmouth; but as the coast of Norfolk was a Weather-shore, we hull'd as close Cromer as we durst lie, here we road Wednesday and Thursday, the 24th and 25th of November'. The protection offered by the low cliffs and hills – 'the High-land about Cromer' as the skipper of the *John and Mary* reported to Defoe – indicates a southerly storm veering to WSW as the depression moved away towards Scandinavia.

The *Callenburgh* meanwhile, battling ineffectually against a succession of south-westerly gales, had been forced northwards and by the evening of the 25th was in the northern North Sea, in the latitude of southern Norway, being buffeted by the storm from which the *John and Mary* had earlier sought shelter. Defoe himself, in London of course, remarks that the fury of the storm on the 25th was such that it 'would have passed for a great wind, had not the great storm followed so soon'. A few miles to the south-west of Oxford at about four in the afternoon there was a tornado, 'a spout marching directly with the Wind', as it was reported to Defoe, possibly triggered by the passage of a cold front. By daylight on Friday the 26th this extensive storm system appears to have been moving away towards the Baltic and the ships being escorted by the *Callenburgh* were able to regroup. By his time, however, something far more ominous was happening off the west coast of Ireland.

Exactly how the Great Storm developed is still the subject of debate and, indeed, given the paucity of records, is unlikely ever to be resolved. C.E.P. Brooks, an eminent British meteorologist writing in 1954, was happy to pick up the idea of a West Indian hurricane – the 'unusual Tempest' – perceptively suggested by Daniel Defoe. Brooks accepted Defoe's suggestion that such a system had travelled up the coast of Florida and out into the Atlantic. It is, he believed, ' a reasonable conjecture that it maintained some of its force until it came within the orbit of the larger storm and attached itself to the southern margin of the latter as a deep secondary depression'. This is not an unreasonable idea and indeed it is not at all likely that Brooks would have made it if it had been. Most autumns witness the passage across the British Isles of decaying, but usually harmless, Caribbean hurricane systems. That such a system might be reinvigorated and as such be the cause of renewed destruction is by no means improbable. A notable example was one which hammered the west of Ireland on 16 September 1961. Better remembered, at least in southern England, was the infamous 'no hurricane' report delivered by the TV weatherman Michael Fish on the eve of the devastating storm of 16 October 1987. Unfortunately for Fish his reference was to just such a West Indian hurricane, still in the western Atlantic, which he predicted would not reach the British Isles. He was right, but, of course, a quite exceptional storm was developing much nearer home.

Another meteorologist of the Great Storm, H.H. Lamb has pointed to the fact that Defoe's speculative remark is the only evidence suggesting a hurricane on the eastern seaboard of America at that time. Defoe himself does not offer a source for his information and neither of the modern lists of early American hurricanes indicate one which might have hit the Florida coast in the period before the Great Storm. What is more, the overwhelming majority of hurricanes occur before the middle of November and it is worth reminding ourselves that had the modern Gregorian Calendar been in use in England at that time (it was not introduced until 1752) the Storm would be dated 7–8 December not 26–27 November. This does not mean that there is no possibility of the Storm having a hurricane origin but of the 1300-plus American hurricanes known to have taken place between 1500 and 1955, only three occurred in December. It could be, as Lamb points out, that the Storm began life as a hurricane that followed a more easterly track, avoiding the Atlantic seaboard and passing, for example, over Bermuda but to accept this is to ignore the only piece of evidence, Defoe's report of the Florida 'Tempest', pointing to a hurricane.

There is nevertheless some indirect evidence indicating that the Great Storm did indeed begin life as a tropical hurricane. The typical mid-latitude depression is characterised by the convergence of polar and tropical air masses along a zone of discontinuity known as a front . Along such fronts the lighter and more buoyant warm air tends to be pushed upwards, the water vapour within it cooling and condensing, frequently giving rise to rainfall. The passage of fronts is also typified by an abrupt veering of the wind, that is to say, as we have seen, a shift in a clockwise manner from, for example, south to south-westerly. By contrast, the Great Storm, in common with tropical hurricanes, appears to have had a relatively calm centre and to have been non-frontal, there being no sudden veering of the wind and little rainfall. Furthermore, as Lamb suggests, the Storm moved across the British Isles, the North Sea and the Baltic at a steady speed of about 40 knots (or 20 m per second) uninfluenced by the older, still deep depression over Norway. This is consistent with the theory that a tropical cyclone was brought close to cold North American air close to the coast of Florida four or five days before, producing a strong jet stream in the upper atmosphere. The rapid, inexorable progress of the Storm is indicative of such an exceptionally strong jet stream and hence with a tropical origin.

The low pressure centre of the Storm followed a track to the south of the coasts of Cork and Waterford, across Cardigan Bay, Mid-Wales and the north Midlands and by 4 o'clock on the morning of the 27th was probably somewhere in the region of Nottingham with a pressure of approximately 950 mb. Although a packet boat at Parkgate in the Dee estuary was 'staved to pieces', places to the north of this track do not in general appear to have experienced very exceptional weather. A hard gale with some rain and lightning was reported at Kinsale on the coast of county Cork on the 26th but there is no further suggestion of particularly bad weather and the experience of shipping on the east coast of Ireland and on the coast of North Wales seems to have been similar. While there was certainly considerable disruption of shipping in the Humber and HMS *Dartmouth* in Grimsby roads logged a 'violent storm', ports further north in Yorkshire appear not to have experienced notably bad conditions and inland there was no report of a storm at Leeds. At midnight, the *Deal Castle*, homeward bound from Archangel, reported fair weather as she set sail from Scarborough for Yarmouth but four hours later was sailing into the teeth of the Storm, for to the south matters were very different.

The estimated pressure at the centre of the depression at the height of the Storm – 950 mb – although low is well above the absolute minimum recorded in the British Isles, 926.5 mb in Perthshire on 26 January, 1884. The key factor in determining wind speed is not the depth of the low but the pressure gradient, the difference in pressure between one place and another. To the south of the cyclonic centre the anticlockwise circulation of the system and the direction of movement of the depression combined to produce a remarkably steep pressure gradient. At about 3 o'clock in the morning, when the Storm was at its height in south-east England a barometer at Nottingham would have shown the equivalent of about 950 mb, one in the capital about 970 mb while on the Sussex coast the glass may have read as high as 990 mb. H.H. Lamb has compared the barometric readings taken at Towneley, Upminster and Paris between 25–29 November, making the corrections necessary for reduction to sea level and the probable height of buildings and assuming unheated rooms. All three bear witness to the passage of a deep depression. Of the English locations the change of pressure was especially abrupt at Upminster where the rise from the minimum was of more than 12.7 millibars in three hours. On the polar side of the depression, by contrast, while Richard Towneley must have experienced strong winds at Burnley they were not exceptional. Another Lancashire Catholic squire, Nicholas Blundell of Crosby, at the mouth of the Mersey, writing in his *Great Diurnall*, records only that he entertained the Apostolic Vicar, making no reference to the weather.

How much thunder, lightning and rain accompanied the Storm is difficult to assess. Derham, who can probably be relied upon, refers to having seen 'Corruscasions or Flashes . . . which some took for Lightning'. Such lightning as there was, however, appears to have been limited both in time and space. Derham was certainly more impressed by the excessive dark than any occasional illumination and this seems to have been the general experience; indeed, the great majority of accounts make no reference to either thunder or lightning. Later descriptions, perhaps on the assumption that any storm worthy of the name must necessarily be accompanied by the added drama of convective activity, probably embellished the truth. Even serious commentators often perpetuated this notion. Isaac Schomberg in his *Naval Chronology* of 1802 thus writes that:

> On the 26th November [1703] about eleven at night, a most dreadful storm arose from the west south-west, attended with dreadful flashes of lightning and peals of thunder. It continued with unabated fury until about seven the next morning.

Earl Stanhope, writing later in the nineteenth century, may have swung a little too far in the opposite direction in pronouncing that the wind was:

> so high that between the gusts it sounded like thunder in the distance. Of real thunder and lightning there was none, but in some places the air was full of meteoric flashes which resembled the latter. In general however the darkness added to the terror, for it was just New Moon.

It does seem to have been the case that lightning and some brisk showers were experienced around the Thames estuary but neither appears to have been of much significance elsewhere.

The Irish Sea was presumably a good deal quieter than the Channel, where surface winds probably reached 80–90 knots and gusts may well have exceeded 120 knots. Winds defined as of Hurricane Force (Force 12) on the Beaufort scale are achieved when a speed of 64 knots (32.7 m/sec) or more is sustained over a period of at least 10 minutes, and it seems likely that in the Channel, the Straits of Dover and the southern North Sea such a force was reached over widespread areas during the early hours of 27 November. In the early eighteenth century, of course, the term 'hurricane' did not carry either of its more modern meanings, that of a tropical cyclone or that of a wind of force 12 on the Beaufort Scale. As used by Defoe and others it simply referred to an exceptionally severe storm. Thus *The Observator* newspaper of 1–4 December 1703 reported: 'never was such a storm of wind, such a hurricane and tempest known in the memory of man, nor the like to be found in the histories of England'.

An indication of the speed of the wind at sea is provided by a story in *The Storm*. At about midnight of 26/27th, when the weather in the south-west was at its most violent, a tin ship with only a man and two boys on board was torn from her anchors in the Helford River in Cornwall. Then, 'without Anchor, Cable or Boat', she was driven out of the river and up the Channel, the small crew's involuntary voyage ending at 8 in the morning with the vessel wedged between two rocks on the coast of the Isle of Wight. Defoe concluded that 'a Run of so short a time is almost incredible; it being near 80 leagues in 8 hours'. Not, however, impossible for if the necessary average speed of 18–19 knots were to be achieved, given that there would have been much wind-driven surface water, Lamb calculates that the surface wind speed must certainly have been in excess of 60 knots, possibly nearer 90; figures not inconsistent with those suggested by the isobaric reconstruction (see Figure 1, p. xiv). The miracle lay not so much in the wind speeds achieved, great as they were, but in the survival of the crew, unwitting holders surely of a remarkable water speed record!

Inland the average wind speed would have been significantly lower because of the greater frictional effect of a rougher surface but storm force winds (56–63 knots) were nevertheless probably sustained over much of southern England for several hours and furthermore the turbulence caused by the uneven land surface would have given rise to more, and more damaging, gusts.

By daybreak on the Saturday morning the Storm was battering the coast of Holland, breaching the Friesland dykes and flooding huge areas of low-lying land. Delft had experienced 'a night of dreadful storm' and, by eight in the morning, it was recorded that the barometer had never been seen so low, albeit that Delft probably lay somewhat to the south of the Storm centre. From the Hague came an account of 'the most dreadful Storm that has been in these parts in the Memory of Man'. Thus as Edward Shipman examined the wreckage of his West Window at Fairford, the burgers of Utrecht ventured out to behold a devastated cathedral. The lee coasts of Holland and Jutland were littered with the wrecks of ships blown ashore and inland great damage was inflicted upon Antwerp, Liège and Cologne. As the Storm centre hurtled on across the Baltic, it left in its wake toppled church towers, including those of Wismar, Rostock and Stralsund. Hanover experienced a 'dreadful storm, scarcely a house but received damage, and the country round suffered worse' while from Hamburg came a report that the 'Damage by a prodigious Storm here and hereabouts is incredibly great'. According to a report from Dantzig dated 1 December, there was on 'Saturday about Noon a most violent storm of wind at WSW which continued about an hour and a half and has doubtless dispersed the Swedish convoy'. The report went on to record much damage 'at Memel, Coningsbergh and other places along this coast'.

Nor did the Queen's enemy escape. Severe weather was experienced on the French coast from La Rochelle to Dunkirk while in Paris on the Saturday morning, as the pressure in the rear of the storm system rose dramatically, possibly by as much as 20 mb in 3 hours, 'a most violent hurricane of wind' was reported. If God had intended to punish those whom Oliver Cromwell had called 'His Englishmen', whether High Church or Low, His aim had been devastatingly indiscriminate.

The centre of the Storm appears to have moved relentlessly north-eastwards across northern Europe at a speed of about 40 knots, eventually passing out of harm's way across northern Finland on the Sunday. The speed with which the Storm system tracked away to the north-east is not, of course, to be confused with the far higher speeds at which the winds hurtled in towards its gyrating centre.

In addition to the high wind speeds, three other phenomena, two factual the other almost certainly the product of understandably enlivened imaginations, were associated with the Storm. A number of the accounts which Defoe received suggested that an earth tremor had occurred at the climax of its passage. It is not unusual for such reports to be made during storms. Typical is the entry in the diary of the Norfolk clergyman Parson Woodforde for 1 January 1791:

> Billy Bidewell brought my Papers from Norwich, and am sorry to find by the Papers that much damage and many Lives lost by the late violent Storm of Wind with most terrible Thunder and Lightning on Thursday Morn' December 23, 1790. It is thought by many that it was attended by a slight shock of an Earthquake.

Even though it was 'the received opinion of abundance of people that they felt, during the impetuous fury of the wind, several movements of the earth . . .', Defoe was sceptical:

> . . . as an earthquake must have been so general, that everybody must have discerned it; and as the people were in their houses when they imagined they felt it, the shaking and terror of which might deceive their imagination, and impose upon their judgement . . .

This he finds perfectly understandable, 'since nothing is more frequent, than for fear to double every object, and impose upon understanding . . .'. Today, of course, we know that the chances of an earth tremor, itself a considerable rarity in the British Isles, coinciding with the kind of Storm that probably occurs once every three or four hundred years is extremely remote, there being no causal link between the two events. More credulous minds, alert to the imminent possibility of Armageddon, would have been less surprised by such a coincidence. Indeed, a biblically highly literate nation would have automatically made the link between the two phenomena, remembering the famous lines from the First Book of Kings:

> And, behold, the Lord passed by, and a great and strong wind rent the mountains, and brake in pieces the rocks before the Lord; but the Lord was not in the wind: and after the wind an earthquake; but the Lord was not in the earthquake.

Daniel Defoe, who certainly knew his Bible as well as the next man, once more displays a remarkably modern cast of mind in rejecting the likelihood of wind and earthquake coinciding.

In some parts of the country, however, the words of the Psalmist would have been all too apt: 'The floods are risen, O Lord, the floods have lift up their voice: the floods lift up their waves.'

Those low-lying stretches of the coastline where inlets of the sea opened out to the south and south-west were especially prone to inundation as high waves, driven in by storm force winds, topped such coastal defences as existed, and banked up the tide causing rivers to overflow. This was a particular problem where the fetch of the waves, that is to say the distance of open ocean across which they had travelled, was greatest. The configuration of the Severn estuary meant that it was especially vulnerable and hundreds of acres of land on both the Somerset and Monmouthshire sides of the estuary were flooded and, as the waters receded seagoing vessels were left stranded great distances from the shoreline.

A third phenomenon associated with the Storm also excited much interest among both the farming and scientific communities. This was the effect the hurricane-force winds had in spreading salt spray far beyond the coastal strip normally affected. Near to the coast the concentration of salt deposits was, of course, greatest so that Stephen Gawen of Hastings referred to the leaves of trees and bushes being 'as Salt as they had been dipped in the Sea'. But even miles inland the presence of precipitated salt was remarkable. From Cranbrook in Kent 'at least 16 miles from the sea and above 25 miles from any part of the sea to windward' came news of 'brackish' rain accompanying the Storm.

Two letters on the same lines were printed in the *Philosophical Transactions* of the Royal Society. One, from Mr Denham, concerned a physician who, shortly after the Storm was travelling from Lewes, in Sussex, to Ticehurst and 'as he rode pluckt some tops of Hedges and chawing them found them Salt'. The writer himself observed that the grass on the [South] Downs 'was so salt that the sheep in the Morning would not feed till hunger compelled them and afterwards drank like Fishes'.

Another letter came from the distinguished Dutch microscopist Anton van Leeuwenhoek who pointed out that on the morning following the Storm at Delft, windows were found to be 'darkened by water with small parts of Chalk or Stone'. He was inclined to dispute the theory that 'the scattering of this Salt water by the Storm will do a great deal of harm to the Fruits of the Earth . . . for I believe that a little salt spread over the surface of the earth, especially when it is heavy Clay ground, does render it exceedingly Fruitful'. Although regular exposure to salt spray is poisonous to many plants, van Leeuwenhoek was right in suggesting that sodium, in limited quantities, can increase yields. Grain crops, roots and fruit all benefit in this respect although the probability must be that the salt deposited by the Storm had all been leached from the soil by the time the next growing season began. That such a topic was under discussion was certainly testament to the scientific inquisitiveness of the age.

The Saturday morning thus discovered a landscape shattered – a favourite term used by Defoe's correspondents – by the Storm and in places ruined by flood. Uprooted trees everywhere, massive branches of forest giants snapped off like matchwood, the debris of the violence strewn everywhere across city streets and country lanes. As Edward Shipman of Fairford, and thousands like him, ventured out to examine the devastation, he would have been only too well aware that the true cost of repairing the damage to buildings weakened and exposed would depend upon what the weather had in store over the days and weeks ahead.

5

HURRY-DURRY WEATHER

Sir Cloudesley Shovell had had a miserable time in the Mediterranean. Although some of his aims had been achieved, he had no glorious victory over the French to report when he arrived in the Downs on 17 November. Had he returned laden with treasure and prizes he may have hurried off to London and a hero's welcome. As it was he stayed with his ships and their sickening, ill-fed crews to face an enemy far more destructive than the French fleet.

A state of war had existed since the spring of the previous year. The War of the Spanish Succession, which was to last until 1713, was in part at least, as its name suggests, an attempt to achieve by war what diplomacy had failed to produce – a successor to the imbecile King Charles II of Spain acceptable to the great powers of Europe. Of the three claimants, a Bavarian prince, a grandson of Louis XIV of France and a son of the Emperor Leopold of Austria, the Bavarian had the broadest support among the powers. Unfortunately for the peace of Europe, neither the Austrians nor the Spanish would accept the partitioning of the Spanish Empire in order to compensate the 'losers'. This intransigence proved to be folly when first the Bavarian prince predeceased the mad king and then, in 1700, when Charles eventually died and was found to have left a will bequeathing his undivided empire to Philip, the grandson of *le Roi Soleil*. The will contained a proviso which virtually guaranteed war: if it was not acceptable then the crown should pass to the Emperor's son, another Charles.

Acquisition of power over the Spanish Empire appears to have inspired the French monarch with what the historian H.A.L. Fisher called 'a new spirit of arrogant intemperance' which, in

1701, led to a rapid deterioration of relationships with his maritime neighbours in particular. He sent troops pouring over the frontier into the Spanish Netherlands (the biggest part of modern Belgium) to occupy the massively fortified towns of the so-called Dutch Barrier. He insisted that the Spanish grant the French the lucrative *Asiento*, the right to trade in slaves between Africa and Spanish America.

Opposition to this sudden expansion of French power took the form of the Treaty of Grand Alliance. This was the work especially of John Churchill, the Earl of Marlborough, representing William III, and the Dutch Grand Pensionary, Heinsius, but it was signed by Austria as well as England and the United Provinces (more or less the modern Netherlands). No sooner had the Grand Alliance been established than Louis rubbed salt into English wounds by appearing beside the deathbed of the deposed James II, exiled in France, and reneging on an earlier agreement, acknowledging his son as the future king. A few days later, on the ex-King's death, James III, the future Old Pretender, was proclaimed the new King of England at St Germains. All but the most extreme Jacobite opinion in England was affronted, for only three months before a Tory parliament had passed an Act of Settlement guaranteeing 'Succession of the Crown in the Protestant line'. The by now inevitable war broke out in the spring of 1702. Max Emanuel, the Elector of Bavaria and father of the dead candidate, who had ambitions on the Austrian Empire, threw in his lot with France.

In the first season of campaigning Marlborough, who commanded the combined Anglo-Dutch army in the Low Countries, succeeded in expelling the French from the valleys of the Maas and Lower Rhine and in capturing Liège. He was created duke in December 1702. At sea, a naval expedition under Sir George Rooke failed abjectly to capture Cadiz but, on its return, fell upon a combined Franco-Spanish fleet in Vigo Bay, inflicting huge losses on the enemy. In the West Indies, meanwhile, a page was added to English naval history when a squadron under the command of Admiral John Benbow conducted a running battle with the French off Santa Marta on the Spanish Main. Benbow ensured his immortality when, his right leg having been smashed by chain shot, he had the carpenter of his flag-ship, the *Bredah*, rig up a cradle on the quarter-deck from which he continued to conduct the fight. Infamously some of his captains refused to join the battle and were subsequently court-martialled and shot. Benbow died of his wounds.

For northern European land and sea forces alike, warfare was confined to the summer half of the year when armies could operate without men and baggage trains disappearing in the mire and fleets could avoid the winter storms. The policy with respect to the armies on the continent had much to be said for it but, with regard to the Navy, opinions were divided. There were those, and King William had been one, who wished to see English bases in the Mediterranean where the fleet could re-fit and spend the winter, protecting merchant trade with the Levant and avoiding the need to run the gauntlet of Biscayan storms and French privateers operating out of Brest and other Breton ports. Sir George Rooke, commander-in-chief of the Anglo-Dutch fleet, had little sympathy with this view, preferring the traditional policy of wintering in home ports.

Opinion was also divided about how the war should be conducted. The High Tories, for whom the very idea of an alliance with the Dutch was deeply distasteful, tended to support the 'blue-water school' whose belief was that the war should be fought entirely at sea in defence and furtherance of English trade with the Americas. Given the fact that Marlborough's military genius was still unproven, they had a case. Even after the great land victories had been won, there were those, including Jonathan Swift in *The Conduct of the Allies*, who clung to this view. Swift's aim was to secure peace, since 'Ten glorious campaigns are passed, and now at last, like the sick man, we are just expiring from all sorts of good symptoms.'

The year 1703 was one of mixed fortunes for the Allies. Marlborough was thwarted by the timidity of the Dutch who were reluctant to take the war to the aggressors. He did succeed in taking Huy, Limburg and Bonn, significant prizes the capture of which made possible, in the following year, his audacious dash across southern Germany to the Danube, victory at Blenheim and the salvation of Vienna. But by the end of the campaigning season of 1703 this was still in the future and he was aware of the danger to the Alliance posed by the French Marshal Villars who, by striking eastwards had joined forces with the Bavarian Elector, thus securing Max Emanuel's continuing loyalty to the French cause. The Duke, by contrast, had been devastated earlier in the year by the loss of his son and heir, a victim of smallpox at Cambridge, seen his plan to capture Antwerp frustrated by the incompetence of Dutch generals and, like Harley, another moderate Tory, was angered by the divisive debates over Occasional Conformity at home.

Likewise at sea there had been nothing to compare with the Battle of Vigo Bay. Sir Cloudesley had shown his flag in the Mediterranean but although his appearance off the Ligurian coast may have persuaded Duke Victor Amadeus of Savoy to abandon Louis in favour of the Allies, he had been unable to bring succour to the French protestants of the Cevennes and had failed to tempt the French navy out of Toulon. Earlier in the year, he had been greatly assisted by the signing of the Methuen Treaty with Portugal, which put the magnificent harbour of Lisbon at his disposal, as well as condemning the country's gentry to a century of port-drinking and gout. The Portuguese, in turn, insisted that an Iberian front be opened up, that the Emperor's son be proclaimed Charles III of Spain and that he come to the Peninsula to fight for his kingdom.

By the end of October, Charles was on the coast of Holland en route for Lisbon via Portsmouth. Sir George Rooke with a squadron of English men-of-war was to provide the escort but the Austrians objected that Rooke lacked the superiority needed to deter a French squadron based at Dunkirk, which they feared might intercept the English admiral and his precious Habsburg cargo. By the time Rooke's force was strengthened valuable time and a fair wind had been lost and the foul weather preceding the Great Storm had set in. The English merchants who traded with Spain were making preparations to present Charles, on his arrival at Spithead, with a gift appropriate to his station and future influence. They were to have a long wait.

Although the bulk of Shovell's fleet was back in the Downs on or about the 17 November, some of the ships were a week or more behind, having received orders to complete further duties before leaving the Mediterranean. A small squadron under George Byng was sent to renew treaties with the Dey of Algiers, a mission which was successfully accomplished only after riding out a severe storm off the coast of Minorca. Before passing through the Straits more ships detached themselves from Shovell's fleet to make similar agreements with the Alcaid of Tangier.

On their return these Moroccan gunship diplomats – of the *Orford*, *Warspite* and *Lichfield* – were further delayed by an action against the French 52-gun vessel *Hasard*. The Frenchman held out bravely for 6 hours against the greatly superior firepower of the English but was eventually compelled to surrender and was taken prize. These delays ensured that both the Algerian and Moroccan ships would arrive in English waters as the Great Storm and its mountainous seas tore up the Channel.

Of the five ships which Rear Admiral Byng had taken to Algiers, the last to arrive off the coast of Cornwall is today the best known. The 70-gun *Hampton Court*, a veteran of the famous victory off Barfleur in 1692, is the subject of one of the finest paintings of the great Dutch maritime artist William van de Velde the Younger. Van de Velde's picture of the *Hampton Court*, to be seen in Birmingham City Art Gallery, depicts the ship in stormy weather against a background of towering black clouds, suggesting worse to come. A tattered union flag streams from the sprit topmast, the fore course flapping furiously as the crew fight to haul it in. This was the golden age of ship adornment and the bow and such as we can see of the stern are richly adorned with carving and gilding, greater attention being paid to such decoration than to efficient handling and battle worthiness. The stern taffrail of the first-rate* *Royal Sovereign*, rebuilt in 1701, for example, included 'an effigie of his majesty [William III] on a horse trampling on the seven-headed hydra. Near him Prudence and Fortitude and two boys holding a Laurel at one end, Neptune sitting on a Fish with his Trident on the other and Arion with his harp sitting on a Fish with the other work such as a

* The rate of a sailing warship referred to the number of guns mounted. At this time it was as follows: first-rate: 100+ guns; second-rate: 84–98 guns; third-rate: 64–80 guns; fourth-rate: 50–60 guns; fifth rate: 32–44 guns; sixth-rate: 20–30 guns. Ships of more than 60 guns were seen as fit to be in the battle line and were classed together as 'ships of the line'. Fourth- and fifth-rates were known as 'frigates'.

Lion, Fox trophies'. The Navy had, according to the maritime historian L. G. Carr Laughton, fallen 'into a slough of meretricious splendour'. The *Hampton Court*, as befits a ship with such a name, was no exception.

By the 25 November 1703 the *Hampton Court*, under Captain Charles Wager, was in the Western Approaches. The usual problems of navigation, especially of fixing longitude, were exacerbated by the atrocious weather in advance of the Great Storm. Land, 'ye Barbary Coast', had last been seen eleven days before and another ship spoken to – a Hamburger bound for Lisbon – on the 19th. Wager's log, from which this information comes, is in a neat, even beautiful, hand – the tails of his 'ds' flying away to the left of the page like pennants from his topmasts – but it lacks something of the power of expression of those of two of his lieutenants. The logs of William Houlding and James Collier, although typically tight-lipped and understated, provide a remarkably robust line to the dramatic events of the hours ahead. A fine sprinkling of dust and particles of soot cover the logs, hinting, even today in the hushed and polished atmosphere of the National Maritime Museum Library, at the 'galley-pepper' which inevitably 'flavoured' the sailors' rations of salt pork and biscuit and doubtless found its way aft into the Officers' Mess and even into the confined quarters of the two lieutenants. They would usually have been written up at the end of each (generally four-hour) watch. Each log is divided into columns recording 'Date', 'Wind' (direction), 'Latitude', 'Longitude' and 'Remarkable Observations and Accidents'. The convention at sea in the early eighteenth century was that the date changed at noon preceding the midnight at which it changed on land but, to avoid, confusion, the date ashore is employed below.

Plotting a course in such dirty weather was a matter of intelligent guesswork or 'judgement', the *Hampton Court*'s position being estimated in relation to that of what English sailors referred to as 'Cape Spratt' or 'Sprate' otherwise Cap Spartel to the west of Tangier, at the entrance to the Straits, the common practice at this time being to express longitude in degrees east or west of a known point of departure. Only with the publication of Maskelyne's *Nautical Almanac* in 1767 did navigators begin to calculate their longitude from Greenwich.

By the end of the eighteenth century the loss of ships in the open sea was virtually unknown, but a hundred years earlier shipwrights were less skilled and navigation was less refined. As the weather worsened, the sailors on board the *Hampton Court* would have been by no means confident that, even if they escaped shipwreck on the treacherous, still unlocated coast of Cornwall, their floating home would not simply break up under stress of weather. Sometimes losses at sea were on a massive scale. All but the youngest cabin boy aboard would have heard with dread of the loss of Sir Francis Wheler's Mediterranean convoy off the coast of Malaga ten years before. Christopher, Viscount Hatton, the Governor of Guernsey described what happened in a letter:

> Mar 27 1693/4
> . . . this day a most dreadful account is come of the Turkey fleet. The *Sussex*, a new 3rd-rate shippe, in which Sir Francis Wheler went Admiral, with all the men except two moors were lost. Sir Francis his body was afterwards found cast ashore.
> The *Cambridge* and *Lumley Castle*, both men-of-war, the *Fortune* fire shippe, the *Serpent* a bomb shippe, the *Mary* and *William*, both tender ketches; 4 merchant shippes bound for Turkey, the *Great George*, the *Aleppo Factor*, the *Indian Merchant*, the *Berkshire*, all bound for Scanderoon [Iskanderun]; the *Golden Frigate* bound for Leghorn; the *William* for Venice; 2 Dutch merchant-men bound for Turkey and one for Leghorn, were all cast away at Gibraltar by a hurricane which happened there, February 19 . . . and all the rest of the fleet terribly shattered and disabled. Besides the shipps and goods which perished, 15,000 sailors were drownded. God make us so truly penitent for our sins as may induce Him to avert His judgements.

In 1744, in an autumn gale far less destructive than the Great Storm, the *Victory*, the Navy's newest first-rate and flagship of Admiral Sir John Balchen, disappeared in the Channel with the loss of 1,100 officers and men.

By the 25 November when Houlding completed his log the *Hampton Court* was reckoned to be some 52 nautical miles (about

60 conventional miles) to the SSW of the Scillies, the weather was squally with bursts of rain, the wind blowing hard and a 'great sea'. During Collier's watch, which ended at eight in the morning, it was still possible to take a sounding using the deep sea lead line, a depth of 80 fathoms indicating that the ship was still not in the relatively shallow water of the Channel proper.

On the morning of the 26th the *Hampton Court* was somewhere in the Chops of the Channel, probably off the Lizard, and experiencing what Houlding ominously summarises as 'thick hurry-durry weather' with a great sea still running. It was probably as day broke that the ship's crew realised that they were no longer in sight of the other vessels of Byng's small squadron, Collier recording that they had 'lost sight of all ye shipping'. In the worsening weather more and more sail was taken in until, eventually, making progress was sacrificed to the exigencies of saving the ship. The order was given to 'lay by a-hull', manoeuvring so that, with the helm lashed to leeward, the wind was on the weather bow in which position she would make no headway but would ride most safely. Not to have taken this precaution but to have run before the gale would have meant that the speed of the ship would have been more or less that of the following sea, the rudder would be rendered useless and there would have been a strong possibility of being 'pooped', the sea crashing over the stern and throwing the vessel off course, until, broadside on to the waves, she would have been in great danger of being rolled over. Furthermore, the stern, with its considerable extent of glazed windows, was a point of weakness in such massively built ships which, once breached, might allow in huge quantities of water.

If such measures proved ineffective it might be necessary to further reduce wind resistance by lowering, or striking, the yards and topmasts and, in the most extreme circumstances, the lower masts would be cut off at deck level – 'cut by the board' – to minimise all resistance above deck. Even on a comparatively small, fourth-rate man-of-war, the 85-ft main mast would rise more than 50 ft from the deck and have a diameter of two feet or more; cutting it down would not have been an easy task. Indeed, how easy it would have been in a howling wind with giant seas breaking over the bow and the decks awash with water to issue such orders, still less to carry them out, is hard to envisage; even the high-pitched tones of the boatswain's pipe being drowned out by the wind shrieking through the rigging, the battering seas and the continual creaking of the ship's timbers.

By the early afternoon, however, the crew of the *Hampton Court* seem to have been offered some respite as the storm moved away northwards. Sails were set and the homeward voyage resumed in seas which at last allowed Henry Winstanley to put out from Plymouth to relieve the beleaguered Eddystone lighthouse.

If the crew of the *Hampton Court* thought that the worst was over they were soon to be violently disabused, for by the late evening they were being brutally savaged by the teeth of the Great Storm itself. In little more than an hour the proud 70-gun man-of-war was reduced to little more than a wave-tossed hull, her deck littered with a tangle of fallen rigging and the splintered remains of masts and yards. James Collier tersely described the events:

> Very hard gales with thick weather . . . at 11 it began to blow Extream hard, lowered our yards but the sails blew all away as did our Main and Mizen topmasts with the violence of the wind. Also the sprit sail which was furled . . .

The likelihood is that the wind was now blowing at force 11 (gale force) or force 12 (hurricane force), most probably the latter. *The Marine Observer's Handbook* describes the appearance of the sea in such conditions. Force 11 means a wind speed of 53–63 knots and:

> exceptionally high waves. The sea completely covered with long, white patches of foam lying along the direction of the wind. Everywhere the edges of the wave crests are blown into froth. Visibility is affected and small and medium sized ships may be lost from view behind the waves.

Force 12 involves winds of 64–71 knots:

> the air is filled with foam and spray. Sea completely white with driving spray: visibility very seriously affected.

'Thick hurry-durry weather' probably describes it just as well.

Neither lieutenant says as much but the probability is that the *Hampton Court* was now being driven before the wind completely out of control, with huge seas breaking over her stern. This appears to be the implication of an entry in Houlding's log:

> . . . abt 2 [on the Saturday morning] shipped a sea over all as well as ye poops, had 5 ft of water in ye Storeroom & much between Decks etc.

Collier, however, refers specifically to water in the 'storerooms forward'. Whatever was the case, the ship must at this point have been in great danger of foundering but, by virtue of what must have been some furious pumping and bailing, good luck and a gradual moderation of the weather, she remained afloat. Although there was still 'stormy weather and a great sea', on the Saturday afternoon they were able to get up a makeshift – or jury – main topmast and rigging and find the shelter of Torbay. The newspaper the *Post Man* carried a report from Dartmouth dated 30 November to the effect that 'the *Hampton Court* is just into Torbay much shattered in her Masts and Rigging in the late Terrible Storm'. The survival of Captain Wager was to have an important, perhaps critical, influence on the outcome of the war.

Although the ships of Queen Anne's navy undoubtedly suffered from design faults, the experience of the *Hampton Court*, with its massive oaken timbers, was probably typical of the ships, both of the royal and merchant navies, caught in the open sea: although badly damaged, most survived, so that during the days following the Storm disabled vessels were struggling into ports all along the Channel coast. From Cowes on the 29th came the report, carried in the *London Gazette*, of the *Nottingham*, a Guernsey privateer, 'who off of Portland was obliged to cut down his Main and Mizen masts, [and] the *King David* of Amsterdam, bound for Santa Cruz who had lost all her masts . . .' Likewise, from Falmouth, came an account of the *Good Intent* of London, Master George Palmer, which arrived on the 29th from Pennsylvania 'laden with furs and tobacco having lost all her Masts which she was forced to cut by the board in the late great storm'. There were also some 'miraculous preservations'; according to Defoe:

> a Guernsey Privateer lost his Fore-top mast and cut his main mast by the Board [and] 12 men washed overboard and by the toss of another immediate sea three of them was put on board again and did very well . . .

the ship eventually finding its way into Lymington River.

Matters were worse for shipping closer inshore, even in what might normally be regarded as safe havens. Many of the most powerful gusts during the passage of the Storm up the Channel would have come from the south-west quarter so that much of the south coast of England would have formed a lee shore, a coastline on to which the wind was blowing. Any ship in the offing of a lee shore was in danger of being blown on to the coast and wrecked. The nature of the coastline itself was of crucial importance in determining the consequences of such stranding. To be thrown up on a beach of sand or shingle or cast on to a salt marsh or mudflat did not mean inevitable destruction but much of the south coast is made of hard, cliff-forming strata, beneath which lie jagged, hull breaking platforms of wave-cut rock. In the kind of seas generated by hurricane-force winds, ships stranded on such coasts, pounded by huge waves, would be rapidly broken up. To run aground on offshore shoals or sandbanks would likewise mean virtually certain destruction. A further hazard was from other disabled, uncontrollable ships being driven before the wind. In such a collision one or both vessels might be holed below the waterline or their rigging and timbers become inextricably entangled, uniting the fate of the least with that of the most severely damaged craft. While such collisions could happen anywhere, the greater density of inshore shipping rendered coastal waters more susceptible to such accidents.

As the Storm blasted its way up the Channel one port after another suffered losses. In the South West even the fine natural harbour of Falmouth – described in *The Pilot's Guide to the English Channel* as 'the safest harbour along the Devon and Cornwall coasts' – with its deep water inlet, protecting hillslopes and the high natural breakwater of Pendennis Point, although accustomed to frequent Atlantic gales, reported 'the most tempestuous weather that hath been known in the memory of Man'. Several ships in the harbour were driven from their anchors and thrown on shore, while on the Pendennis peninsula, perched high on the headland, Henry VIII's castle, the last royalist stronghold in Cornwall to surrender in the Civil War, suffered 'great Damage' as did many of the houses in and about the town of Falmouth.

In the days ahead most of the vessels blown ashore were re-floated, although a packet boat, the *Mansbridge* was feared lost, and scattered ships of the Virginia fleet, separated from their convoy, the men-of-war *Guernsey* and *Oxford*, 'in a storm about 300 leagues from the Capes', continued to struggle into port. The warships themselves were no longer in a position to offer assistance. The *Guernsey* had encountered the Great Storm as she headed east for the Channel. According to the ship's log, at nine o'clock on the Friday evening she met with:

> a violent storm of SW by W insomuch that all our topsails blew loose from the yards, we lost our foretops and foretopmast spritsail, topsail and topmast skysail which blew all in pieces. At 11 lowered mainyard, at 12 [midnight] our ship would not live with a foresail and we splitt and clew from the yard, we shipped a great sea which washed away all our powder in the lower room. The fish room was also filled with water and we lost a great deal of Oyle. We had in the body of the ship, 4 foot and a half of water . . . we lay a-hull the wind bearing to the west. At 10 [on the morning of the 27th] the wind abated . . .

Two or three degrees eastwards the experience of the *Oxford* was similar. She encountered a 'very violent gale of wind pticularly [sic] from 8 till twelve at night'. The foresail was split and she subsequently endured other, unspecified 'accidents'.

From Plymouth itself came news of what has proved the most enduring story of the Storm – the loss of the Eddystone lighthouse. As well as the personal tragedies involved, to which we will return, this was a loss, 'a considerable damage' in Defoe's words, which threatened the future prosperity of the port and the effectiveness of the Royal Navy. At Plymouth itself, near to which a naval dockyard had been established in 1696 and at Dock, later, more euphoniously, Devonport, three or four merchant ships were 'castaway and one was stranded but many of the men saved'. This latter was probably the *George of London*, a brigantine commanded by Samuel Lawrence and bound for Guinea and therefore, in all likelihood, a slaver which, by the end of November had been 'got off without much damage'. Of the two warships at anchor in the Sound when the Storm struck, the *Mermaid* rode out the weather but the *Mark* was driven near to the shore and her captain was obliged to cut all her masts by the board to save his ship. Even in the Hamoaze Channel, sheltered by Torpoint, several men-of-war drew from their moorings and the 61-gun *Defiance* was driven ashore.

The county town of Devonshire, although some distance from the open sea, suffered extensively in the Storm. According to the 1731 revision of Richard Izacke's *Remarkable antiquities of the city of Exeter*, '. . . about eleven at night there arose a most terrible tempest of wind, which continued till past four in the morning . . . Most of the houses in the City . . . felt the effects thereof, several stacks of chimneys thrown down, beating in the very roofs before 'em: but by the good providence of God, not one person hurt.'

The approach to Exeter is today protected by the substantial sand spit of Dawlish Warren which projects across the mouth of the Exe estuary for a distance of 1½ miles from the western shore between Dawlish and Starcross. In the early eighteenth century, however, the Warren extended westwards from the eastern (Exmouth) shore so that the opposite bank of the estuary was exposed to storm attack. The sea driving into the estuary on the night of the Storm dammed up the waters of the Exe and caused widespread flooding of the lowland around Powderham to the south-west of the city. A similar effect was repeated on a far greater scale about the coasts of the Bristol Channel.

Plymouth and Falmouth are both fine natural harbours but, further east, the far smaller port of Lyme Regis is a man-made harbour originally created in the reign of Edward I – the *rex* of the town's title. The port was formed by the building of the Cobb, a pier initially of wood but later of stone, which serves as both a breakwater and quay. It was, of course, in a fictional future, to be the site of Louisa Musgrove's dramatic and fateful fall in Jane Austen's *Persuasion*. Eighteen years earlier it was here that the Duke of Monmouth had landed at the beginning of that disastrously ill-starred adventure. This event was, doubtless, uneasily recalled by Defoe on opening a letter from his correspondent Stephen Bowdidge of Lyme informing him that five boats were driven out of the Cobb and one of them lost in the Storm. The writer reflected that 'had the Hurricane happened at High Water the Cob must without doubt have been destroyed and all the vessels in it lost'. Today, it should be said, the harbour very nearly dries out at low tide and consequently affords very little shelter in bad weather.

Five or six miles to the east of Lyme, beneath the cliffs below Golden Cap an 8-gun Guernsey privateer was driven ashore and only three of the crew of forty-three saved. For Lyme Regis itself further disaster lay ahead; the War so disrupted her trade that an irreversible decline set in. Only when she re-emerged as a seaside resort at the end of the eighteenth century did the town's fortunes begin to recover.

Further up the Channel the waters about the Isle of Wight, including as they do the approaches to Southampton and Portsmouth as well as the island harbours of Cowes and St Helen's (Bembridge), were, as they still are, one of the busiest parts of the English coastline. There were some navigational aids. At the western side of the entrance to Lymington River there is a beacon, a timber post with cagework, known as Jack-in-the-Basket. It, or rather its ancestor, enjoying exactly the same name, was already there in 1698 when it appeared in a survey of the south coast carried out at the behest of Government by the Surveyor-General, Edward Dummer, and Captain Thomas Wiltshaw.

Such navigational aids were, however, few and at night-time and in bad weather when landmarks were obscured, places such as the Needles Channel at the western entrance to the Solent were fraught with danger. At the eastern side of Christchurch Bay lie the Shingles, an especially hazardous shoal which rises abruptly from the floor of the Channel. Then, protruding out a mile and half into the sea from the Hampshire coast to the east of Milford, is the Hurst Castle spit. Running NW to SE this shingle bank, created by the easterly drift of beach material, had reached the very edge of the deep water passage and lay across the course of vessels seeking the safety of Lymington or Cowes. Celia Fiennes recognised the dangers posed by the Needles themselves, describing them as 'severall Great Rocks on that side of the island, craggy, and severall stand out in to the sea which makes it very hazardous for shipps to pass there especially in a Storme'. Furthermore, dangerous ledges of rock form an abrupt edge to the safe channel and while the white chalk stacks of the Needles are at least conspicuous, they are surrounded by submerged reefs. A ship such as the third-rate man-of-war the *Monmouth*, which had been off Start Point when the Storm broke but by daybreak was approaching the Needles in weather that was 'almost inexpressable', with all her sails blown away and tiller rope broken, was clearly in a precarious position.

The Storm wrought havoc all about the Island; dismasting, wrecking and sinking ships, drowning whole crews and washing men overboard. One of the first reports to reach London, dated 27 November, came from Portsmouth:

> Last night we had a very violent Storm of Wind which held at the height from 12 till about 5 this morning. We have in sight 6 or 7 wrecks, 4 or 5 of them to the eastward of Southsea Castle and 2 upon Gilkicker Point. We hear that all our transports from Ireland ride it out except the loss of some of their Masts which will be easily repaired.

This, somewhat complacent account, which appeared in the *London Gazette*, was followed by a far more alarming report, also from Portsmouth, in the rival *The Post Man*:

> On Friday it blew here a perfect Hurricane which has done so much damage to the houses of this place that 10,000 pounds will not make good the same and there is scarce a Man of War at Spithead which has not received damage. We have an account that about 12 sail of stout ships have been driven ashoar and staved. There are at Spithead 10 sail of men of War.

The same newspaper carried news from Cowes that the *Swallow*, a ketch from Lisbon and a transport ship with soldiers aboard bound for Ireland had been driven from the Roads and were still unheard of. From Lymington Defoe learnt of the *Assistance* of 200 tons from Maryland, laden with tobacco, 'cast away upon Hurst Beach'; one of the mates and four sailors were lost. According to another account 'the master, mate and all men' were lost, including four who got ashore but appear to have died of exposure.

From Newport on the Isle of Wight Defoe also heard, albeit rather imprecisely, of wrecks on the south coast of the island, a notorious lee shore in a south to south-westerly gale such as the Great Storm. 'Several ships are stranded on the south and south-west coasts of our island . . . some say 7, others 8, 12 and some say 15.' One of this indeterminate number was almost certainly the tin ship blown from her anchors in the Helford River in Cornwall and driven, '80 leagues in 8 hours' according to Defoe, eventually to be 'miraculously run in between two rocks' on the back of the island and the crew – of two boys and a man – 'all preserved'. There is, perhaps, a greater chance that its cargo was retrieved than that of the *Swallow* which had disappeared from Cowes Roads. This ketch, 'laden with wines from Lisbon', was blown across the Solent running aground in Stokes Bay near Gosport. Rather more exotically, another Portuguese vessel, driven from anchor off Newlyn in Cornwall was cast ashore near Marazion with a cargo of oranges and lemons.

Others were less fortunate than the crew of the tin ship. Of the men-of-war at Spithead, the 638 ton, 50-gun *Newcastle* and the *Lichfield Prize* were feared lost on the Dean Sands at the entrance to Langston Harbour. The fireship *Vesuvius* was driven on shore near Southsea Castle, while another fireship, the *Firebrand*, and a hospital ship, the *Jeffreys* were driven on to the Spit Sand but later got off again. The *Lichfield Prize* was eventually re-floated but the *Newcastle* sustained the greatest casualties; of the 50-year-old ship's complement of 233, 197, including the commander, Captain William Carter, were lost.

On the 26 November the third-rate warship *Resolution*, Captain Thomas Lyell, was anchored off Bembridge Point unable to take advantage of the relative shelter and secure holding ground of St

Helen's Roads owing to the high wind. Soon after midnight she lost both anchors and was driven before the wind, striking 'at least five times' the dangerous shoals of the Owers, off Selsey Bill but, fortunately, continuing to drive eastwards until she was eventually thrown ashore between Beachy Head and Hastings. All of her crew of 211 survived but the *Resolution* was lost. Had she been stranded on the shoals – the Outer Owers are five miles offshore – the sailors' chances of telling their Great Storm yarns would have been slim.

Even at Southampton, 'one of the finest harbours in the world . . . so well protected as to prevent the rise of any very rough sea', according to *The Pilot's Guide*, the Storm had devastating effects. George Powell, Defoe's correspondent, wrote:

> We had most of the Ships in our River and those laid off from our Keys blown ashoar, some partly torn to Wrecks and three or four blown so far on Shoar with the Violence of the Wind, that the Owners have been at the Charges of unloading them and dig large channels for the Spring Tides to float them off, it being on a soft sand or Mud, [they] had but little Damage . . . few or no houses have escape't . . .

South coast towns more exposed than Southampton to the fierce onslaught of the Storm as it tore in from the sea suffered devastating damage, sometimes adversely influencing their economic fortunes for decades. The mile and a half separating Christchurch from the sea seems to have afforded the town little protection. Defoe's correspondent, William Mitchel, informed him that:

> We had a great part of the Roof of our Church [the Priory] uncovered which was covered with very large Purbick-stone and the battlements of the Tower and part of the leads blown down, some stones of a vast weight blown from the Tower, several of them between two and three hundred weight were blown some Rods or Perches distance from the Church; and 12 sheets of Lead were rouled up together, that 20 men could not have done the like, to the great Amazement of those that saw 'em.

The uncovering of the slate roof of the nave in fact created a hole 30 ft long by 12 ft wide. Something similar occurred in the severe storm of January 1990.

In Sussex the coastal towns of Shoreham and Brighton [then Brighthelmstone] were both badly damaged. At Shoreham, at the mouth of the Adur, the Market House, 'an Antient and very strong building' was 'blown flat to the ground and all the Town shattered'. At some time before 1720 the nave of the magnificent church of St Mary de Hawra (meaning 'of the harbour') collapsed and it is tempting to suggest that this may have been, in part at least, a consequence of structural harm inflicted by the Storm. By 1720 a passing traveller noted 'the ruins of many large buildings', suggesting that the town had still not recovered from the blasting it had received earlier in the century.

Prior to the building of modern sea defences and the stabilisation of the beach by the construction of groynes, Brighton was always susceptible to the depredations of the sea. In 1340 the village and 150 acres thereabouts was inundated and there were a number of sea floods early in the seventeenth century. Today all that remains of the medieval settlement is the Old Steine, where the fishermen dried their nets, and the church of St Nicholas, built on a hill to the north-west of the original site along the shore. There was no port, the boats being hauled up on to the shingle. By the time the Great Storm struck, Brighton was already in decline; the population of about 1,450 being less than half of that of the year 1580. Although the Storm severely damaged the fabric of the little town, turning up the leads on the church roof, flattening two windmills and causing such widespread devastation that 'the town in general looked as if it had been bombarded', the loss of life, especially in the light of the demographic crisis, may have had a worse long-term effect. A correspondent of Defoe's listed the casualties:

> Derrick Pain, Junior, Master of the *Elizabeth* Ketch of this Town lost, with all his Company. George Taylor, Master of the Ketch called the *Happy Entrance* lost and his Company, excepting Walter Street, who swimming three days on a Mast between the Downs and north Yarmouth was at last taken up. Richard

West, Master of the Ketch called the *Richard and Rose* lost with all his Company near St Helen's. Edward Friend, Master of the Ketch called *Thomas and Francis*, stranded near Portsmouth. Edward Glover, Master of the Pink called *Mary* driven over to Hamborough [Hamburg] from the Downs having lost his Anchors, Cables and Sails. Robert Kitchen, Master of the *Chomley* Pink of Brighton lost . . . with 9 men. Five men and one boy saved by another vessel.

Two years later, Brighton was hit by another, more local, storm which demolished the lower town, engulfing the wreckage of the houses in shingle. Lacking any great benefactor or patron to inject the kind of capital needed to revitalise the place, Brighton's decline continued. By 1744, of 455 houses, 336 were exempt from property taxes because of poverty. Only with the arrival, in the 1750s, of Dr Richard Russell with his *Dissertation concerning the Use of Sea Water in Diseases of the Glands*, did the fortunes of the town begin to change and the collection of impoverished fishermen's hovels begin the makeover that would transform it into 'Old Ocean's Bauble'.

Back at Portsmouth the responsibility for organising the retrieval and repair of the Navy's scattered and shattered assets about Spithead fell to George Byng, recently returned from Algiers. The newspaper reports of the condition of the ships arriving in the Channel ports after the Storm often tell a good deal less than the full story. The dry as dust, official government newspaper the *London Gazette* in particular seems to have aimed, wherever possible, to understate the degree of damage suffered by the fleet (in Paris, by contrast, the impression was given that scarcely an Englishman remained afloat). The report, for example, carried in the *Gazette* and dated 29 November that 'Rear Admiral Byng came to St Helen's the 28th [sic] instant with H.M. Ships *Ranelagh*, *Monmouth* and *Montague*' neglects to mention the state of the vessels and the means by which their crews brought them safely into harbour.

Byng's flagship the *Ranelagh* had, if anything, endured an even greater mauling at the mercy of wind and waves than had the

Hampton Court. Having sighted the Lizard early on the day of the Storm, she was probably off Start Point late on the Friday night when the violence of the weather suddenly started to increase and within a short space of time had lost all her sails and, as the fury of the weather increased, Byng was obliged to issue the order to cut down the main and mizen masts. A succession of disasters then ensued. A gun broke lose and, careering about the gundeck, holed the ship's side, adding to the amount of water rapidly filling the hold. Then, with all hands pumping and bailing, the chain pump broke. With the level continuing to rise, a crewman, later rewarded with a gunner's warrant, dived under water to mend it. By daybreak the wind was beginning to ease but then the tiller broke at the head of the rudder, necessitating several hours of repair work. In the afternoon of the 27th, the shattered ship, with its exhausted crew, dropped anchor in St Helen's Road.

Byng sent a letter to the Navy Board detailing the damage done to his and other ships at St Helen's and, on the grounds that he was ill, requested permission to go up to London. Permission was refused: 'the damages Her Majesty's Ships have received at Spithead making it necessary for [him] to continue at [his] Duties'. It was perhaps as well for Byng who was made flag officer in charge. It was certainly as well for two seamen, condemned to death for desertion but pardoned by Byng on the grounds that the service could not afford to lose another man. They were the first of several, both sailors and civilians who, over the months ahead, were to substitute a life at sea for death at the end of the hangman's rope.

Devastating as had been the Storm in the Channel, many men, ships and cargoes had been lost but it was for the loss of one man that the Storm would be remembered.

6

This Fatal Piece

The 'Protestant' easterly wind which, in 1688, had allowed William of Orange to sail down the Channel and land at Torbay while trapping King James's navy in the Thames, had demonstrated the inadequacy of that river as a centre for naval operations. At the same time, greatly improved French west coast ports, such as Brest and Rochefort, posed a threat to English shipping, which demanded the establishment of a major base to the west of Portsmouth. The decision to locate that new base at Plymouth, or, more precisely, on the Hamoaze, part of the Tamar estuary to the west of the town, at what was to be known as Dock, was taken in 1690.

The greatest drawback to the use of the Devon base, however, was the presence 14 miles south of Plymouth Hoe, of the deadly Eddystone Rocks. Consisting of three reefs, the Western, Southern and Northern, and other isolated rocks, at low water they occupy an area of about one square mile, and at high water spring tides all are submerged. They are jagged, steeply inclined gneissic rocks, ideal keel-ripping material, and extremely difficult to build on.

Within little more than a year of the decision to build a Royal Naval dockyard at Plymouth, the Elders of Trinity House, the authority responsible for navigational aids, were approached with a proposal to build a lighthouse on the Eddystone. Trinity House could not itself grant permission to build – that could only come from the Crown – but a proposal which did not come via the 'Corporation of Trinity House on Deptford Strond' stood little chance of success. The petition came from a man of whom little is known other than that he was called Walter Whitfield and that his petition was successful. Once the light was in place and functioning, dues could be collected from the passing shipping: one penny per ton on all outward- and inward-bound vessels and twelve pence per voyage on coasters.

Having received the royal patent in June 1694, Whitfield, inexplicably, delayed the beginning of building work which, in any case had to be confined to a relatively short, with luck, storm-free, summer season. The summer of the following year came and went and still no progress had been made. There then occurred an event which would trigger rapid and dramatic developments. On Christmas Eve, 1695, yet another ship, the *Constant*, struck the Rocks. Ship, crew and cargo were lost to the dismay of the ship's owner, an Essex businessman, Henry Winstanley. Winstanley, who had all the qualities that Whitfield appeared to lack – ability, dynamism and, not least, an incredible nerve – entered into partnership with the patent-holder who rapidly ceased to play any further part in the project. Although a wave-swept lighthouse had existed on the Cordouan Rock at the mouth of the Gironde estuary for over a century, the reef connecting rock to shore is exposed at low tide. This was to be the first ever genuine off-shore lighthouse.

If Winstanley was rash in taking on such a daunting scheme, his impetuosity was not that of youth. His fiftieth birthday was already behind him; he had been baptised at Saffron Walden in Essex on 31 March 1644. Although Henry never received any kind of architectural training he had been brought up in an environment of remarkable architectural singularity, his father being head steward in the great house of the Earl of Suffolk at Audley End. It may well have been Winstanley senior who showed Samuel Pepys around the house in 1660:

> . . . the housekeeper showed us all the house; in which the stateliness of the ceilings, chimney pieces, and form of the whole was exceedingly worth seeing. He took us into the cellars where we drank most admirable drink, a health to the King. Here I played on my Flagelette, there being an excellent Echo. He showed us excellent pictures; two especially those of the Evangelistes and Henry 8th. After that I gave the man 2s for his trouble . . .

Revisiting Audley End in 1667 Pepys was rather less impressed: 'the house doth appear very fine, but not so fine as it hath heretofore to me'. It had, in fact, been badly damaged in the storm of 'Windy Tuesday', 18 February, 1662.

The Audley End we see today is only a fragment of the seventeenth-century pile; Celia Fiennes, who visited in 1697, gives an idea of the Gormenghast-like scale of the building which Winstanley knew so well:

> Then we went to Audleyend a house of the Earle of Sussex [sic] which made a noble appearance like a town, so many towers and buildings of stone within a parke which is walled round . . . its built round 3 Courts, there are 30 great and little towers on the top and a great Cupilow in the middle, the roomes are large and lofty with good rich old furniture, tapestry etc . . . there are 750 roomes in the house.

The satirical humourist Ned Ward may not have been greatly exaggerating in suggesting that 'it is a day's work for a running footman to open and shut the windows'. Such was Audley End, the largest house in England, where Henry Winstanley grew up. Before he reached adulthood he was himself on the payroll, initially, it appears, as a porter. Eventually he became estate manager.

At some stage in his early life he had learnt to draw and by the time he was twenty-five he had developed the skills of an engraver and had commercially produced a set of 'geographical playing cards'. The suits of the pack represented the four continents of Europe, America, Asia and Africa, the individual cards each representing a country, the chief characteristics of which are described on the face of the card. Winstanley's ingenuity combines with what was very probably a genuine enthusiasm for learning in the suggestion that 'to make them profitable to a youth that shall desire them, I would give them one by one to him as he shall have learnt them by heart'.

In 1688 he combined his interests in engraving and architecture by publishing *Plans, Elevations, and Particular prospects of Audley End* which consists of twenty-four line drawings of the house. A surviving 'advertisement', circulated by Winstanley, offered to make copper-plate engravings of the 'mansion houses' of the nobility and of gentlemen, 'to be printed for composing a volume of the Prospects of the principal Houses of England', claiming that he had seen 'most of the famosest houses in France, Italy and Germany'. This sounds like a rather extravagant boast but it does appear that Winstanley, probably in his late teens, had travelled on the continent, possibly accompanying one of the young gentlemen of the Howard family on a grand tour. When it came to designing his lighthouse he certainly showed a familiarity with the architecture of classical and more recent, Mediterranean lighthouses.

On marrying his wife Elizabeth in the early 1670s, Henry embarked upon the building of his own house in the nearby village of Littlebury. It was here that his individuality and inventiveness perhaps found their truest expression. House and garden were laid out as a kind of prototype theme park; visitors, who passed through a turnstile, were charged one shilling for entrance and then treated to a tour of all manner of clockwork and water-driven contrivances. A German traveller, Zacharias Conrad von Uffenbach, described 'a water theatre in which tea and coffee were laid on in pipes and cups presented to the company. At the close all the pipes threw jets of water.' Celia Fiennes visited Littlebury, 'a house with abundance of Curiosityes all performed by Clockwork and such like', after going round Audley End in 1697. The 'Master' being absent at the time of Miss Fiennes' visit (given the date he would have been in, or on his way to, Plymouth) she was able to see no more than the chair on rails which conveyed the visitor from house to garden. As well as the Littlebury attraction, popularly known as the 'Smiling House', Winstanley combined his skills in hydraulics and showmanship to create 'Winstanley's Waterworkes', near Hyde Park in London, a spectacular entertainment of fountains, waterfalls and other fluvial delights. From this background as a kind of hydraulic impresario Winstanley was to move into an altogether harsher aquatic environment.

Work on the lighthouse had actually begun in July of 1696 by which time he had surveyed the Rocks, chosen the site – on the Western or, as it was to become known, House Rock – and completed his designs. The task of construction was by no means a simple one. Keeping a foothold on slippery, steeply-inclined, wind- and wave-swept rock could not have been easy and even to reach and successfully land at the site could pose major difficulties. Winstanley had the assistance of a man-of-war, the *Terrible*, which, ideally, would sail within a short distance of the Rocks allowing the workmen and their equipment to be rowed to the reef in a long boat. In practice, as Jason Semmens, the most recent historian of the Eddystones, has pointed out, matters were rarely so straightforward. On some days the weather was so calm that the *Terrible* could get nowhere near the Rocks, entailing either a long, time-consuming and exhausting row or the abandonment of work altogether. In bad weather it was impossible to land on the rock and progress was again held up. The first season's work was confined, in Winstanley's words, to:

> . . . making twelve holes in the Rock and fastening twelve great Irons to hold the Work that was to be done afterwards, the Rock being so hard and the time so short by reason of the Tides and Weather and the distance from the shore and the many Journeys lost that there could be no landing at all and many times glad to land at our return at places that if weather permitted would take up the next day to get to Plymouth again.

By mid-August the holes had been painstakingly drilled and the rods, about twelve feet long and three inches in diameter had been dropped into them and set in place with molten lead. Such seems to have been the sum of the first season's endeavours.

The second building season, that of 1697, seems to have got off to a good start. The *Terrible* was still assisting Winstanley and his men and the two weeks following 10 June saw uninterrupted progress. On 25th of the month the Admiralty's resident Commissioner at Plymouth, George St Lo, went out to inspect the work. The weather was fine and settled and Winstanley felt confident that he and his men could now be left overnight on the rock, the building now being high enough to offer some protection from the sea. St Lo agreed and returned to Plymouth: the *Terrible* went off cruising. Although the Nine Years' War with France was shortly to be concluded, at this point the Treaty of

Ryswick was some months from being signed and French privateers were still active in the Channel. Alas for Winstanley, the comings and goings about the Eddystone had probably already attracted interest and no sooner had the *Terrible* disappeared over the horizon than a Frenchman hove into sight, raided the island and made him a prisoner of King Louis.

Once the Admiralty learnt of Winstanley's capture they reprimanded St Lo and began negotiations for the prisoner's return. The French monarch, who took a personal interest in the affair (in piquant contrast to the presumably shame-faced 'Engineer' who, in his written account of his work, makes no mention of his kidnapping), took the enlightened view that that the lighthouse would be of benefit to mankind in general and not to his enemies in particular and the builder was quickly released and returned. Within a fortnight of his capture work had resumed and, by the end of the summer, Winstanley described how his time had been spent:

> . . . in making a solid Body or kind of round Pillar twelve foot high and fourteen feet Diamiter and then we had more time to work at the place, and a little better landing, having some small shelter from the Work and something to hold by but we had great trouble to carry off and land so many Materials, and be forced to secure all things as aforesaid every night and time we left work, or return them again in the Boats.

In the third year Winstanley and his men were able to stay on the rock for a prolonged period, greatly increasing the length of the working day and, consequently, far more was achieved than in the previous years:

> . . . the aforesaid pillar was made good at the Foundations from the Rock to sixteen foot Diamiter and all the work was raised to the Vain which was Eighty foot, being finished . . .

Winstanley, no doubt anxious to receive a revenue in return for a very considerable outlay, had worked on through the autumn and eventually, on 14 November 1698, the 60 candles in the lantern room were lit and the first Eddystone lighthouse sent out its beneficent rays across the approaches to Plymouth Sound.

The weather immediately turned unpleasant and it was not until three days before Christmas that Winstanley and his men were relieved and the first offshore lighthouse-man and his wife took up their duties.

Henry Winstanley was by no means the kind of fly-by-night entrepreneur to disappear as soon as the work was completed. If anything he was a perfectionist who wanted to reassure himself that all was well. He would conscientiously visit the Eddystone every spring and autumn. When he returned to the rock in the spring of 1699 he discovered signs of deterioration at the base of the pillar, where the cement may not have ever properly dried out, while the lighthouse-men reported the occasional 'burying' of the lantern by the sea, 'although more than sixty Foot high'.

Winstanley immediately set about encasing the house in 'a new Work of more than four feet thickness from the foundation, making all solid nearly 20 foot high and taking down the upper part of the first Building and enlarging every part in its proportion, I raised it 40 feet higher than it was at first'.

Winstanley's construction was quite unlike the modern conception of what a lighthouse, especially one on a wave-swept reef, should be like. With its baroque cupola and lantern, ornamental exterior candlesticks, saluting gallery and cranes, it looks like nothing so much as a product of the inventively absurd genius of William Heath Robinson. Still smarting under his ignominious treatment at the hands of the French in 1697 he even included 'a moving Engine Trough, to cast down stones to defend the landing place in case of need'. Neither wind- nor wave-resistance seems to have figured prominently in Winstanley's design. The protruding beams, chutes and ornaments were conceived with anything but aerodynamic efficiency in mind and, although the 1699 modification replaced what was originally an eight-sided building with one of twelve sides, it would still be inclined to meet rather than deflect the full force of the waves. In at least one respect, however, history has underrated Winstanley's lighthouse; it is often, misleadingly, referred to as a wooden structure. The Victorian historian Earl Stanhope described it as 'not of stone but of timber; and judging from the designs of it that remain, it resembled in some degree a Chinese Pagoda.' Had it been entirely of wood it is difficult to imagine that it would have survived one, let alone five, Channel winters. In fact, the lowest 45 ft of the 122 ft tall structure was of stone.

The point has often been made that Winstanley's fatal error was to build a Mediterranean-style lighthouse of a kind that might have been suitable in a tideless sea with limited wave energy, in an exposed, high energy Atlantic environment to which it was totally unsuited. Two points must, however, be kept in mind: first, the extent to which Winstanley, in managing to build any kind of structure on so difficult a site, was an innovator; secondly, that the lighthouse survived five 'normal' winters and the Storm which toppled it was altogether exceptional, in terms of frequency-magnitude, perhaps the 500-year storm, possibly rarer even than that. Henry Winstanley was, without doubt, a very unlucky man.

Perhaps it was the very fact that the weather in advance of the Great Storm had been so bad that the conscientious Winstanley was persuaded to visit the lighthouse in November, 1703. Half a century later John Smeaton, who built the third Eddystone lighthouse, was told in Plymouth that Winstanley, prior to setting out for the light, had boasted that the strength of his lighthouse was such that he wanted nothing more than to be there 'in the greatest storm that ever blew under the face of the heavens'. How true the story is it is impossible to say although it certainly has those elements, of hubristic aptness, which are often, under such circumstances, the hallmarks of invention.

There must have been a sufficient lull in the weather between the passage of the preceding storm, Lieutenant Houlding's 'thick hurry-durry weather' and the arrival of the Great Storm to allow Winstanley on the morning of the 26 November to sail for the lighthouse in the supply ship, to disembark and allow the ship to return to Plymouth. As night fell and the violence of the weather again increased, those remaining on the Rock – Winstanley and two others, according to Stanhope – could have been in little doubt as to the danger they were in. At some time that night the 60-ft high waves shattered the lantern and the frail wooden superstructure and dislodged the great supporting beams, sea water pouring down through the interior of the lighthouse. At what stage Winstanley and his companions succumbed to the waves we shall never know.

Nor do we know a great deal of what his fellow countrymen thought of Henry Winstanley, although his 'ingenuity' was often praised, and the nature of his death means there is no alabaster monument to record his virtues. When we consider his works, however, from the novelty 'geographical playing cards' to the 'Smiling House' and the 'Waterworkes' and most of all when we contemplate his beautiful engraving of the 'Edy-Stone Light-House', dedicated to Prince George, the Lord High Admiral, we cannot but admire him, for they seem to contain a love of life and a hugely attractive combination of utility and entertainment. To the engraving of the lighthouse, Henry's wife, Elizabeth, had a small amendment made; the following words:

The Light House was built
Stood untill that Dreadfull
Storm of 27th of November
1703 which destroyed both
it and the Ingenious Projector
Henry Winstanley, Gent.

Many delightful Curiosityes
of his Invention Severall
Drawings and Engravings
of Copper plates, he has left
which are Preserved.
This Fatall Peice which was
His last Work, may serve for his
Monument, the House being his
Tomb the Sea his Grave.

The story is told that not only was the lighthouse itself destroyed during the Great Storm but so too was a model of the lighthouse which featured among the attractions of the 'Smiling House'. The Eddystone historian Jason Semmens describes as a 'colourful tradition' the story that for as long as the model stood so too did Elizabeth's faith in the durability of the lighthouse proper but that as soon as the model blew over 'she knew that she had become a widow and would not be shaken from the conviction that the Eddystone lighthouse was no more'. 'Colourful' as this tradition may be, however, it does seem likely that the model was in fact destroyed. The story of the loss is certainly reported by Defoe within a few months of the event.

Daniel Defoe, in telling the story of the destruction of the Eddystone lighthouse, concluded, with less than his usual prescience, ''tis very doubtful whether it will ever be attempted again'. In fact, of course, Winstanley's monument has been the succession of lighthouses which have stood on the Eddystone Rocks, the next only six years after the Great Storm. His pioneering work initiated an enterprise which, over the course of three centuries, must have prevented many hundreds of lives being lost.

The value of a light on the dangerous Eddystone reef was made almost immediately and devastatingly clear when, just two nights after the Great Storm, the *Winchelsea*, an armed merchantman of 22 guns and 28 men, part of the widely dispersed Virginia fleet, with a cargo of 450 hogsheads of tobacco, was lost on the rocks. Only six of the crew, including Captain Reed, survived. During a storm in the winter of 1881/2 when the present lighthouse was being built on a low rock some 45 yards to the south-east of House Rock, the remains of a cannon were thrown up which may well be, as the workmen who found it believed, a last fragment of the *Winchelsea*. It must certainly have served to remind them of the vital importance of their life-saving work.

A nineteenth century authority on lighthouses, W. J. Hardy, summed up the impression which the loss of Winstanley and the first Eddystone light had on the nation's collective memory: '. . . the memory of this terrible gale lingered long in the minds of those who experienced it, the papers of the day are filled with accounts of pitiable disasters and of hairbreadth escapes; but no incident made a deeper impression in the mind of the public than the overthrow of Winstanley's lighthouse. . . .'

7

THIS FAR THE WATERS CAME

The 26 of November, at night, 1703 a very Tempestuous wind which did strip, and blowe down houses and mills; and Churches received hurt and in the morning being Satterday the sea broak in and drowned the Parishes – Pawlett, Huntspill, Burnham Brean, Lympsham grounds and both Brents – very much hurt by loss of goods.

(From Overseer's Book, parish of Mark, Somerset)

As the Storm roared in from the south-west it caused huge problems around the shores of the Bristol Channel and from Milford Haven to the head of the Severn estuary. In terms of the damage inflicted upon property and livestock this was very probably the worst affected part of the kingdom. The nascent insurance industry being at this time almost exclusively concerned with marine and fire policies, it is not possible to use insurance claims, as we do today, as a guide to the extent and geographical impact of the Storm*. Initial estimates certainly placed the losses sustained at Bristol far above those of other provincial towns and cities. A report from there carried by the *Post Man* and dated 27 November, while quite probably over-

* The Storm of 15–16 October 1987, for example, which affected a rather less extensive area than that of the Great Storm, produced insurance claims of £860 million. If an estimate for uninsured loss is added, total losses probably exceeded £1000 million.

estimating the extent of the losses, explains why the damage received was so great:

> Last night a violent storm of wind happened here, which blew down a Church and did damage to several other Fabricks, killing several persons and the Tyde flowed so high in the streets that several hogsheads of tobacco were found floating insomuch that the damage sustained in this City and by the shipping in harbour is computed at £150,000.

This compares with estimates of £12,000 at Gloucester, £10,000 at Portsmouth and £3000 at King's Lynn. The figure for London was thought to be in excess of £1 million. The particular problem in Bristol was the flooding of warehouse cellars, many of them recently re-stocked as the West Indian and Virginian fleets had arrived. Indeed it was said that 'there was never known so great a quantity of sugar, tobacco etc. accumulated in the City as at this time'. According to Defoe, 1,000 hogsheads of sugar and 1,500 of tobacco were spoiled. Summarising the damage done 'by the Tide on the banks of the Severn', Defoe estimated the loss of '15,000 sheep on one level, multitudes of cattle on all sides and the covering of lands with salt water' at 'above £200,000'.

Guarding the entrance to the Bristol Channel on the northern, Welsh, side lies the long, deep harbour of Milford Haven, then a naval base and an important link with Ireland. Despite the fact that the anchorage is protected by the high headland of the Dale peninsula, the Storm created havoc among the shipping. A 'heavy gale' blew at S by E till two on the Saturday morning. There was then 'exceeding much wind' and at 3 a.m. in a squall the wind veered suddenly from S by W to WNW at which point one of the naval ships, the *Cumberland* drove: 'We could perceive all over the Harbour various Wrecks and ships lost, no possibility of any help to be had for them, the Storm being so violent'. By seven the gale began to moderate and daylight revealed the extent of the devastation.

The log of the *Dolphin* laconically records, 'Storm so very dreadful', but, on board, Captain Josiah Soanes, commodore of a squadron of six men-of-war convoying about 130 merchant ships 'bound about the land', wrote to Defoe to describe 'what this place felt . . . tho' a very good harbour'. He records that with 'the violentest of the weather' the *Cumberland* broke her sheet anchor and the *Rye*, with but one anchor left, was 'wonderfully preserv'd from the Shoar' by attaching a gun to the broken anchor cable and pushing it overboard. Above the roar of the Storm could be heard the booming sound of the guns fired by ships in distress, 'though 'twas impossible to assist each other, the sea was so high and the darkness of the night such'. By daybreak, Soanes wrote:

> . . . it was a dismal sight to behold the Ships driving up and down one foul of another, without Masts, some sunk and others upon the Rocks, the wind blowing so hard, with Thunder Lightning and Rain that on the Deck a Man could not stand without holding . . . By computation nigh 30 Merchant ships and vessels without Masts are lost.

This included a number of ships 'shelter'd under the land' at Dale, which were driven from their anchors and 'split to pieces, the Men all lost'.

In the Pembroke River, an arm of Milford Haven, a captured enemy ship was thrown up on to the mill dam across the tidal creek beneath the North Gate of the town. The vessel was got off again and the startled crew probably had an easier time than did that of the *Express*, off the Devon coast near Appledore, on the southern side of the Bristol Channel when the Storm broke. The ship's log records that:

> Almost 10 att night ye storm came very violent and a little before 12 ye best bower cable parted. The very violence of the wind carried away our Bowsprit which was presently followed by our Foarmast.

The ship was driven onshore and the crew were obliged to spend several days in a makeshift tent.

Eastwards of Milford Haven the towns of South Wales variously suffered. Although at Swansea 'the greatest part of the houses in the town were uncovered, more or less', the tide 'did not much damage' but, at Cardiff, 'a considerable breach was made in the Town Wall', part of the church steeple was blown down, houses were untiled and, on the marshes, many sheep and cattle were drowned.

The principle problem around the Bristol Channel was that great seas generated by the Storm blowing in from the south-west burst through the earthen sea defences of the low-lying parts of the coast while, especially at high tide, the wind-driven surface water dammed up rivers such as the Usk, Wye, Avon and the Severn itself. The effect was much the same as that of the kind of North Sea surge against the effect of which the Thames Barrier is designed to protect London.

At the beginning of the eighteenth century Bristol was enjoying the dawning of what might be called its golden age. Its Merchant Venturers stepped out confidently around the new Queen's Square, with its fine equestrian statue of their hero, William III, as their ships ploughed the oceans to the Indies and North America as well as, notoriously, to Africa on the first leg of the slave trade triangle. They traded 'with more entire independency upon London than any other town in Britain', Defoe was to write in his *Tour through the whole Island of Great Britain*, the port's hinterland included not only the West Country but also great parts of the Midland counties. 'As for the city itself, there is hardly room to set another house in it,' Defoe wrote, 'except in the great Square about which is little too subject to the hazard of inundation: so that people do not so freely enlarge that way.' A lesson, no doubt, having been learnt from the flooding that accompanied the Storm.

Although the damage inflicted by the wind to the city's buildings – especially the Cathedral and St Stephen's church – and to the great trees about College Green, was considerable, 'the greater damage,' wrote Daniel Jones, 'was done by the violent overflowing of the tide [which] did abundance of damage to Merchants' Cellars'. The vestry minutes of St Stephen's record that the floor of the church was six feet under water and boats are said to have been rowed in Thomas and Temple streets and other low-lying parts. One 50-ton vessel was washed up on to the wall of the quay.

Just as the Avon was dammed up by the waters of the Severn estuary, so too did the Avon cause flooding along its tributaries and at Henbury, on the Hazel Brook, a girl was forced to climb on to the roof of her house. As the waters continued to rise the house was swept away but, managing to cling to the branches of a tree, she was eventually rescued. Her parents, whose name was Nelmes, and three other children perished. In the neighbourhood of Henbury 'almost every house . . . was stripp'd of its covering', the price of helm, for re-covering roofs rose to 20 shillings per dozen and it was two years before there was sufficient available to complete the repair work.

A not dissimilar story to that of the Nelmes child came from Highbridge, near the mouth of the Brue on the Somerset Levels. As the rising tide invaded the ground floor of a house there, the man and woman are said to have run upstairs but the water eventually, 'undermining' the house, it fell and they were killed, 'but the Child floated out of the house before it fell in the cradle it lay in . . . so that when the flood abated it was found alive'.

As the wind had veered round to WNW, so the shipping in the King and Hang Roads, the deep water channel off the mouth of the Avon, between Avonmouth and Portishead, found itself off a lee shore. The *London Gazette* contains news of three ships driven aground, the *Richard and John*, 'lately come from Virginia', and the naval vessels *Suffolk* and *Canterbury*. The *Canterbury*, a storeship, Captain Blake, broke to pieces with the loss of all but fourteen of her crew of forty. At about one o'clock, the *Suffolk*, a hospital ship, Captain Watkins, lost her best bower and she was cast up close to the *Canterbury* but, although by seven o'clock her hold was 7 ft deep in water and the ship was lost, Watkins and all his crew of eighty survived. The *Richard and John* and two other merchantmen, the *George* and the *Grace*, also sank, 'the number of people lost variously reported'.

In terms of loss of life, however, Severnside had known worse. On 20 January 1606 about 2,000 people had been drowned when the sea poured over the defences. On the wall of Nash church, on the Gwent moors, a plaque marks the level of the floodwater and at the nearby church of St Mary Magdalene, Goldcliff, a brass memorial plate reads:

> 1606
> ON XX DAY OF JANVARY EVEN AS IT CAME TO PAS IT PLEASED GOD THE FLVD DID FLOW TO THE EDGE OF THIS SAME BRAS AND IN THIS PARISH THEARE WAS LOST 5000 AND OD POWNDS BESIDES, XXII PEOPLE WAS IN THIS PARRISH DROWN.

Across the Usk estuary, at St Bridget's Church at St Bride's, Wentlooge, where the water was about five feet deep, a stone tablet records 'The great Flvd 20 Janvarie in the morning 1606 . . .'

In 1703 the Gwent moors were again inundated, the event described in some detail in a letter sent to Defoe by the Revd Thomas Chest of Chepstow.

> . . . the Wind throwing the Tyde very strongly into the Severn and so into the Wye on which Chepstow is situated. And the Fresh in Wye meeting the Rampant Tyde, overflowed the lower part of our Town. It came into several houses about 4 foot high, rather more; the greatest damage sustained in houses was by the makers of Salt, perhaps their loss near £22.
>
> But the Bridge was a strange sight . . . built mostly of Wood, with a Stone Peer in the midst, the centre of which divides the two Counties [Monmouthshire and Gloucestershire] there are also stone platforms . . . over these are Wooden standards fram'd into peers 42 Foot high . . . the Tyde came over them all . . . most of planks on Monmouthshire side carried away, the Sleepers (about a Tun by measure each) were many of them carried away.
>
> All the level land on the Side part of Monmouthshire called the Moors was overflow'd. It is a tract of land 20 miles by as much as 2½. This Tyde came 5 Tydes before the Top of the Spring . . . many of the cattle got to shore and some dy'd before landed . . . they lost in hay and cattle between 3 and 4000 pounds. 'Tis thought most of their land will be worth but very little these 2 or 3 years, and 'tis known that the repairing of the sea walls will be very chargeable.

> About 70 seamen were lost out of the Canterbury, Storeship and other ships that were stranded or wrecked . . . Mr Churchman, that keeps the Inn at Betesley [Beachley], a passage over the Severn and had a share in the passing Boat, seeing a single Man tossed in a Wood-buss [a sailing vessel; in this case perhaps used for carrying timber from the Forest of Dean] off in the River, prevailed with some belonging to the Customs to carry himself and one of his Sons and two servants aboard the Boat which they did, and the Officer desired Mr Churchman to take out the man and come ashore with them in their Pinnace. But he, willing to save the Boat as well as the Man, tarried aboard and sometime after hoisting Sail, the Boat overset and they were all drowned, viz: the Man in the Boat, Mr Churchman, his Son and a Servant, and much lamented . . .

From all along the coast on both sides of the Severn estuary and the Bristol Channel came news of the sea walls being broken. The low-lying parts of the Vale of Berkeley, on the Gloucestershire bank, suffered widespread inundation. The Vicar of Berkeley informed Defoe that 'hereby the Severn was let in above a Mile over part of the parish'. In one place the water swept away 'a gentleman's stable', with its equine inhabitant, 'into the next Ground' where it fell to pieces 'and so the Horse came out'. At nearby Slimbridge, 'the Tide drowned the greater part of the Sheep on our Common' and at Rockhampton, one of the parish books contains the following memorandum:

> Nov 28th In the year 1704 [sic] by a great storm of wind the sea overflowed the walls, a great part of the countery was drowned. A great many people lost their lives besides Cattell and sheep.

– to which someone has added the correction 'it should be 1703'.

In the early eighteenth century the Somerset Moors, or Levels, were still largely undrained marshland. Piecemeal drainage had been undertaken by individuals since the Middle Ages, including the tenants of the monks of Glastonbury, Muchelney and Athelney and the canons of Wells Cathedral. In the large parish of Yatton, most of which lay on the marshes between the Yeo and the Kenn, advantage had been taken of the Edwardian Reformation in the mid-sixteenth century, to sell the church's great silver processional cross and with the £18 realised by the sale, invest in 'the makyng of a sirten skusse [sluice] agenste the rage of the salt water'.

From islands in these fens – villages such as Mark, Wedmore and Weston Zoyland, built on land a little above the level of inundation – reclamation had gradually taken place; rivers had been embanked and sea walls built. Traditional wild-fowling, fishing, reed- and turf-cutting were carried out around the unreclaimed meres and dairying, for Cheddar cheese-making, on the drained pastures. Large-scale, systematic drainage, however, would await the passing of parliamentary enclosure acts later in the century. At this time there had been sufficient work to ensure large losses of livestock but insufficient to prevent it. In the *Tour* Daniel Defoe summarises the consequence for the area of the Storm:

> This low part of the country, between Bridgwater and Bristol, suffered exceedingly in that terrible inundation of the sea, which was occurred by the violence of the wind in the great storm of 1703, and the country people have set up marks upon their houses and trees, with this note upon them, 'This high the waters came in the great storm'; 'This far the great tide flowed up in the last violent tempest'; and the like. And in one place they showed us, where a ship was, by the force of the water and the rage of the tempest, driven up from the shore, several hundred yards from the ordinary high water mark, and was left in that surprising condition upon dry land.

This is one of numerous references Defoe makes to the Great Storm in the *Tour*, written some twenty years later. Unusually, in the case of Minehead, the sea port on the western side of Bridgwater Bay, he appears to have forgotten what he had already written in *The Storm*. In the earlier book he had reproduced a letter informing him that:

> Three seamen were drowned in the Storm, and one Man was squeez'd to Death last Wednesday by one of the Ships that was

> forc'd Ashoar, suddenly coming upon him as they were digging round her, endeavouring to get her off. Our Peer also was somewhat damaged.

By contrast, in the *Tour* we read:

> Minhead, the best port, and safest harbour, in all these [south-western] counties, at least on this side: and they told me that in the great storm anno 1703, when in all the harbours and rivers in the country, the ships were blown on shore, wrecked and lost, they suffered little or no damage in the harbour.

At Barnstaple the quay was 'almost destroyed'.

As in Gwent, extensive flooding had occurred in Somerset in 1606 and in the church at Kingston Seymour, on the Yeo marshes, next to a plaque recording that event, is one telling how the gales and subsequent floods had led the parishioners of Yatton to take out a lawsuit against those charged with maintaining the sea walls which had been breached in 1703; the plaintiffs having lost cattle, sheep and harvested corn and salt water having 'invaded the land'.

Further south, Huntspill, near Highbridge, was the home of Sam Wooddeson, 'as we suppose, the minister of the place' wrote Defoe to whom he had sent the following, splendidly detailed account:

> SIR, – The parish of Huntspill hath received great damage by the late inundation of the salt water, particularly the west part thereof suffered most: for on the 27th day of November last, about four of the clock in the morning, a mighty south-west wind blew so strong as (in a little time) strangely tore our sea walls: insomuch, that a considerable part of the said walls were laid smooth, after which the sea coming in with great violence, drove in five vessels belonging to Bridgewater Key out of the channel, upon a wharf in our parish, which lay some distance off from the channel, and there they were all grounded: it is said, that the seamen there fathomed the depth, and found it about nine foot, which is taken notice to be four foot above our walls when standing; the salt

water soon overflowed all the west end of the parish, forcing many of the inhabitants from their dwellings, and to shift for their lives: the water threw down several houses, and in one an antient woman was drowned, being about fourscore years old: some families sheltered themselves in the church, and there stayed till the waters were abated: three window leaves [shutters] of our town were blown down, and the ruff cast scaled off in many places: much of the lead of the church was damnify'd; the windows of the church and chancel much broken, and the chancel a great part of it untiled: the parsonage house, barn and walls received great damage; as also, did some of the neighbours in their houses; at the west end of the parsonage house stood a very large elm, which was four yards a quarter and half a quarter in circumference, it was broken off near the ground by the wind, without forcing any one of the moars [roots] above the surface, but remained as they were before: the inhabitants (many of them) have received great losses in their sheep, and their other cattle; in their corn and hay there is great spoil made. This is what information I can give you of the damage this parish hath sustained by the late dreadful tempest. I am, Sir, Your humble servant, Sam Wooddeson

Wooddeson was indeed 'the minister of the place' and had been since 1679, having, as a boy, been a chorister at Magdalen College, Oxford.

This graphic account, powerfully evoking the forlorn scene on the bleak Parret marshes, is a reminder not only of the extent of physical damage to buildings, challenging enough for people with limited means of making repairs, but also, and more desperately, the loss of sources of food and income. The prospect of the winter ahead must have been grim indeed. According to Edith Conyers of Wells, who confirmed the death of the old woman, three or four of the vessels that had been driven ashore 'cannot be got off'.

Thomas Scott Holmes, the Victorian historian of *The Parish and Manor of Wookey*, another marsh edge village to the west of Wells, quotes from the parish records:

1703. Thomas Randell was buried the 26th November and the same night a mighty hurricane of wind which rent and spoiled

> many dwellings together with outhouses, and threw down innumerable multitudes of trees and drove many ships out of the sea into the meadows by reason of the very great tempest at night.

Holmes points out that until 1703 the only collections that could be made in the parish church were those for the poor at holy communion and those authorised by royal brief. He lists the collections made at Wookey over the years – nearly all 'for loss by fire' – but it may have been this change in the law which made possible a payment to 'a man of Huntspill . . . that has lost his goods by the breaking in of the sea'.

Finally from the hard-hit Somerset Levels, a reminder that, in addition to the beaching of ships and flooding of farmland, the wind roaring in from the sea across the flat, open moors also caused damage to more buildings than the Bishop's Palace at Wells. John Gill of Badgworth, recording expenditure on the fabric of the church, notes in the Churchwarden's Book:

> This is to repair the breeches of the dredfull Tempest done to our Church and Tower, which apered with Wonderfull violence both by sea and land on the 27th November, 1703. To our Tower was blown down all the west Batelments, and the t[w]o west Penicels and half ye Batelments south side ye Belfery Window to pieces. The Church tile blown all of, and all new lasted and laid; much of the Rou[gh]cast Beat down all new laid and a great deal of ye Plaistering and all of it new done. This was Amazing, and God grant that there never be the like while the world lasteth.

8

About Three Hundred Sail of Colliers

It was England south of the Trent that suffered most from the ravages of the Great Storm, the part of the country which Daniel Defoe in his *Tour* was to describe as 'the most populous part of the country and infinitely fuller of great towns, of people and of trade'. The supremacy of London among the 'great towns' was one of the most frequently repeated themes of the *Tour*. Supplying food and drink, clothing and heating to over half a million people drew, in days when overland transport was notoriously difficult, a vast amount of shipping to the Thames. Since the Glorious Revolution standards of living had been rising, in a stuttering, inequitable and uncertain way to be sure, but incomes were increasing. At the centre of the consequent rise in consumption was the apparently inexhaustible appetite of London. Much of the capital's inward-bound trade, especially in bulky goods such as coal, corn, timber, smoked herring (by the barrel), pitch, tar and beer, came either down the east coast or from across the 'German Ocean', from Scandinavia and the Baltic. Vast fleets converged on the Thames from all parts of the North Sea.

As trade increased the road system continued to deteriorate. Although the first Turnpike Act had been passed in 1663 little improvement had so far taken place and the responsibility for the upkeep even of roads of national importance still lay with the individual parishes through which they passed. Where a road ran across a well-drained limestone plateau or chalk downland the going might be tolerably good but in the clay lowlands in winter the 'highway' might be little more than a morass of indeterminate width. In the words of Sidney and Beatrice Webb, writing of the roads converging on London:

> The constant tramping of droves of cattle, herds of sheep and pigs, and flocks of geese and turkeys, the incessant stream of walking pack-horses, the galloping relays of post-horse and fish-carriers, all tended to keep the track in a perpetual slough of mud.

The state of the roads rendered sea- and river-borne traffic especially important. Although, as yet, the canal-building era had not begun, the navigation of many rivers had been improved to the benefit of the ports at their mouths. Forty years earlier, what Samuel Pepys had drunk as 'Hull ale' had in fact been brewed at Burton, carried down the Trent to Hull and then shipped, coastwise, to the capital.

It was, however, coal that dominated this east coast traffic. The largest ports, excluding London itself, were Scarborough, Sunderland, Newcastle, King's Lynn, Great Yarmouth and Whitby, all of which were involved in the coal trade. At the beginning of the eighteenth century nearly half the nation's coal was mined in the north-east (Northumberland and Durham) and most of that was taken down the east coast to London. Typically, the colliers involved were small brigs, two-masted vessels rarely carrying more than 300-400 tons of coal, which meant that great fleets of vessels were needed to meet the growing demand. Some 3,000 voyages per year were required, despite the fact that the trade to the capital was heavily taxed, the revenues being used to rebuild London's churches, including St Paul's, following the Great Fire.

Another major feature of east coast shipping was a large, if fluctuating, export trade in corn. Especially important was the transport of barley and malt through the Norfolk ports of King's Lynn, Blakeney, Wells and Great Yarmouth. At the time of the Great Storm there were probably as many as several hundred sail of colliers voyaging between the Tyne and Wear and the Thames as well as the busy corn trade with the continent and a great fleet from Russia under the convoy of three of Queen Anne's men-of-war. Although the danger which most of these ships faced was of being blown from their anchorages out to sea, ships off the Essex coast would have been on a lee-shore in the early hours of the Storm while later, as the wind veered round to WNW and NW, shipping off the coast of north Norfolk would have been in similar jeopardy. The sheer number of ships also increased the danger of vessels dragging their anchors running foul of one another.

The probability is that the worst weather was experienced in the rear of the Storm depression as the low pressure centre moved across the coast and out over the North Sea, while ports to the north of Hull escaped significant damage. On the coasts of Norfolk and Lincolnshire the worst of the Storm appears to have been shortly before daybreak. In Grimsby Road the *Rochester Prize* noted that at 5 a.m. 'the wind shifted and blew a violent storm' while further south the *Martin*, a naval vessel anchored off Boston, rode out the weather until 6.30 when she lost her small bower cable*. Around the Norfolk coast off Happisburgh, the *Tilbury* logged strong winds at 2 a.m. and the storm increasing and at 6 a.m. it was 'very violent from the SSW' when it began to veer north-westwards, remaining violent until 11 on the morning of the 27th.

About the mouth of the Humber itself, although wind speeds were almost certainly less than further south, the estuary probably had a funnel effect, exaggerating local velocities. Furthermore, sandbanks and, extending halfway across the estuary, the great curving sand and shingle spit of the Spurn, were particular hazards to ships out of control.

Defoe received a graphic account of what happened thereabouts from a 'Minister of Hull' who had the story from Peter Walls, 'Master of the Watch Tower called the Spurn light'. As the coast of Holderness has steadily been eaten back by the North Sea, so the spit attached to it has gradually been pushed

* Although larger ships would have carried a sheet anchor for use in emergency, should the main bower anchors fail, smaller vessels would only have had two anchors, the best bower on the starboard bow and the small bower on the port side. Despite their names, they would have been of similar weight and quality. Ships' logs make frequent mention during the Storm of best bower cables being let out or the small bower 'coming home' (that is, dragging).

north-westwards, its narrow neck periodically breached and the point itself washed away. What Defoe describes as 'Mr Wall's Pharos (which is about 20 yards high)' was Justinian Angell's lighthouse, built in 1674, a little over a mile to the north-east of the present Spurn Point. There was also a lower lighthouse, to serve as a leading mark but in the conditions that prevailed on the night of the Great Storm, with terrific waves breaking over the spit, that had been abandoned. Walls was expecting that his own lighthouse would be toppled at any moment. In the event, the fire in the brazier which provided the light, was blown by the wind so fiercely that it 'melted down the iron bar on which it laid like Lead'. The lighthouse-men were compelled to quench the light, put in a new bar and rekindle the flame which they were able to keep alight until daybreak, when Walls distinguished:

> . . . about six or seven and twenty sail of ships all driving about the Spurn Head, some having cut, others broke their cables, but all disabled and rendered helpless.

(A ship's hemp anchor cables, up to 20 inches in circumference, were cut with axes if, under, stress of weather, weighing anchor proved impossible and the ship threatened to capsize.)

The distressed ships were 'some from Russia and most of 'em colliers to and from Newcastle'. Three were driven on to the sandbank known as the Den or Old Den which lies on the landward side of Spurn Point. No sooner had the first of these ships run aground than she turned turtle. Of the crew of six all but one unfortunate – in the shrouds when the vessel struck – were able to save themselves and were picked up by the boat of one of the other stranded vessels. The company of the third ship was picked up by the same boat which made for the spit and the lighthouse-man's house where they met with 'good fires and good accommodation necessary for them in such a Distress'. As they huddled around Mr Wall's fire the shipwrecked sailors all agreed that they had never before been out in 'so dismal a night'.

The three ships wrecked on the Den were probably part of a fleet of about eighty which had been anchored in Grimsby Road.

Many of these ships appear to have broken their cables, many running foul of one another, three sinking in the Road itself, their crews all lost, others disappearing out to sea.

The other major concentration of east coast shipping on the day of the Storm was at Great Yarmouth. At one o'clock in the afternoon of the 26th, a little after the flood tide, the *John and Mary*, which had spent the previous two days sheltering beneath 'the High land about Cromer', dropped anchor in Yarmouth Roads. She joined a large fleet of ships, 'about 300 sail of Colliers . . . and a great fleet from Russia under the Convoy of the *Reserve*, frigate, and two other Men of War: and about a Hundred sail of Coasters, Hull-men and such small craft'. Hardly had the skipper 'set all to rights' than the wind began to strengthen and an ominous, black sky started to build up to windward. The *John and Mary*'s crew, in common no doubt with those of other ships in the Roads, struck the top mast and yards, battened down the hatches and prepared to sit out the oncoming storm. The night was excessively dark – a point made by observers all round the coast – and from eight until ten a storm blew before abating for a short time and then returning with redoubled ferocity. By one o'clock with a 'dreadful Storm' blowing, the skipper had veered out more cable and let go a sheet anchor. Although the anchors held well, the ship was in great danger of foundering as huge waves crashed over her. At two, 'the Sea fill'd our Boat as she lay upon the Deck and we were glad to let her go overboard for fear of staving in our Decks'.

There follows an especially interesting part of the account, a reference to the kind of dispute between desperate men which must, in reality, have commonly occurred during the Storm at sea but which is never hinted at in the logs of Royal Naval vessels:

> Our mate would have cut our Mast by the board but I not willing and told him I thought we had better slip our Cables and go out to sea, he argued she was a deep ship and would not live in the sea and was very eager for cutting away the Mast; but I was loathe to part with my Mast and could not tell where to run for shelter if I lost them.

At about three o'clock 'abundance of Ships drove away, and came by us; some with their masts gone and foul of one another'. Members of the crew claimed they saw two such ships founder and a 'Russia Man' and a collier which were locked together were later reported to have sunk. The men-of-war and some of the Russian ships were firing their guns to attract help 'but 'twas in vain to expect it; the Sea went too high for any Boat to live'.

The *John and Mary*'s anchors continued to hold for a further two hours but at about five o'clock a ship's long boat 'came driving against us', striking the bow with such force that the master thought he had been hit by another ship. Whether the long boat contained men or not nobody on board could tell, the sea being too high for any member of the crew to be on the fo'c'sle where they might have been able to see into her before the impact staved the long boat to pieces. Immediately and perhaps as a consequence, the ship's sheet anchor cable gave way and the *John and Mary* herself was driven before the wind. Fortunately, for her crew, the ebb tide had now begun to flow and the waves although still 'exceeding high' were 'somewhat abated'. Eventually the wind lessened and they were able to stand in for the shore being in the shelter of 'the Cliffs near Scarbro'. In a matter of only a few hours they had travelled 150 miles. 'Such a Tempest as this,' the master concludes, 'there never was in the World'.

The bad news from Yarmouth travelled fast – or, at least, attempted to. No sooner had the Storm passed over than news of it was dispatched to London. The public post, carried by postboys on horseback and furnished with bag and horn, would have been taken to the General Post Office in Lombard Street. An express service was in existence and doubtless this was how the initial news of the Storm about the coast first reached the capital. The journey from Yarmouth would not have been easy. Strong winds were still blowing, the road must frequently have been blocked with fallen trees and other obstacles, and the job of clearing up the devastation in towns such as Beccles and Stowmarket would have been far from complete by the time the post passed through.

Detailed news of the state of affairs at Yarmouth did not reach Sir David Mitchell at the Admiralty Office until the Tuesday following the Storm, suggesting that the post took longer than the normal two days. The Navy Board minutes contain the note that on the evening of that day Sir David went to the house of Mr George Churchill (the *de facto* manager of naval affairs acting in the name of the Lord High Admiral, the Queen's husband, Prince George of Denmark) 'upon the occasion of an Express from Yarmouth'. This contained letters from Captain Jepson of HMS *Portland* and from the Mayor of the town.

The Yarmouth correspondents of both the *London Gazette* and the *Post Man* put pen to paper when the terrifying sound of the Storm whistling about their chimney pots was still fresh in their ears. Even the Storm, however, was not sufficiently great an event to cause their editors to break with the convention that diplomatic news came first. Thus the first edition of the *Gazette* to carry news of the disaster, that for Thursday 25 November to Tuesday 29, leads with the news from Rome (some weeks old) that 'The Venetian Ambassador had a long Audience with the Pope yesterday, upon the Occasion, it is said, of the Duke of Savoy declaring for the Allies'.

The contents of the letters read by Churchill and Mitchell can probably be summarised in the words, lower down the page, of the next day's *London Gazette*:

> Yarmouth 27th Nov. – Yesterday and last night we had a very violent Storm, the wind changing from SSW to W and WNW and in the morning we found that of the 500 Ships that lay in our Roads many were missing which we suppose were drove off to sea: some were forced on the sands and others have lost all their Masts. HM Ship the *Reserve* foundered about 11 this morning and all her men were lost; but the *Lyn* and *Margate* ride out and the wind is much abated and tho' still high that no boats can be sent out to them.

In his haste to get his copy to London, the *Post Man*'s Yarmouth man got his story a little confused:

> The *Reserve*, *Lyn* and *Nightingale*, Frigots, were forced on shoar, and this morning to our great surprise the *Reserve* sank, and all

the men perished, and most of the Men of War besides much damaged with several merchant ships the particulars of which is not yet known.

In fact, the warships still in difficulty were the *Lyn* and *Margate*, as stated by the *Gazette*, rather than the *Nightingale*. News that these two ships were in distress must have crossed with orders from the Admiralty that they were to join the search for Sir Cloudesley Shovell who had already been reported missing. According to a contemporary Admiralty official, Josiah Burchett, whose *Complete History of the most remarkable transactions at sea* was published in 1720, the *Reserve* had been seen about eight o'clock in the morning 'with all her Masts gone and only her Ensign staff standing', firing a gun to attract help which, however, no other ship was in a position to provide. At about noon she foundered and 'not one Soul belonging to her was saved'. The *Lyn* and *Margate*, according to Burchett, had been damaged by other ships 'driving on board them', had cut their masts and were riding dangerously near to St Nicholas Sand. The *Lyn* took up the crew of 'a rich merchantman bound for the Scaw' which sank within three hours of being driven on 'the said sand'.

The letters from Captain Jepson and the Mayor supplied Churchill and Mitchell with information that triggered a broadside of orders. Jepson was to take the *Advice* under his command and convoy the merchantmen bound for Holland; then to proceed to the Dutch island of Goeree and join up with Admiral Rooke (still waiting to escort the uncrowned King of Spain to Portugal). The *Nightingale* was to stay by the crippled *Lyn* and *Margate* and assist them into Harwich. The *Triton*, also in Yarmouth Roads, was to look for Sir Cloudesley off Aldeburgh.

Mitchell and Churchill appear to have been the principal decision-makers in the Admiralty in the days following the Storm and their contrasting antecedents and personalities deserve some attention.

Sir David was a Scot of such obscure origins that the year of his birth is uncertain, but he was probably in his early fifties in 1703. He joined the merchant navy as a boy and in 1672 was pressed into the Royal Navy, according to one story, having been pulled from under the coals on a Newcastle collier. This was the making of him. Within ten years he had his own command and soon came to the attention of Admiral Edward Russell, who became his patron. Mitchell commanded Russell's flagship, the *Britannia*, at Barfleur in 1692 – the Admiral's success in that action usually being credited to the advice he received from Mitchell and the Master of the Fleet, Benbow. For his conduct in that action Mitchell was appointed one of King William's grooms of the bedchamber, promoted to rear-admiral and entrusted with convoying the king to Holland. Six years later he was given the task of convoying Peter the Great to England on the famous 'western embassy'. Mitchell impressed the Czar who tried, unsuccessfully, to entice him to Russia: in Peter's words, 'it is a much happier life to be an Admiral in England than to be Czar in Russia'.

With the accession of Queen Anne, her husband, Prince George, 'a kindly, negligible mortal', in Trevelyan's words, became Lord High Admiral. Mitchell was appointed to his Council and, certainly at the time of the Storm, fulfilled his duties conscientiously and with apparent efficiency, appearing in the Office day after day receiving letters from commanders, issuing orders and making recommendations for action to the Prince and the Navy Board. Occasionally he was accompanied by Mr Brydges (later Lord Chandos) but usually he was alone with the clerks.

The contrast with George Churchill could scarcely have been more stark. Churchill owed his position to a combination of opportunism and influence. Although an arch-Tory, he had been one of the first naval officers to offer his services to the Prince of Orange. After commanding the *St Andrew* at Barfleur, he seems to have relied principally upon his elder brother, John, the future Duke of Marlborough, for advancement. When Queen Anne, already greatly indebted to the Marlboroughs, came to the throne, George Churchill was appointed to Prince George's Admiralty Council. His first act was to promote himself Admiral of the Blue, hoisting his flag at Portsmouth just long enough to qualify for the pay. He had not been at sea since 1692. His influence upon the weak Prince continued until the consort's death in 1708, by which time his rapacity, ignorance and incompetence incited the greatest contempt. Following the success of French privateers in the Channel, a fellow Tory, Lord Haversham, said of Churchill in the Lords:

> Your disasters at sea have been so many, a man scarce knows where to begin. Your ships have been taken by your enemies, as the Dutch take your herrings, by shoals on your coast: nay, your Royal Navy itself has not escaped. These are pregnant misfortunes and are big with innumerable mischiefs.

The historian of Queen Anne's navy, R.D. Merriman, asserts that at the beginning of her reign the service had become 'a profession with a rapidly rising *esprit de corps*'. Mitchell would appear to have been more typical of this improved professionalism than the more powerful, deeply disliked Churchill. Fortunately for the shipwrecked and distressed victims of the Storm and for the immediate future of the Royal Navy in 1703, it was Mitchell who seems to have shouldered the burden of responsibility at this crucial time.

So far as the public was concerned, the position at Yarmouth was further clarified in the next edition of the *London Gazette* in a report dated the 29th:

> HM Ships the *Portland*, *Advice*, *Triton* and *Nightingale* which were in our Road in the late great Storm have received no damage but the *Lyn* and *Margate* were obliged to cut all their Masts by the Board. A merchant ship called the *Golden Peace* of Dantzig which was bound thither was cast away on our Sands but all her men were saved. About 200 sail of laden colliers sailed hence yesterday southward.

Normality was gradually returning, although ships driven from their anchors about the mouth of the Thames were still appearing in the waters around Yarmouth and casualties were still being reported. On the Tuesday following the Great Storm, a Yarmouth ship, the *Robert and Elizabeth*, Master John Humphreys, from Archangel and, presumably part of the scattered Russian fleet, so leaky as a consequence of the damage she had received, was forced to run aground at Winterton Ness, north of the town, in order to save her cargo.

There was slightly better news of the 54-gun man-of-war, the *Reserve*, the *Post Man* reporting;

> the *Reserve* had 190 Sailors perished on board her, but the Captain [John Anderson], Chyrugeon and second mate with 25 sailors (who came on shoar the evening before the storm, in two barks for some Provisions . . .) are here and report that they left on shoar at Shields, the Master, the purser and a midshipman and, of the Marines, Captain Sanderson and two of his Lieutenants.

At Harwich, to the south of Yarmouth, the *Diligence* had struck her yards and topmast at eight on the evening of the Storm but at five the following morning was driven ashore and was probably one of the vessels referred to in the log of the *Adventure* in which was noted 'Vessels ashore. Blowing an extraordinary storm all night whereby most of the town of Harwich suffer'd.' At Maldon in Essex, where the church spire collapsed, several ships in the harbour were badly damaged especially a vessel laden with corn for London which was stranded and her cargo, 'to the value of 500 pounds', lost. The crew 'narrowly escaped', being rescued by a small boat next day.

On 4 December, a Committee of the Commons was asked to consider 'the excessive price of coals' and the following day, a week after the Storm, Sir David Mitchell in Whitehall received a dispatch from Captain Trevor of the *Triton*, ordered to search the debris-strewn southern North Sea. The news could only have been alarming – and not only about the price of coal.

9

Damage Most Tragicall

Winds from the Aeolian Hall
Roar through the Woods, and make whole forests fall!
(*Odyssey*, Alexander Pope)

Death at sea during the Storm must often have approached with a gradual awareness of the awful inevitability, the realisation that the boat would not reach the shore, that the ship upon the rocks was breaking up, that the tide was rising and no help was at hand. On land the *coup de grâce* came more abruptly, terror breaking in suddenly on a more general feeling of disquiet – the falling tree, the collapsing chimney stack, dislodged roof timber or skull-breaking tile. The fatal blows also tended to be less concentrated, with a sleeping couple here, an unlucky waggoner or miller's boy there. Because of the highly sporadic nature of the incidence of such mortalities on land and the absence of any kind of national recording agency, it is impossible to guess with any degree of accuracy how large was the death toll ashore. If Defoe's estimate of 8,000 deaths overall is a close approximation, then the number killed across the country must have run into thousands. It is, however, an assumption. Many of his correspondents, often after describing the amount of damage done to the fabric of buildings, write of the 'miracle' of how few succumbed to death or injury. 'The escape of all persons here from Death being generally miraculous', was the view from Ely and in Wokingham in Berkshire it was regarded as a matter of much surprise that there was 'not one person killed nor hurt'. Although Northampton was terribly hard hit, 'yet through the Goodness of God, no Person killed or maimed'. Despite the fact that the abbey roof at Tewkesbury was 'strangely ruffled', 'Not one of our Town was kill'd (although Mr W.M., wife and child escaped when a chimney fell through the roof into their bed chamber).' When lives were lost the 'miracle' was often that more were not. Thus from Reigate Defoe received from Thomas Foster a letter recounting how:

> In the Parish of Capel by Darking [Dorking] lived one Charles Man, who was in Bed with his Wife and two children and by a fall of part of his House, he and one child were killed and his Wife and one child miraculously preserv'd.

At Swyre in Dorset, between two hills and looking out over Lyme Bay, the wind must have come in off the sea with terrific force so that at about midnight the Revd Jacob Cole had gone out 'to give orders to my servants to secure the house and ricks of corn and furze'. Shortly afterwards he returned to the house and:

> I heard something of great weight fall behind me and a little after going out with a light to see what is was, I found it to be the great stone which covered the top of my chimney to keep out the wet; it was a yard square, and very thick weighing about an hundred and fifty pounds. It was blown about a yard off from the chimney, and fell edge-long, and cut the earth about four inches deep exactly between my foot steps.

The anonymous author of A *Wonderful History of All the Storms, Hurricanes, Earthquakes* etc. published in London in 1704, tells of Thomas Lanier of Cranbrook in Kent, where:

> a great stack of chimneys falling on his Mansion House broke through and beat the floors to the cellar wither he was carried with his bed, and yet neither himself or any servants in the house hurt.

Those who lived to tell such tales naturally did so.

England was still thinly peopled. Of the total population of little more than 5 million, 500,000 lived in London but 80 per cent lived in rural locations, the overwhelming majority south of a line from the Severn to the Humber, the area affected by the Storm. Of the population of Wales, about 300,000 in total, the majority again lived in the southern lowlands between Pembrokeshire and Monmouthshire, with coastlines open to the full force of the tempest.

A high percentage of the rural population made a living either directly or indirectly from the land, and exports of corn and wool contributed significantly to the country's rising prosperity. Although most farms were 'mixed', having evolved from a subsistence economy, they produced primarily for the market and, while there was a broad division between an arable south and east and pastoral north and west, more specialised regional distinctions had emerged. Furthermore, despite the low population density, when compared to continental neighbours the country was intensively farmed. Although large areas around Ely and between March and Whittlesey remained under water, most of the Fenland was by now drained and productive and, while the Surrey heathlands were still 'a sandy desert'*, Daniel Defoe, in the *Tour*, was proud to quote a 'foreign gentleman' who observed to him 'that England was not like other countries, but it was all a planted garden'.

The 'planted garden', with its windmills, haystacks, thatched buildings, open fields and scattered woodlands was indiscriminately ravaged by the Great Storm, the bad weather in advance of which had already caused considerable damage, weakening man-made structures and, in an expression of John Evelyn's, subverting the woods. One of the most graphically evocative letters received by Defoe concerned a tornado which ripped across the Berkshire-Oxfordshire border on the afternoon

* Defoe, writing in the *Tour*, regarded Bagshot Heath as a moral affront, 'a foil to the beauty of the rest of England; or a mark of the just resentment shew'd by Heaven upon the Englishman's pride . . . a vast tract of land some of it within 17–18 miles of the capital city, which is horrid and frightful to look on, not only good for little but good for nothing, much of it a sandy desert, and one may frequently be put in mind of Arabia Deserta'.

of 26 November, some eight or nine hours ahead of the Storm itself. Tornadoes – violently rotating whirlwinds with distinctive funnel-shaped clouds – occur on an average of about eight days a year in Britain, where they tend to be smaller and less destructive than on the Great Plains of the USA. The letter in *The Storm* eloquently describes a typical British tornado:

> Sir,
>
> Meeting with an advertisement of yours in the Gazette of Monday last (28th November), I have much approved of the Design, thinking it might be a great motive towards making People, when they hear the Fate of others, return Thanks to Almighty God for his Providence in preserving them. I accordingly was resolved to send you all I knew. The place where I have for some time lived is Besselsleigh in Barkshire, about 4 miles south-west of Oxon. The wind began with us about One of the Clock in the morning, and did not do much harm, only in untiling Houses, blowing down a chimney or two, without any Person hurt and a few trees. But what was the only thing that was strange, and to be observed, was a very tall Elm, which was found the next Morning standing, but perfectly twisted round; the Root a little loosen'd, but not torn up. But what happened the Afternoon preceding is abundantly more surprising, and is indeed the intent of this Letter.
>
> On Friday the 26th of November, in the Afternoon about Four of the Clock, a Country Fellow came running to me in a great Fright, and very earnestly entreated me to go and see a Pillar, as he call'd it, in the Air, in a Field hard by. I went with the Fellow; and when I came, found it to be a Spout marching directly with the Wind: and I can think of nothing I can compare it to better than the Trunk of an Elephant, which it resembled only much bigger. It was extended to a great length and swept the ground as it went, leaving a Mark behind. It crossed a Field; and what was very strange (and which I could scarce have been induced to believe had I not myself seen it, besides several Country-men who were astonish'd at it) meeting with an Oak that stood towards the middle of the Field

snapped the body of it asunder. Afterwards crossing a Road, it sucked up the Water that was in the Cart-ruts: then coming to an old Barn, it tumbled it down, and the Thatch that was on the Top was carried about by the Wind, which was then very high, in great confusion. After this I followed it no farther, and therefore saw no more of it. But a Parishioner of mine going from hence to Hincksey, in a Field about a quarter of a mile off of this place, was on the sudden knock'd down, and lay upon the Place till some People came by and brought him home: and he is not yet quite recovered. Having examined him, by all I can collect both from the Time and Place, and Manner of his being knock'd down, I must conclude it was done by the Spout, which, if its Force had not been much abated, had certainly kill'd him: and indeed I attribute his Illness more to fright, than the sudden Force with which he was struck down.

I will not now enter into a Dissertation on the Cause of Spouts, but by what I can understand they are caused by nothing but the Circumgyration of the Clouds, made by two Contrary Winds meeting in a point, and condensing the Cloud till it falls in the Shape we see it; which by the twisting Motion sucks up Water, and doth much mischief to Ships at Sea, where they happen oftener than at Land. Whichever of the two Winds prevails, as in the above-mentioned was the S.W., at last dissolves the Cloud, and then the Spout disappears.

This is all I have to communicate to you, wishing you all imaginable Success in your Collection. Whether you insert this Account, I leave wholly to your own Discretion; but can assure you, that to most of these things, *tho' very surprizingly*, I was my self an Eye-witness. I am,

Sir,
Your humble Servant,

Dec. 12, 1703 Joseph Railton

The way in which the elm tree was contorted suggests that it may have been a casualty of the tornado rather than the later Storm.

The tornado itself was probably related to instability along a cold front associated with a secondary low moving away to the NE in advance of the Storm system. Later in the day whirlwinds were observed at Delft in Holland. There is some evidence, too, of a whirlwind at Whitstable in Kent, from where Defoe received a report of 'a Boat belonging to a Hoy [which] was taken up by the violence of the Wind, clean off from the Water, and being blown in the air, blew turning continually over and over in its progressive motion, till it lodg'd against a rising Ground, above 50 Rod [250 m] from the Water, in the passage it struck a Man, who was in the way, and broke his Knee to pieces'. As the Storm occurred at night it is unlikely that the boat's flight would have been so clearly observed, or the unfortunate man have been in its path, at that time of day.

During the Storm all kinds of man-made structures were susceptible to damage. The kind of harm inflicted on churches has already been summarised. Windmills, invariably wooden structures often located on the parish's windiest hilltop, were especially vulnerable to the depredations of excessive wind. Defoe's frequently repeated statistic is that 400 windmills were destroyed in the Storm. Statistics are not Defoe's strong point – he recognised their power of persuasion without having the means properly to assemble them – and all that can be said is that the number probably could be counted in hundreds. By 1703 the total number of windmills in England was approaching its all-time peak of approximately 10,000. In the seventeenth century Cornelius Vermuyden, employed by James I to reclaim the Fens, had built hundreds of wind-powered drainage mills. Most windmills, however, were used for grinding corn and were most commonly found in the cereal-producing counties of the south and east. Windmills, in other words, were particularly characteristic of the counties worst affected by the onslaught of the Great Storm.

A fundamental feature of all but the most primitive windmills is a mechanism for moving the sails to face the quarter from which the wind is blowing. At the time of the Storm the great majority of windmills were of the relatively simple post mill type. The body of the post mill pivoted on a massive central oak post and was luffed into the wind manually by means of a tailpole. The fantail, which moves the mill automatically, was not invented until 1745. This meant that as the wind veered or backed during a storm the miller would have to brave the elements to ensure the sails remained at right angles to the wind. All windmills at this time used canvas sails tied in a variety of ways across the stocks, the main sail timbers. As the wind increased, the area of sail would be reduced by reefing it in something like the manner employed on sailing ships. The spring sail with its hinged wooden shutters was not introduced until 1772. Again, the task of adjusting the sails had to be performed manually by the miller.

Various disasters could overtake a post mill in a storm. If the mill was not, or could not be, turned into the wind, it might be tail-winded, in which case the sails and windshaft – the massive near-horizontal oaken shaft carrying the sails – would counter-rotate with gathering speed until forced from their bearings. The rapidly rotating sails would then crash into the body of the mill and the tail end of the windshaft, would lift up smashing through the roof of the mill. Furthermore, when operating normally the ladders of a post mill are on its leeward side and provide a degree of stability but, if the mill were to be tail-winded, the mill could be blown over.

Fire was also a danger in tar-coated, dust-laden mills. The friction created by a fast rotating windshaft could cause it to catch fire, as could the application of the brake intended to slow the mill down. Feeding the mill with grain also served to retard it but this too required the presence of the miller. William Derham the clergyman-scientist of Upminster, in his account of the Storm written to the Royal Society, specifically mentions that because his weather-vane had been blown down he was unable to pronounce with certainty on the direction of the wind and, therefore, after the event had gained his information from 'Millers and others that were forced to venture abroad'.

Defoe devotes part of his book to 'The dreadful Storm of Wind, accompanied with Thunder, Lightning, Hail and Rain' of 18 February 1662, so-called 'Windy Tuesday'. There he tells the tragic story of the destruction of Mr Roberts's windmill at 'Langton' in Leicestershire. The Langtons – there are four of them, Church, East, Thorpe and Tur Langton – lie about ten miles south-east of Leicester, a few miles north of Market Harborough. The enclosure map of 1792 shows a windmill in a small field south of the Kibworth Beauchamp – Welham road and about half a mile south-east of Church Langton, to which it is connected by footpath. This may well be the site of the mill that on 'Windy Tuesday' blew down killing one man outright, breaking the back of another and severing the leg (or arm, Defoe is unsure) of a third. The two men who survived to be discovered, unsurprisingly, died of their injuries.

In 1703, Defoe was sent the story of the miller at Charlwood in Surrey, who, as the wind started to rise, got up from his bed in order to go to his mill 'resolving to turn it towards the Wind and set it to work, as the only means to preserve it standing'. On his way from his house to the mill, however, he felt in his pocket for the key and found that he had left it at home. Setting out from his house a second time he looked up only to see that the mill was no longer there: it had been blown down so that his 'lucky forgetfulness' had saved his life.

Feeding the mill with grain was not, of course, an option available in the case of the Fenland drainage mills where one man might operate a number of mills. At Wisbech, where a vessel laden with oil – probably whale oil – was forced ashore, four windmills were blown down and several of the drainage mills on the Isle of Ely appear to have been allowed to turn with such fury that 'the Timbers and wheels have heat and set the rest on Fire'. The author of *An Exact Relation of the Late Dreadful Tempest* tells of a mill, belonging to Francis Cherry Esquire of the parish of Shottesbrooke in Berkshire which 'by the swift turning of the sails took fire, as some conclude', others arguing that it had been struck by lightning, 'that darted prodigious Flashes through the gloomy Night'.*

Although it was not uncommon for old mills with decaying timbers to be blown down in a storm, the destruction of a mill at Portsdown, near Fareham in Hampshire, was thought worthy of mention because 'it had not been up many years'. Two mills were 'overthrown' at Brighthelmstone and three in the badly hit town of Northampton where 'the mighty upright post below the floor of the mills' was 'snapt in two like a Reed'.

* The author of *An Exact Relation* . . . also tells of a far worse fire at Lodden in Norfolk, where 'the Flames being terribly driven the people were so amazed and heartless in the double calamity that for want of Diligence used to extinguish the fire, the great part of the town was burnt down'.

The implications of this large scale destruction of post mills are difficult to assess. Re-building would have been a comparatively easy task in most cases. It may, however, in some instances, have provided the opportunity to convert to the recently introduced, more substantial and more easily manoeuvred smock mill. Such mills, in common with the later, brick-built tower mills, have a relatively small rotating cap carrying the windshaft and sails. The operation of manually moving the mill to face the wind was, consequently, easier so that the mill could be built higher and greater wind speeds be taken advantage of.

Agricultural buildings generally less well maintained than many other structures, were particularly susceptible to damage; but although numerous instances of the harm sustained by barns and outhouses survive, most were probably regarded as unworthy of record. The thatched roofs so common on such buildings, especially in the clay lowlands, would have been particularly vulnerable.

A feature of most farms was the rickyard, often near to the granary where the corn was threshed and stored. There the straw and hay was stacked on staddle-stones or on a bed of brushwood. Such winter feed and bedding material, was of crucial importance to the farming economy and, even in the best of times, was usually in short supply. Many accounts refer to the devastation caused by the Storm to this crucial harvest: 'several stacks of corn overturn'd by the violence of the wind in the parishes of Roysily [Rhossili] and Largenny [Llangennith] in Gower'; 'Hay recks in abundance . . . torn to pieces' about Witney, Oxfordshire; and so on. From Marton in Warwickshire comes evidence of both a well-made rick and the strength of the wind:

> a good Rick of Wheat blown from its staddle and set down without a sheaf remov'd or disturb'd (20 yards away).

After the 1662 storm 'A Gentleman of good Account' who took a ride out from Ipswich in Suffolk to examine the damage caused by the wind, described how 'within a very few miles' of that town 'above 30 Barns, and many of them with Corn in them, were blown down'. If such a density of agricultural destruction was anything like

St Michael's, East Peckham, Kent. A spire was blown down in the Great Storm and replaced by the spirelet shown. The weather vane carries the date 1704. *(Author's collection)*

All Saints', Leamington Hastings, Warwickshire, where a great many sheets of lead were 'roll'd up like a piece of cloth'. Over the South Porch is the date 1703. *(Author's collection)*

Lady Rachel Russell. *(© National Portrait Gallery, London)*

The Kidder memorial, Wells Cathedral. *(Dean and Chapter of Wells Cathedral)*

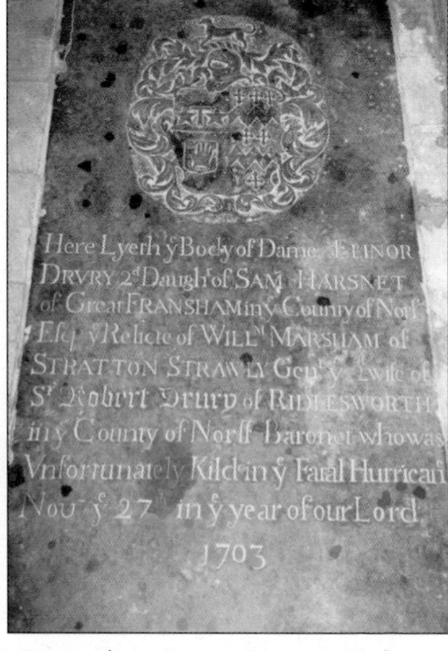

Memorials to Mary Fisher and her aunt, Dame Elinor Drury. *(Yvonne Bird)*

The ‘ingenious’ Henry Winstanley (1644–1703), self-portrait as a young man. *(© Saffron Walden Museum)*

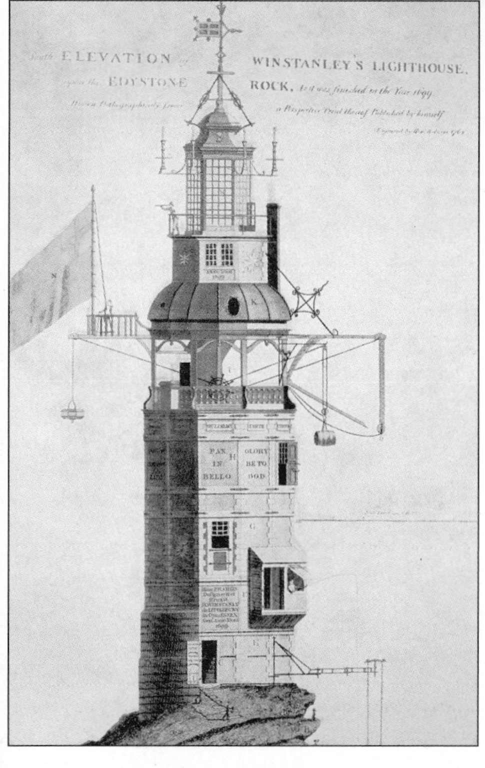

Winstanley’s Eddystone lighhouse, as modified in 1699 and destroyed in the Great Storm. *(© The British Museum)*

HMS *Hampton Court*, by Willem van de Velde the Younger. The ship survived the Storm 'much shattered in her Masts and Rigging'. *(© Birmingham Museums & Art Gallery)*

HMS *York*, by Willem van de Velde the Elder. 'In blowing weather the 23rd of November [the ship] was broken all to pieces.' *(© National Maritime Museum)*

Sir Cloudesley Shovell, Admiral of the White, for a long time believed lost.

John Leake, relieved 'by the invisible Hand of Providence'. *(© National Maritime Museum, London)*

George St Lo, resident commissioner at Plymouth during the building of Winstanley's lighthouse and, later, at Chatham. *(© National Maritime Museum, London)*

'The Great Storm, Novber 26, 1703. Wherein Rear Admiral Beaumont was lost on the Goodwin Sands . . .'. A fanciful contemporary print. *(© National Maritime Museum, London)*

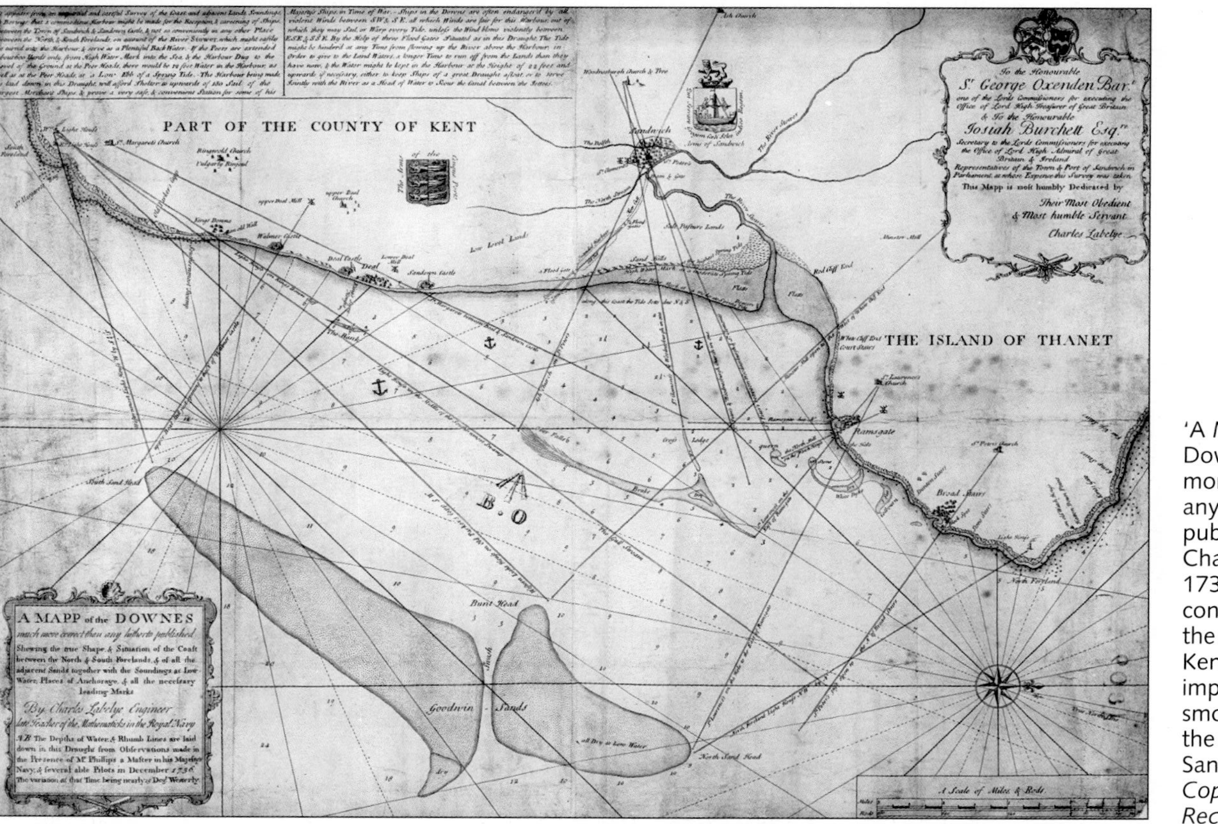

'A Mapp of the Downes, much more correct than any hitherto published' by Charles Labelye, 1736. Note the contrast between the detail of the Kent coast and the improbably smooth outline of the Goodwin Sands. *(Crown Copyright, Public Record Office)*

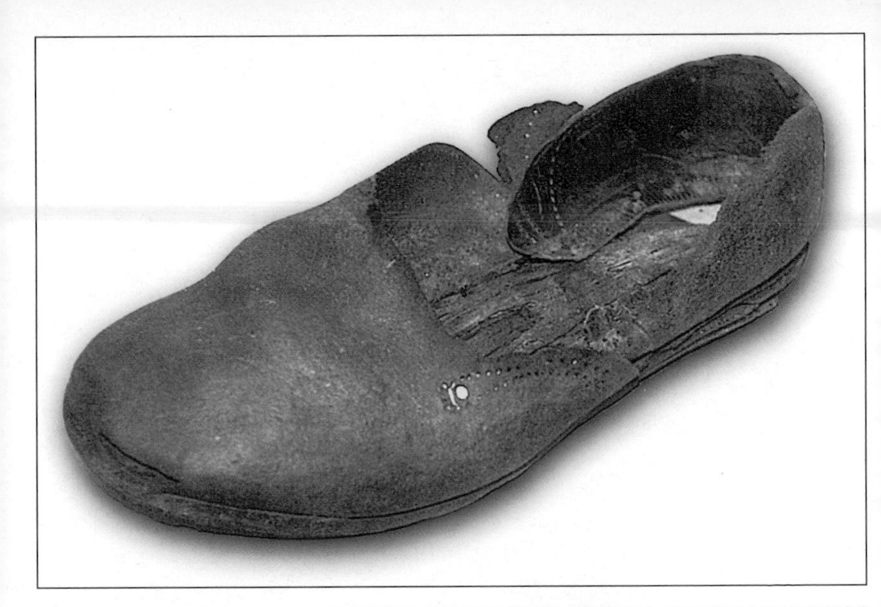

Numerous objects have been retrieved from the Great Storm wrecks on the Goodwin Sands including this 14cm-high brass candlestick and a virtually complete leather shoe, both from the *Stirling Castle*. *(© Ramsgate Maritime Museum)*

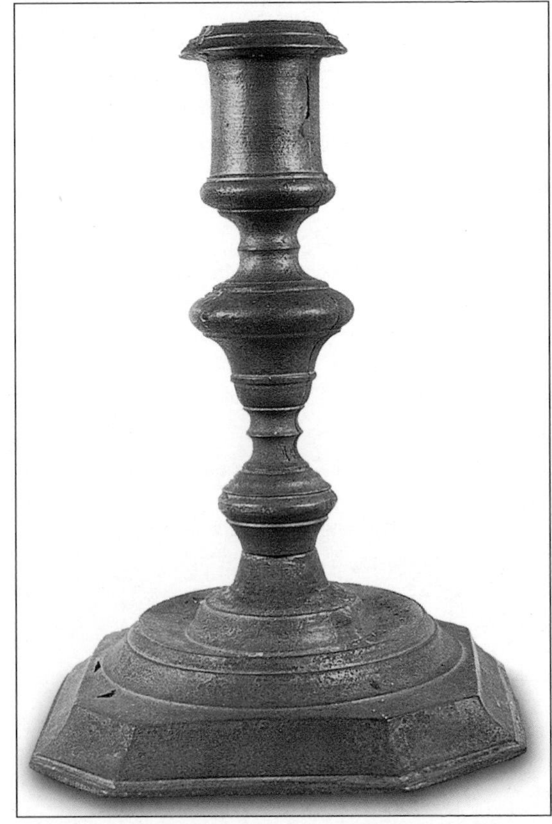

typical of the south of England as a whole it must have constituted a major disaster for the whole farming community.

In 1703 on the opposite side of the same county lived William Coe, a farmer and malster of the Brewhouse, West Row, near Mildenhall, who kept a diary in which he devoted special attention to his 'sinnes' and to 'Mercyes Received'. In the first category are found such colourful confessions as 'Filthy and obsceene discourse att Mr Bradbury's', 'Drank too much att Mr Challings' and 'Too many idle and rash words att Bury'. In 1703 William was fortunate to be able to count surviving the Storm among the 'Mercyes Received' for on the 4 June he had had a narrow escape of a very different kind:

> I stood near a lyon (which came about for a sight) with my back to him, and he rose up (as I am told by some that called to me) to mischief me, and I stept forward the same moment out of his reach and God knows what the event might have been.

On 'November 26 att night and 27 in the morning', however, he suffered more than a fright for there was:

> a very high wind and blew down severall houses and trees and killed severall persons, but blessed be God who spared our lives and limbs, and though I sustained a considerable loss and damage, my cowlodge was blown down and killed 3 cows, yet if God's great mercy had not intervened, it had proved a great deal worse.

A mercy was certainly received by one John Dicer of Bruton in Somerset who, according to Hu. Ash:

> lay the night as the tempest was, in the barn of John Sellar [and] the violence of the wind broke down the roof of the barn, but fortunately for him there was a ladder which staid up a rafter, which would have fell upon the said John Dicer, but he, narrowly escaping being killed, did slide himself through the broken roof and so got over the wall without any great hurt.

Generally speaking, it was the poor who suffered the worst miseries, as another of Ash's stories reminds us. This is from Evercreech, only about four miles from where John Dicer had his lucky escape:

> a poor woman begged for lodging in a Barn of one Edmond Peny that same night that the storm was, she was wet the day before in travelling, so she hung up her cloaths in the barn where she lay in the straw; but when the storm came, it blew down the roof of the barn where she lay, and she narrowly escaped with her life, being much bruised, and got out almost naked through the roof where it was broken most, and went to the dwelling house of the said Edmond Peny, and they did rise and did help her to something to cover her, till they could get out her cloaths . . .

The kind of damage done in rural areas across the country can be appreciated by reference to a small area, about 32 miles square, centred on Ilminster in Somerset, and to an individual estate owned by Christ's Hospital, in north-west Kent. Although the account which Defoe received from Ilminster is anonymous it contains the kind of detailed knowledge of the area that can leave little doubt as to its authenticity. In the *Tour* he mentions relatives living at nearby Martock at the time of Monmouth's rebellion, one of whom may be the source of the following:

> IMPRIMUS. At Ashil [Ashill] parish, 3 miles west from this town, the stable belonging to the Hare and Hounds Inn was blown down, in which were three horses, one killed another very much bruised.
> 2. At Jurdans [Jordans], a gentleman's seat in the same parish, there was a brick stable, whose roof, one back, and one end wall were all thrown down, and four feet in depth of the fore wall; in the stable were four horses, which by reason of the hay loft that bore up the roof, were all preserved.
> 3. At Sevington [Seavington St Mary], three miles east from this town, John Huthens [probably Hutchings] had the roof of a

new built house heaved clean off the walls. Note, the house was not glazed, and the roof was thatched.

4. In White Larkington [Whitelackington] park, a mile east from this town, besides four or five hundred tall trees broken and blown down, (admirable to behold, what great roots was turned up) there were three very large beaches, two of them that were near five foot thick in the stem, were broken off, one of them near the root, the other was broken off twelve feet above, and from that place down home to the root was shattered and flown; the other that was not broken, cannot have less than forty wagon loads in it; a very fine walk of trees before the house all blown down, and broke down the roof of a pigeon house, the rookery carried away in lanes, the lodge house damaged in the roof, and one end by the fall of trees. In the garden belonging to the house, was a very fine walk of tall firrs, twenty of which were broken down.

5. The damage in the thatch of houses, (which is the usual covering in these parts) is so great and general, that the price of reed arose from twenty shillings to fifty, or three pound a hundred; insomuch that to shelter themselves from the open air, many more people were glad to use bean, helm* and furze, to thatch their houses with, things never known to be put to such use before.

6. At Kingston [Kingstone], a mile distance from this town, the church was very much shattered in its roof, and walls too, and all our country churches much shattered, so that churches and gentlemen's houses that were tiled, were so shattered in their roofs, that at present, they are generally patched with read, not in compliance with the mode, but the necessity of the times.

7. At Broadway, two miles west of this town, Hugh Betty, his wife, and four children being in his house, it was by the violence of the storm blown down, one of his children killed, his wife wounded but recovered, the rest escaped with their lives. A large almshouse had much of the tile blown off, and

* Helm or haulm – collectively the storks or stems of peas, beans or potatoes without the pods or tubers, sometimes used for thatching.

other houses much shattered; a very large brick barn blown down, walls and roof to the ground.
8. Many large stacks of wheat were broken, some of the sheaves carried two or three hundred yards from the place, many stacks of hay turned over, some stacks of corn heaved off the stadle, and set down on the ground and not broken.
9. Dowlish walk [Dowlish Wake], two miles south-east, the church was very much shattered, several load of stone fell down, not as yet repaired, therefore can't express the damage. A very large barn broken down that stood near the church, much damage was done to orchards, not only in this place, but in all places round, some very fine orchards quite destroyed; some to their great cost had the trees set up right again, but a storm of wind came after, which threw down many of the trees again; as to timber trees almost all our high trees were broken down in that violent storm.
10. In this town Harry Dunster, his wife and two children, was in the house when it was blown down, but they all escaped with their lives, only one of them had a small bruise with a piece of timber, as she was going out of the chamber when the roof broke in. The church, in this place, escaped very well, as to its roof, being covered with lead only on the chancel; the lead was on the top of the roof heaved up and rolled together, more than ten men could turn back again, without cutting the sheets of lead, which was done to put it in its place again: but in general the houses much broken and shattered, besides the fall of some. This is a short, but true account. I have heard of several other things which I have not mentioned, because I could not be positive in the truth of them. . . . At Henton [Hinton] St George, at the Lord Pawlet's [Poulett's], a new brick wall was broken down by the wind for above 100 foot, the wall being built not above 2 years since, as also above 60 trees near 100 foot high. At Barrington, about two miles north of this town, there was blown down above eight score trees, being of an extraordinary height, at the lady Strouds [Strode's].

In 1703 the former Augustinian priory of Lesnes Abbey in Kent was in the possession of the Blue Coat School (Christ's Hospital) which at that time was still located in Newgate Street in London. Lesnes lies between Woolwich and Erith on land overlooking Erith Marshes. The Abbey had, with the Pope's permission, been suppressed by Wolsey in 1525 in order to help endow the college – Cardinal College (subsequently Christ Church) – which he was building at Oxford. After the fall of Wolsey the college's estates were confiscated by the Crown and Lesnes was sold, passing through numerous hands until in 1633 it was bequeathed to Christ's Hospital. By this time all the monastic buildings had been pulled down, with the exception of the Abbot's lodging, the Abbey House, which served as the manor house. The estate was leased to the executors of Croschild Draper and sub-let to the occupant, John Rudman.

After 27 November the representatives of the Christ's Hospital charity do not appear to have viewed the property until 11 April 1704 when they discovered 'abundance of mischief done to these premises by the late Storme'. At the Abbey house itself a stack of chimneys had fallen through a roof and had done 'a great deal of damage to Tileing, Rafters and ceiling of one of the chambers which now lyes open'. The roof of the stable was 'much damnifyed', the Carthouse blown down and the Barn 'much damnifyed in the thatch roof' and a little tenement next to the house was also damaged. The palings about the Abbey wood, which survives to this day, were also in need of repair. To make good the damage done to the buildings would involve at least seven loads of timber and the Governors of Christ's Hospital instructed Captain Bodenham, Mr Draper's executor, to carry out the repair forthwith, 'according to the covenant in the lease'.

The damages sustained at Lesnes were by no means the only losses endured by the charity as a consequence of the Storm. The principal buildings in London were, as we shall see, severely hit, as too were the barns and other outbuildings leased to Richard Wareing at East Bedfont in Middlesex. There a great timber-framed barn of five bays was removed to the manor yard for repair and Wareing was advised to replace the wall between the orchard and the garden, which had been blown down 'in seasonable time', with a quickset hedge.

Prior to the Storm the diarist John Evelyn had noted that 'Corne and Provisions' were 'on the sudaine so cheap that farmers are unable to pay their rents'. Then came the Storm and the same farmers abruptly found themselves faced with a very different problem: crops which the day before had been all but worthless, rose rapidly in value and, where barns had been unroofed or corn stacks destroyed, as Defoe points out, 'the Country People were under a necessity of Threshing out their Corn with all possible speed least if a Rain had followed which at that time of year was not unlikely, it might have been all spoil'd'. In fact, for three weeks, by 'a special providence' there was very little rain. Straw was also at a premium for purposes of re-thatching. Unsurprisingly, the price of wheat rose. At Cambridge the price shot up from the average for the period of 24*s* per bushel in the summer to 40*s* by Christmas following the Storm. It did not return to 24*s* until after the following harvest. A load of hay or straw, which had cost 14/6 a load in London on 30 October was, by 18 December, fetching 28*s*. The destruction of windmills would also have created some local bottlenecks in the food supply chain. A shorter term interruption came on the morning after the Storm when, according to Defoe, the wind was still blowing so strongly that the milk maids who carried the milk into London from the surrounding villages 'were not able to go along with their Pails on their heads'.

Since the sixteenth century the diminution of woodland had been the cause of spasmodic bouts of national neurosis. The depredations of the Civil War and the demands of the Admiralty meant that by the beginning of Anne's reign the Royal Forests were much depleted and only the New Forest, the Forest of Dean and Alice Holt (in Hampshire) continued to play a significant part in meeting the demands of the Navy for oaken hulls. Fir masts were imported from the Baltic and, increasingly, from New England.

Alarmed by the shortage of timber, the Navy Board recruited John Evelyn to their cause and in 1664 he published his *Sylva, or a Discourse of Forest Trees*, a work aimed, with much success*, at

* In the 1679 version of the book, which ran to many editions, Evelyn claimed indirect responsibility for the planting of many millions of trees.

encouraging the nobility and gentry to plant trees on their estates as a matter of national duty. Most of the country's best timber was now to be found in the parks and woodlands of such estates. The contemporary statistician Gregory King estimated that of the 39 million acres of land in England and Wales, 3 million consisted of woods and coppices and a further 3 million of forests, parks and commons. And the most thickly wooded areas of Great Britain were the worst affected by the Storm.

Within a few days of the Storm Daniel Defoe set off on a 'circuit . . . over most parts of Kent' and counted 17,000 fallen trees before, 'being tired', giving up. Hardly surprising! He also states that over twenty-five parks had over a thousand trees blown down and that in the New Forest in excess of 4,000 trees had been lost, but he adds, judiciously, that these figures are 'rather under than over the real truth'. A comparison with recent storms suggests that the total number of trees broken and uprooted probably ran into millions. In the storm of 16 October 1987, which affected a very similar part of the UK, some 15 million trees were lost, over 2,000 of the 6,000 trees in the 120 acres of Sheffield Park, East Sussex, alone. In the *tempête* of 26 December 1999 in France, admittedly a much larger and more densely wooded country, a staggering 360 million trees were destroyed.

Wind speed is not, of course, the only factor governing a storm's ability to flatten woodland. One of the remarkable things about the 1999 French storm was that it occurred in winter when the trees of the, largely deciduous, forests had lost their leaves and, consequently, presented less resistance to the wind. As Oliver Rackham has pointed out, the 1987 storm in England caused exceptional damage to woodland whereas that to buildings was only 'moderate', the reason being not only that the trees were still in leaf but also that 'the ground had been weakened by weeks of heavy rain'. This second factor, although not of course the first, was almost certainly of significance in the uprooting of so many trees in 1703. The summer in the south of England had been, as William Derham recorded at Upminster, exceptionally wet. Plenty of rain had also accompanied the gales which preceded the arrival of the Storm.

Particular note was taken of the fall of tall, old trees, such as the 'five hundred tall trees broken and blown down' in Whitelackington park* and, at nearby Barrington Court, where 'above eight score trees being of an extraordinary height' belonging to Lady Strode came down. Of course, as trees age and grow taller not only does their susceptibility to windblow increase but so too does the drama of their fall and the likelihood that their loss will be thought worthy of record. In Sir Thomas Samwell's park near Northampton 'a very great-headed Elm was blown over the Park wall into the Road and yet never touched the Wall'. Near Witney in Oxfordshire 'a great Oak of about nine or ten loads was blown down, having a Raven sitting in it, his feathers got between two Bows and held him fast: but the Raven received no hurt'. Well over half a century later the villagers of Gilbert White's Selborne recalled that it was in the Storm of 1703 that the great oak on the Plestor (the village square) had been blown down. Shallow-rooting trees such as beech would have been especially vulnerable and the elms of southern England, tall, often isolated hedgerow trees, were said to have given up 'without a struggle'.

A man who must have been very much aggrieved at the effect of the Storm upon his woodlands was William Kingscote of Kingscote, near Tetbury, Gloucestershire. According to Henry Head, the vicar of Berkeley, Kingscote had many woods:

> among which was one grove of very tall trees, being each near eighty foot high; the which he greatly valued for the tallness and prospect of them: but it so happened that six hundred of them, within the compass of five acres were blown down: (and supposed to be at the same time) each tree tearing up the ground with its root: so that the roots of most of the trees, with the turf and earth about them, stood up at least fifteen or sixteen foot high; the lying down of which trees is an amazing sight to all beholders.

* Whitelackington, the home of the Speke family, had been visited in 1680 by the Duke of Monmouth who had sat beneath a tree in the park to touch people for the King's Evil. This tree survived into the nineteenth century.

Nobody, however, could have been more upset by the devastation the Storm had wrought upon the country's woodlands than John Evelyn himself. He was by now an old man, in his eighty-fourth year, still very much concerned about public affairs but saddened by the loss, four years before, of his only surviving son and his elder brother who left him the family house at Wotton in Surrey, a couple of miles west of Dorking. Earlier in the Storm year he had also lost his good friend Sam Pepys, 'a very worthy, industrious and curious person'.

Evelyn also had houses in Dover Street, London and at Sayes Court at Deptford in Kent but at the time of the Storm he was staying at Wotton. His record of what happened is worth quoting in full:

> 26* The dismall Effects of the Hurecan & Tempest of Wind, raine & lightening thro all the nation, especial[y] London, many houses demolished, many people killed: & as to my owne losse, the subversion of Woods & Timber both left for Ornament, and Valuable materiall thro my whole Estate, & about my house, the Woods crowning the Garden Mount, & growing along the Park meadow; the damage to my owne dwelling, & Tennants farmes and outhouses is most Tragicall: not to be paralleled with anything in our Age [or] in history almost, I am not able to describe, but submitt to the Almight[y] pleasure of God, with acknowledgements of his Justice for our Nationall sinns, & my owne, who yet have not suffered as I deserved to: Every moment like Jobs Messengers, bring[s] the sad Tidings of this universal Judgement. We hourly dread to he[a]re what has happened at sea during the Tempest & even in our very harbours.

On 7 December Evelyn travelled with his family to the London house and:

* E.S. de Beer, editor of the definitive edition of Evelyn's Diary, places this entry under 26 November but points out that the date has been altered 'on or to 27'. The nature of the entry is such that it could not have been written before the 27th. Evelyn usually wrote up his diary, from odd scraps of notes, some time after the event.

> saw the lamentable destruction of Houses & Trees thro all the Journey: & observed it had least injured those trees &c which grew in plaine exposed & perflatil [= exposed to the wind] grounds & places; but did most execution where it was pent in by the villages & among the bottom of the hills.

It was not until 10 February that Evelyn managed to get down to Sayes Court, his house near Deptford. The sight of the damage done to his house and gardens must have been especially troubling as the property had been quite wantonly desecrated by Peter the Great when he had been tenant there during his visits to the shipyards in 1698. The sight reawakened the diarist's sense of loss and he launched into a kind of sylvan threnody:

> Methinks I still hear, and am sure feel the dismal Groans of our forests, so many thousands of goodly Oaks subverted by that late dreadful Hurricane, prostrating the trees, and crushing all that grew under them, lying in ghastly Postures, like whole Regiments fallen in Battle, by the Sword of the Conqueror: such was the Prospect of many Miles in several Places, resembling that of Mount Taurus, so naturally described by the Poet speaking of the Fall of the Minotaurs slain by Theseus.

Beneath the formality of the language and the classical allusions there can be no doubt that the old man, 'the father of English arboriculture', as Trevelyan calls him, was truly distressed by what must have seemed like the destruction of his life's work. The 1706 edition of *Sylva*, published in the year of his death, contains a summary of the destruction wrought on the nation's woodlands:

> The losses and dreadful Stories of this Ruin were indeed great, but how much greater the Universal Devastation through the Kingdom! The Publick Accounts tell us, besides innumerable Men, reckoning no less than 3000 brave Oaks in one part only of the Forest of Dean blown down; and in New Forest in Hampshire about 4000; and in about 450 Parks and groves, from 200 large trees to a thousand of excellent Timber, without

counting Fruit and Orchard Trees sans number, and proportionately the same through all the considerable Woods of the Nation; with those stately Groves, Arbours and Vistas. . . .

Sir Edward Harley had One thousand Three hundred blown down; My Self above 2000; several of which torn up their fall, rais'd Mounds of Earth near 20 foot high, with great Stones entangled among the Roots and Rubbish; and this within almost sight of my Dwelling (now no longer Wotton*) sufficient to mortifie and change my too great Affection and Application to this Work; which as I contentedly submit to, so I thank God for what are yet left standing.

Evelyn advised his grandson and heir 'to restore the name of Wotton'.

The regions which specialised in orchard fruit production were hard hit by the Storm. From Littleton in the Vale of Evesham there was news of 'very many fruit trees . . . torn up' and Anne Watts wrote to Defoe from Hereford listing a catalogue of local calamities – a man killed when his house collapsed at Wormsley, the damage to the oaks of 'my Lord Skudamoor [Scudamore]' at Holme Lacy, an 'abundance of tiles off the old houses' in the city and the blowing down of 'some hundreds of fruit trees' in the county. In Sussex many large orchards and cherry gardens were said to be 'lay'd waste'.

The most important area of apple production in the kingdom was the West Country. Commercial apple-growing was already established in the late sixteenth century when considerable quantities of cider were sold for the provisioning of ships. By 1630, Thomas Westcote, in his *View of Devonshire* wrote that the farmers of the south-east of the county were 'very curious in the planting and grafting all kinds of fruit'. In *the Tour* Defoe gives an idea of the scale of production:

. . . there is one article in the produce of Devonshire, which makes good what I have written before, that every county contributes something towards the supply of London; and this

* i.e. 'Wood-town'.

> is, the cider which takes up the south part of the county, between Topsham and Axminster, where they have so vast a quantity of fruit, and so much cider made, that sometimes they have sent ten, or twenty thousand hogsheads of it in a year to London, and at a very reasonable rate too.

It was from Axminster that, after the Storm, Defoe received a 'plain but honest account' stating that 'Our loss in the Apple-Trees is the greatest; because we shall want liquor to make our Hearts merry'. As in the nearby Ilminster area of Somerset, farmers attempted to redeem the situation by replanting the trees – 'the Farmers sate them up again' – but, also as at Ilminster, the wind subsequently blew them down.

Although it was more than half a century since Thomas Hobbes had characterised the life of man as 'solitary, poor, nasty, brutish and short', life expectancy was probably no longer at the beginning of the eighteenth century than it had been in the middle of the seventeenth. Average life expectancy at birth by the time of the Storm was around thirty-seven. This was an improvement on the 1680s when it had fallen to little more than thirty but, even so, death was a frequent visitor not least to households with small children. Rates of infant mortality were still high, 20 per cent of children dying before they reached their first birthday. As Julian Hoppit has pointed out, however, this did not mean that parents were 'desensitised' by the loss of so many children: contemporary memoirs and diaries are full of stories, often heartbreakingly rendered, of the loss of offspring. It may be for this very reason that the record of the Storm contains more references to the remarkable flights of hayricks and uprooted elms and to 'miraculous preservations' than it does to the loss of human life. Unsurprisingly, we know much more of the relatively small number of well-to-do victims than of the many who died intestate and lie in unmarked graves.

10

HER TRUE AND FAITHFUL LOVER

The history of the Storm, like much of the history of England, is a story told of men by men. It reflects the bias that existed against women even at a time when the monarch was a woman. Women were less likely to be literate and therefore to leave an account of their experience, less likely to be engaged in hazardous occupations that exposed them to the vagaries of the weather and it was utterly unlikely they fill the secretarial posts which demanded that they explain the expenditure resulting from Storm damage. The overwhelming majority of Defoe's correspondents were male, Edith Conyers of Wells in Somerset, Anne Watts of Hereford and Elizabeth Lack of Tunbridge being the exceptions. Even Bishop Kidder's wife is reduced to the anonymity and vassal-status of 'his lady', and the monument to her parents erected by their daughter in Wells Cathedral does not even mention her by name. An exception to the general rule of mute ingloriousness in the face of the Storm was one of the most remarkable women of the age, Lady Rachel Russell. She was among the great ladies of the day, a daughter of Thomas Wriothesley, Earl of Southampton and his Huguenot first wife, *la belle et verteuse* Rachel de Ruvigny. Lady Rachel was a prolific letter writer (the English Madame de Sévigné perhaps?) who had numbered among her correspondents Queen Mary, Archbishop Tillotson and Bishop Ken's friend, the non-juror Dr Fitzwilliam. In the year of the Great Storm, however, by which time she was sixty-seven years old, many of her greatest friends were dead. Pre-eminent among them was her husband, Lord

William Russell, who in 1683 had been beheaded for his part in the Rye House Plot, aimed at the assassination of Charles II and his brother, the future James II. During her husband's trial Lady Rachel had sat in court devotedly making notes for the defence and, once the verdict had been passed and the sentence pronounced (initially of being hanged, drawn and quartered but later commuted to beheading) she energetically flung herself into an attempt to save her husband, even to the extent of literally throwing herself at the feet of a merciless monarch. Lord William went bravely to his death earning himself pride of place in that rather slim volume, the Whig Book of Martyrs.

On her father's death in 1665 Lady Rachel had inherited an estate in the tithing of West Stratton at Micheldever, between Winchester and Basingstoke, in Hampshire. Stratton House was reputed to be the Russells' favourite residence. On the death of her elder sister in 1680 Lady Rachel also inherited Place House, an old Premonstratensian abbey, at Titchfield, near Fareham in the same county. It was in this latter house that she was living at the end of November 1703 and from there that she wrote to her daughter, also Lady Rachel, living at Belvoir Castle in Leicestershire, home of her husband, John Manners, Marquis of Granby. The letter was written on Tuesday 30 November. It seems to support the view expressed by the writer of the article on her in the *Dictionary of National Biography* that in managing her extensive estates she proved herself an excellent business woman:

> I have been under great anxiety, so till the post came yesterday, for though Belvoir is so strong a building, I feared accidents there as little as anywhere; yet so many fatal and dismal ones have fallen upon so many, that would justify a mighty apprehension. I bless God we are all well; but the chimney where my son [Wriothesley] and his wife lay, fell, and the bricks and soot coming down the chimney, made them rise at six o'clock and come to my drawing room; the wall of the garden fell next the field, and all the trees beat one side to the very ground; but at Stretton [sic] my loss is worse in all respects, my farms torn to pieces, corn and hay dispersed, seen hanging on the trees, and among trees near the house, the fir grove, as

Richard writes, entirely broken and torn up by the roots. I send Spencer tomorrow to see if it is in nature possible to set up but a row round the ground. Hampshire is all desolation; Devon House escaped better than any house I hear of. Many killed in country as well as in town. Lady Penelope Nichlesse [Nicholas] killed in her bed at their country house, and he, in the same bed, found a piece of timber falling between his legs and kept of the bricks, but it is innumerable the mischiefs and the preservations; sea matters yet too uncertain. So certain Beaumont is lost, and wonderfully lamented, and five ships upon the sand. No news that is to be relied on of Sir Cloudesley Shovel, and we sorry your Lord lost his match; but really the present calamities take up all my thoughts. It is time to dine, so must end this

From your affectionate Mother

Although not of quite such blue-blooded stock as Lady Rachel, Penelope Nicholas too was of an aristocratic background. She was the daughter of Spencer Compton, the Earl of Northampton who had been killed in the Royalist cause at Hopton Heath in 1643 when Penelope was four. She had six remarkably talented brothers of whom the most prominent was Henry, the Bishop of London, and the most able William who, although a committed Royalist, had by his sobriety and godliness, won the admiration of Cromwell. Penelope's own children – she had three sons and a daughter – were civilised and well educated; typical offspring of the Enlightenment.

She had married Sir John Nicholas, who also had sound Cavalier credentials, his father, Sir Edward, having been First Secretary to both Charles I and Charles II with whom he had been in exile. Sir Edward had retired on grounds of age and sickness in 1662 with a pension of £10,000 which he appears to have used to purchase West Horsley Place in Surrey on the death of Carew Raleigh, the son of Queen Elizabeth's one-time favourite, the subsequently executed, Sir Walter.

Sir John Nicholas, born in 1623, accompanied his father into exile during the Interregnum. At the Restoration he became one of the clerks in ordinary to the Privy Council. When his father died in 1667 he inherited the house at West Horsley which John Evelyn, whose brother lived only five miles away at Wotton, described as 'a pretty drie seate on the Downe'. Sir John was a conscientious civil servant, occasionally mentioned by Pepys, who remained in his post until his death. On the night of the Storm, however, as Rachel Russell's letter relates, he was at home and narrowly escaped dying alongside his wife. In fact, the London newspaper the *Post Man* initially reported that it was he who had died, later correcting an error which must have raised some ambitious hopes in the Privy Council office.

Pam Bowley, historian of West Horsley, describes Sir John as 'a careful, precise man' who 'carried his clerkly habits into his private life, jotting down expenses, rents and memoranda into many small books'. One such jotting refers to 26 November 1703 and reads: 'This night was the dreadful storm and tempest wherein my deare wife was killed in our bed by the fall of a chimney, and I was wonderfully preserved by God's Providence.'

According to *An Exact Relation of the Late Dreadful Tempest . . . collected by an Ingenious Hand*, an account, like Defoe's, published in 1704, Sir John, 'a learned and Antient gentleman' was 'taken out of the Rubbish very dangerously hurt' but:

> the Chirurgeons, who viewed the Body of the Lady Penelope gave in their Opinion, that her Ladyship being between 80 and 90 years of Age [she was much younger], was killed by the Fright of that most terrible Storm; and though her leg was broke, yet no Blood nor Matter flowing from it, she was dead before the Fall of the Chimney.

Sir John only outlived his wife by a year and they lie side by side beneath the floor of the south chapel of St Mary's church, West Horsley. Their memorial, a masterpiece of filial devotion, translated from the Latin, reads as follows:

> Here lies JOHN NICHOLAS Knight of the Bath and eldest son of Edward who is buried nearby. After going with Charles II into exile, he was appointed Clerk to the Privy Council. He filled the same position with the utmost distinction in the

reigns of James, William and Anne, famous for her triumphs over the French.

Here too lies his dearest wife Penelope. She was the daughter of Spencer Compton, the Earl of Northampton, renowned for his courage, who was killed by the Rebels near Stafford. By her he had three sons, EDWARD, JOHN and WILLIAM, and an only daughter PENELOPE, named after her mother.

They were both remarkable for the simplicity of their lives, their devotion to each other, their generosity to the poor and their simple devotion towards God. Their souls were received back by their Creator on 26th November 1703 when she died, aged 64, and on 9th January 1704 when he died at the age of 81. This [memorial] was erected to the best of parents by their son Edward.

Lady Penelope's burial, as was the upper-class custom, took place at night and the solemn, candlelit occasion must have had a decidedly gothic atmosphere for, in the digging of the grave, a skull, unattached to a skeleton, had been unearthed, close to the grave of one of Carew Raleigh's sons. It was believed to belong to the executed Sir Walter. The story may well be true for, after the execution in 1618, the head, instead of being put on public display, was placed in a red leather bag, Sir Walter's cloak was thrown over it and it had been whisked rapidly away in Lady Raleigh's coach. It is thought that the loyal wife had kept the head in a cupboard at West Horsley and that, some time after her death, possibly in 1660, it was buried beneath the floor of the church.

Another female victim of the Storm was Dame Elinor Drury of Riddlesworth in Norfolk, who had put her signature to her last Will and Testament on 20 April 1694 in the presence of Henry, Elizabeth and Mary Frith in Rose Street, Covent Garden, London. Henry, one imagines, was her lawyer. She was the second of the five daughters of Samuel Harsnet of Great Fransham also in Norfolk and her will reveals her as a gentlewoman of some independence of both means and spirit. That Elinor had made a will at all was remarkable. A survey of wills proven in the Prerogative Court of Canterbury between 1694–1700 shows that for every 1,000 fewer than nine were made by women.* As Mary Prior has pointed out, considering the position of women in common law, as chattels of their husbands, 'the marvel is that any wives made wills'.

Elinor does not appear to have had children either by her first marriage, to William Marsham of Statton Strawless whom she had married in 1666 but who had died eight years later, or by her second husband, Sir Robert Drury of Riddlesworth. It was this second marriage which brought Elinor to the house in which she would die in the Great Storm.

Under the terms of her second marriage settlement Elinor retained the right to dispose of her personal possessions as she saw fit, a power of which she seems to have taken full advantage. Furthermore, she was anxious to ensure that the, largely female, legatees themselves benefited in person from her will. The three executrices, her sisters, Barbara Fisher, Mary Bowles and Cotton Beck, were also the principal beneficiaries. By the time the will was written another of Elinor's sisters, Anne Strange, was already dead.

Dame Elinor was happy to leave most of the detailed arrangements for her funeral to her sisters but did specify that 'they would expend the sum of forty pounds in Rings to be given to such persons as shall be invited to my funerall' . Another request was that 'they would not use or give any wine or other liquors at such my funerall'. She was clearly concerned to ensure that her interment was a solemn and seemly occasion, further stipulating that the sum of forty shillings be distributed 'among the poor people that shall come in a week after my funerall to prevent trouble at such time of my funerall'. To the parson of Riddlesworth she left the sum of twenty shillings 'for preaching my funerall sermon to buy him a Ring in remembrance of me'. It was also her desire that 'if Parson Denny shall at any time within one year after my decease preach a sermon as for me then I give

* Quoted by Mary Prior in 'Wives and Wills, 1558–1700' in J. Chartres and D. Hey: *English Rural Society: Essays in Honour of Joan Thirsk* (1990).

him for his pains twenty shillings to buy him a Ring in Remembrance of me'. Parson Denny was almost certainly the Revd William Denny, rector of the nearby village of East Harling.

To her sister Barbara, Elinor bequeathed 'all my wearing apparel whatsoever (except my colour'd embroidered petticoat)' and the sum of ten pounds for her 'sole and only separate use'. These bequests were to be disposed of by Barbara 'as she shall think fit', her husband, Edward Fisher, being 'wholly debarred and excluded both in Law and Equity of and from interfering or meddling with the same'.

Beds and bedding had become much more comfortable in the sixteenth century and Shakespeare who famously bequeathed his second-best bed to his wife (the marriage bed rather than the guest bed) was by no means idiosyncratic in that respect. That great local historian W.G. Hoskins suggests that the study of household inventories reveals that a materially comfortable Tudor life revolved around 'a good fire, a good meal and a good bed' and even at the end of the seventeenth century, beds and their hangings, often beautifully embroidered, were still considered a valuable inheritance. It is not then surprising to find that to her sister Mary Bowles, who was widowed, Elinor gave 'my green wrought Bedd and the chayres suitable', specifying, however, that her own husband, Sir Robert, have the use of them during his lifetime, provided that he did not re-marry. Mary was also to receive 'one of my own pictures'. Under the same conditions her sister Cotton, also a widow, was left 'my wrought needlework Bedd cross-stitch embroidered' together with the matching chairs; her dining room hangings and matching cushions in English stitch; and her great looking glass in an oval frame with matching table and stands. The will further specifies that after Cotton's death, she also apparently being childless, these bequests should go to 'my said sister Bowles's daughter' – also called Cotton – 'if then alive if not to such of my Relations as she shall think fit but to none other'. These objects too were to be 'used and enjoy'd by my said husband during his life and widowhood, as aforementioned'. Upon Elinor's death her Sister Cotton was straightaway to receive a diamond gorget. After the death of Sir Robert, Dame Elinor's 'pewter, brass and other household stuff' was to be divided equally between the three sisters 'share and share alike'. To be split up in the same way was a plot of land and two cottages on the common at Knettishall in Suffolk, just across the Little Ouse, the county boundary, from Riddlesworth.

Dame Elinor's two nephews and six nieces were also beneficiaries. Of Barbara's five children, two were to receive twenty pounds apiece; Mary ten pounds; Barbara twenty pounds, some silver salt cellars and spoons; and Ellen, who was married, was to gain a gold watch and 'a share in the linen manufactory amounting to four score pounds upon improvement'. This share could be used as Ellen wished on condition only that her husband be 'wholly debarred and excluded . . . from interfering or meddling in any part thereof'.

The greatest individual beneficiaries appear to have been the two only children of Elinor's sisters Anne and Mary. Mary's daughter Cotton, in addition to receiving the furniture passed on to her aunt Cotton, was also to receive twenty pounds, a silver tankard engraved with the Marsham and Harsnet arms, five silver spoons marked with the Marsham arms and the sky-coloured, embroidered petticoat . On Sir Robert's death she was also to receive a black marble table and stands and a large looking glass in a black frame. Anne's daughter, also Elinor, may have been a particular favourite for she was to receive (in addition to twenty pounds, a silver plate marked with the Marsham and Harsnet arms, five spoons, a silver castor, and three silver-handled knives and forks) one of the two pictures of her aunt. Elinor was also to be given another black marble table and the stands and glass belonging to it but, again, only after Sir Robert had ceased to have need of them. To another nephew, Thomas Marsham, was to be left 'his Uncle's, viz. my first husband's picture'. To each of two god-daughters, Mary Lambe and Elizabeth Barnes, Dame Elinor left twenty pounds to buy pieces of plate.

The relationship between Elinor and Robert appears to have been neither happy nor conventional. Apart from the loan of her furniture during his widowhood, Robert was to receive no more than ten pounds 'to buy him Mourning', no personal token 'in remembrance of me'. He was to get 'my Diamond Ring' but, apparently, in a spirit of resentment rather than love, for this is a ring which 'he took from me to lend to Elizabeth Cook'! What is more, Sir Robert's right 'to use and enjoy' the furniture was itself conditional not only upon him not remarrying but also upon his not dealing with or concerning himself 'on any account with the family of the Cooks our present tenants'.

Elinor's final bequest was the sum of ten shillings to each of 'such servants as shall live with me at the time of my decease'. Two of them, maidservants, were, it was said, in bed in Lady Elinor's chamber on the night of the Storm and it was no doubt they who ventured across the bedroom and among the dust and debris, the wind howling through a gaping hole in the ceiling, discovered the worst. Whether Dame Elinor and her niece Mary Fisher lay in the green bed or in the cross-stitch embroidered one that night we shall never know, only that they lay together – the younger woman perhaps comforting her ageing aunt – and that they were killed by a stack of chimneys falling through the roof.

The Riddlesworth parish register records:

The Ladye Elinor Drury Buryed Nov. 30: 1703:
Mary Fisher her Neece buryed ye same day.

Set into the floor at the east end of the nave of St Peter's church are a number of black slate memorials. One has carved into it the arms of Drury impaled with those of Harsnet below which are the words:

Here Lyeth ye Body of Dame ELINOR
DRURY 2d Daught of SAM HARSNET
of Great FRANSHAM in ye County of Norf.
Esq. ye Relicte of WILLM MARSHAM of
STRATTON STRAWLY Gent ye 2d wife of
Sr Robert Drury of RIDLESWORTH
in ye County of Norf. Baronet who was
Unfortunately Kild in ye Fatal Hurricane
Nov ye 27 in ye year of our Lord
1703

The affectionate words of a distraught husband are conspicuously absent and we are not surprised to find that Sir Robert did indeed marry for a third time for there in the church floor we also find the memorial to Diana Drury, his widow, who died at the age of seventy-two on the 13 August 1744. This, however, is not entirely a tale of loveless tragedy for near to the memorial to Elinor is another, carved with the Fisher hatchment and beneath it the following:

In Memory of the Pious and
virtuous Mrs MARY FISHER
Whose Soul tooke her Flight
to heaven in ye Furious hurricane
on November ye 27th 1703
This Monument of Respect
is Dedicated by her true &
Faithfull lover ANTHONY
DRURY of MENDHAM
in NORFOLK Gent.

Anthony, rather than Robert, Drury must be our representative mourner for the many thousands who died in the Great Storm.

11

Sir Cloudesley is Expected

Sir Cloudesley Shovell, returning from the Mediterranean aboard HMS *Triumph*, had sighted land on 15 November and, as Naval etiquette demanded, had lowered the Union flag and hoisted his own as Admiral of the White*. Two days later the *Triumph* and the accompanying ships of Shovell's squadron dropped anchor in the Downs, an anchorage already thick with the masts of shipping; in the words of Lieutenant Arthur Feild of the *Association*:

> Fresh squalls of wind – we anchored in the Downs in 9½ fathoms. Adm Beaumont with about 10 more sail of Cruising Shipps and many Merchant men riding here.

The Downs lie off the east Kent coast between the North and South Forelands and to the west of the Goodwin Sands, which are

* The fleet was, at least in theory, divided into three squadrons, the red, white and blue in that order of seniority. Each squadron was commanded by an admiral with, beneath him, a vice-admiral and then a rear admiral. The expression Admiral of the Red was not always used because, as the highest ranking officer, he was Admiral of the Fleet. At this time Sir George Rooke was the Navy's senior admiral and Sir Cloudesley, as Admiral of the White, was next in seniority. Again in theory, promotion was from one flag rank to the next, for example, from Rear Admiral of the Red to Vice-Admiral of the Blue. Like most aspects of eighteenth-century official life, however, the system was open to corruption. When George Churchill in effect appointed himself a flag officer he became Admiral of the Blue, thus leap-frogging his arch-rival Matthew Aylmer who was Vice-Admiral of the Red.

four miles offshore. The Goodwins provide shelter from easterly winds while, with the wind in the west, the land forms a protective weather shore. Land batteries also provided defence against a seaborne enemy so that the Downs were a safe and convenient anchorage in which convoys could be assembled, Thames' pilots could be picked up and set down and ships could await a suitable wind to carry them down the Channel.

By Saturday 20 November Sir Cloudesley was, according to the parliamentary diarist Sir Narcissus Luttrell, 'expected this night in town' but fresh gales kept him in the Downs together with four other flag officers, Sir Stafford Fairborne and Sir John Leake, who had been with him in the Mediterranean, the Vice-Admiral of the White John Graydon newly returned from the West Indies and Rear Admiral Beaumont who had spent the summer and autumn escorting Baltic convoys, searching, unsuccessfully, for the French privateer St Pol and blockading Dunkirk.

Basil Beaumont was the fifth son and one of the twenty-one children of Sir Henry Beaumont of Stoughton Grange and Coleorton in Leicestershire where he was born in 1669. Nothing is known of his early naval career but his rise to flag status was as dramatic as his career in general was unspectacular. He was made lieutenant in 1688 and, before reaching his twenty-first birthday, was given his first command, a ship called the *Centurion* which was lost in a violent gale in Plymouth Sound on Christmas Day 1689. No blame was attached to the young captain who by 1692 was in command of the 66-gun *Rupert*, part of the Red Squadron which had borne the brunt of the fighting at Barfleur.

Although he spent the summer of 1696 in the Mediterranean, Beaumont's commissions usually involved cruising in the Channel or the North Sea. Having often been the senior officer at the Nore or in the Downs with, as he put it in a letter to the Lord High Admiral, 'no small trouble and a great deal of charge', he was rewarded by being promoted Rear Admiral of the Blue on 1 March 1703, hoisting his flag on the *Mary* then being re-fitted at Woolwich.

The *Mary* was a fourth-rate ship of 64 guns which by this time was more than fifty years old, having been launched, as the *Speaker*, at Woolwich in 1650. At the Restoration of 1660 Samuel

Pepys had dined on board her and found her 'a very brave ship' and in the same year, in the anti-parliamentarian spirit of the day, she was renamed the *Mary*.

Of Beaumont the man we know little. It would, however, appear that his rapid rise to flag officer (at the age of thirty-four – Rooke and Shovell had both been forty) owed more to merit than to influence. By 1703 he had spent the major part of his naval career cruising the waters off south-east England. Few men, certainly of his age, can have been so familiar with the Thames estuary and its approaches, with its great shifting sandbars, shallow rocky shoals and treacherous tidal currents. The sands and channels of the estuary have a general south-west to north-east trend, some of the banks being up to 30 miles in length and 4 in width and often so steep-sided that, within yards, a vessel that had been in 10 fathoms of water could be banging against the tide-moulded surface of a bank such as the, appropriately named, Kentish Knock.

In the Second Dutch War (1665–1667) Pepys had blamed superior Dutch knowledge of English inshore waters, among other things, for the humiliating defeat of the Battle of the Medway, when de Ruyter had found his way up river, capturing and burning English warships and blockading London. Then, wrote Pepys:

> they managed their retreat down this difficult passage [the Nore to the Middle Ground] better than we could do ourselves in the main sea . . . when the *Prince* and the *Royal Charles* and other great ships came on ground upon the Galloper [in the Four Days Battle of 1666]. Thus in all things . . . in wisdom, courage, force and knowledge of our own streams and success, the Dutch have the best of us.

In fact, de Ruyter was helped by English deserters, their pay months in arrears – thanks to Pepys and the bureaucrats – who acted as pilots.

Nevertheless, knowledge of submarine features – channels and banks – at this time was a good deal less precise than it is today. A survey of the Downs and Sandwich Haven undertaken in 1736 by Charles Labelye, engineer and 'late Teacher of the Mathematicks in the Royal Navy' is notable for the contrast between the accuracy with which the coastline is drawn and the improbably smooth outline of the Goodwin Sands. Three-quarters of a century earlier, sailors such as Beaumont would have had a good general knowledge of the principal offshore features while lacking the kind of detailed knowledge of their precise shape and dynamic nature which hydrographers have been gaining over the last 200 years. Not, of course, that such understanding would have been of very much help to captains whose anchor cables had broken and, under bare poles or even mast-less, were being driven helpless in a sea full of hazards. Little as they could do, the disposition of such sandbanks and shoals would be all important in determining their fate.

On the Wednesday before the Storm, Shovell seems to have taken advantage of the southerly winds in advance of another incoming low, that which was to bring Defoe's storm which 'would have passed for a great wind had not the great storm followed so soon'. No doubt he was hoping for an end to the sequence of storms so that he would be able to reach the Nore and be within striking distance of his wife and home at May Place, Crayford. The *Triumph*, having picked up the 'mud pilot' who would guide her into the river, sailed in company with other warships including the *Association*, *St George*, *Cambridge*, *Russell*, *Dorsetshire*, *Royal Oak*, *Revenge* and a number of smaller ships. Of the warships some were 'great ships', having three gun decks one above the other so that they stood high out of the water. In battle they were the strongest parts of England's 'wooden walls' but in a storm they presented a large surface area to the wind and were thus in particular danger.

That night the *Triumph* anchored in 12 fathoms, 6 leagues* to the north-east of the North Foreland. This would appear to be a somewhat roundabout course but at this date the only known navigable channel for large ships into the Thames was from the north-east, following the Essex shoreline. From the Downs it was

* A nautical league was a twentieth of a degree, equivalent to about 3.456 statute (land) miles.

necessary to sail north-eastwards around the Kentish Knock and the Long Sand Head before turning westwards to the Gunfleet and then running south-westwards into the Thames.

By the morning of the 26th there were thus two major concentrations of warships just outside the Thames estuary. Shovell with the ships under his command was well to the north-east of the North Foreland, the *Association* being in 19 fathoms of water off the Long Sand Head. The other group, including Beaumont's squadron and Leake in the *Prince George*, who was to return to Portsmouth, was still in the Downs where there were also large numbers of merchantmen. Once the Storm arrived and the wind veered round to the west both groups faced a similar hazard – sand to leeward.

In the normal course of events ships in the Downs would not be in danger of a wind blowing off the Kent coast, wind speed being reduced over the land and the cliffs between Dover and Deal providing shelter for the vessels anchored beneath them. Should a ship be driven from its anchors, however, it would be in real danger of being driven onto the Goodwin Sands, the most notorious menace to shipping about the coast of Great Britain. If the Goodwins are defined by the 2-metre submarine contour, they are 9 miles long from the South Sand Head to the North Sand Head, while from west to east across Kellett Gut is a distance of 5 miles. The Sands are thus very extensive and shoal almost all over so that in stormy weather, as the tide falls, they are covered with the white water of breaking waves. With a further fall of the tide large areas of sand dry out. On the flood tide, however, the surface becomes a deadly quicksand as the rising waters push the sand particles apart so that any weight placed upon them – a man, a boat, eventually even a ship – is engulfed, swallowed by the sand.

For Sir Cloudesley's ships further out in the southern North Sea the threat came from the steep-sided sandbank, 15 miles to the east of the Long Sand Head, named the Galloper, appropriately enough, after the height of the waves which broke over it. Even where there is sufficient depth of water for a ship to remain afloat, the height and uneven nature of the pattern of breakers would threaten to capsize it.

As the weather began to deteriorate in the evening of 26 November, captains would have begun to take precautions to ride out another storm. Admiral Sir John Leake was in the Downs and survived the Storm, according to his biographer and relative Sir John Martin-Leake, because of the measures taken:

> This wonderful deliverance, under Providence, was owing to a prudent foresight, in the Admiral and his captain, Captain Martin [Leake's brother-in-law], by providing against the worst, the day before, when it blew very hard; when considering the time of year, the place they were in, and what might happen, they made a snug ship, veering out their longservice to two cables and two-thirds, and doing everything that might enable them to ride out a hard storm; by which precaution they not only saved themselves but the lives of 700 men under their care, with HM's ship; and all this without cutting away a mast, or using any extraordinary means or receiving any damage other than usual in a hard gale of wind.

This reads rather smugly; suggesting, as it does that those less fortunate captains provided less conscientiously for the survival of their ships and ships' companies. Of course, the logs of the ships that perished have not survived but those of ships that barely endured the Storm are full of similar preventative action being taken: 'we veered away to three cables and a half' (*Association*), 'we veered away to two cables and a half' (*Dorsetshire*), 'veered out more than three cables of our best bower' (*Triumph*). When a ship is lying to a single anchor and the weather deteriorates, veering, or paying out more cable, adds to her safety by increasing its scope.

As with ships in deep water, every effort would also have been made to minimise wind resistance by lowering yards and topmasts and, if necessary, cutting masts by the board. There were, of course, many factors over which the captain had no control, such as the quality of the anchor's holding ground, exposure to 'freak' waves and unusually strong gusts of wind, and collision with other vessels. John Leake was without doubt a good sailor but whether his actions in preparing for the Storm were any more creditworthy than those of Basil Beaumont we shall never know.

One of the great ships accompanying Sir Cloudesley and anchored off the Long Sand Head at six o'clock on the evening of 25 November was the *Association*, a second-rate of 96 guns, the flagship of Sir Stafford Fairborne, Vice-Admiral of the Red, who had been with Shovell in the Mediterranean. Fairborne, like Leake, was a future Admiral of the Fleet. There is nothing in his record to suggest other than that he was a highly competent sailor. Beneath Fairborne was Captain Richard Canning. On the 26th not only did the fair wind needed to carry them into the Thames fail to materialise but the wind from the opposite quarter – the SW – grew stronger. The *Association* struck her yards and topmasts and prepared for the worst.

Little could Fairborne and Canning on the quarter-deck or the oldest, most weather-beaten tarpaulin in the fo'c'sle have envisaged the nautical nightmare that was about to begin. It must be remembered that this ship had set sail from Spithead on 1 July and was part of Shovell's Mediterranean expedition of which Sir Narcissus Luttrell had written:

> They say his fleet has been very sickly, several officers of note and seamen dead; and the provisions not being well salted, a great deal of it was spoiled before they arrived in the Streights.

Leake's ship the *Prince George* had lost 70 of 700 to disease and the rest were said to be so poorly that they were barely able to bring the ship into port. While they were in the Downs they would have had the opportunity to take on fresh provisions and set down the most 'sickly' of the crew. Second Lieutenant Richard Clarke of the *Association* had written in his Journal on 18 November:

> This day I had leave from Admiral Fairborne having been indisposed for some part of the Voyage to go on shore for the recovery of my health and to return to my ship as soone as she got to the Nore.

Clarke's leave was to be far longer than he could ever have anticipated. Furthermore, it seems likely that the *Association* was, as the Storm broke about her, severely undermanned, her crew undernourished and, beginning to despair of ever seeing the taverns of Chatham again, of low morale. Such was the unpromising situation aboard Fairborne's flagship on Friday 26 November as she embarked on a new voyage upon the orders of an Authority higher even than that of their lordships at the Admiralty.

Darkness would have fallen early that evening and the *Association* would quickly have been engulfed in the pitch blackness of the moonless night, a rising wind blowing from WSW with squalls of rain. By three in the morning a 'hurricane' was blowing and at five, according to Lieutenant Lewis Billingsley, 'we veered away to 3 cables and ½' but still the best bower cable parted. Canning then let go his sheet anchor the cable of which also promptly parted. The small bower cable then began to drag and the ship, helpless, was driven before the wind.

In no time the *Association* was passing over the northernmost part, the tail, of the Galloper, in first 9 then 7 fathoms of chaotically breaking waves. Amidst the confusion a massive sea broke over her starboard side, smashing in the ports on the upper deck some 20 ft above the water line. A great quantity of water was taken on board causing her to list dangerously. Orders were given to scuttle the decks to let the water drain into the hold from whence it could be pumped away. For a time, however, this huge volume of water was washing perilously about the inside of the vessel, at one stage crashing with such force against the ship's side that two of the lower gun-deck ports were forced open; 'the most hazardous Accident, next to touching the ground, that could have happened to us'. According to the account of the *Association*'s tribulations which Defoe reproduced, the Admiral himself, 'although much indispos'd', took charge of the operation to secure the burst open ports, thereby saving the ship.

Once over the Galloper, the sea was less rough but the hurricane still blew, if anything increasing in force. The Defoe account – from the *Annals of the reign of Queen Anne* – is then especially good on the sheer physical difficulty of giving and receiving orders under such conditions:

> For Words were no sooner uttered than they were carried away by the Wind, so that although those upon Deck spoke loud and close to one another, yet they could not often distinguish what was said; and when they opened their mouths, their Breath was almost taken away.

There is also a graphic description of the effect of the wind upon the surface of the water:

> We plainly saw the Wind skimming up the water as if it had been sand, carrying it up into the Air which was then so thick and gloomy that Day light, which should have been comfort to us, did but appear more ghastly.

Eventually at about one o'clock on the Saturday afternoon the Storm began to abate. The most dangerous threat now was that the *Association* would be driven on to the sandbanks skirting the Flemish coastline but, before this could happen, the Storm having moved away over the Baltic, a degree of control was resumed: 'gott up the Mizen yard and set the sail', so that the great ship was steered north-eastwards along the coasts of Holland and Friesland to the mouth of the Elbe. At one stage she was able to 'speak' to several vessels in a similar plight which had been driven out of Yarmouth Roads.

Then, on 4 December, as they were about to weigh anchor and set sail back across the North Sea, another gale arrived which carried her even further north. The following week must have been one of extreme deprivation and plummeting morale: the ship's provisions were rapidly being exhausted, all wood and candles used up, no beer or 'anything else in lieu' and the crew 'jaded by the continual Fatigue of the Storm, falling sick every day'. On 8 December, twelve days after the Great Storm, they were put on short allowance and one quarter of water a day. As Samuel Pepys had observed in 1677, 'Englishmen, and more especially seamen, love their bellies above everything else . . .

any abatement from them in the quantity or agreeableness of their victuals is to discourage and provoke them in the tenderest point . . .'*

Three days later Fairborne was obliged to seek help in the neutral port of Gothenburg. This was probably an exigency he would have preferred to avoid. The diplomatic ramifications of a warship's arrival could be complicated and unpredictable and Charles XII of Sweden, although young, was notoriously bad tempered and unreliable. In a letter written from there to Josiah Burchett at the Admiralty, he described his predicament: three anchors lost, five cables, likewise the long boat and pinnace and the greatest part of the provisions used or ruined and lacking 'other Necessaries in that cold Country', all of which, according to Burchett, 'mightily pinched the poor Man who had suffered so much'. If the Admiral was 'mightily pinched' the state of the common seamen must have been grim indeed.

Provisions and fresh water were, however, obtained without creating an international incident and the *Association* proceeded to Copenhagen where anchors, cables and 'other necessary things for the security of the ship were not only obtained but furnished 'in a very friendly manner'. (Although Denmark, too, was neutral in the War of the Spanish Succession much of her first-class army was on loan, at a price, to the Allies.)

There was a further real threat in these northern waters at this time of year: the ports could become ice-bound. The writer of the Defoe account specifically mentions 'the great care and diligence

* Pepys had just drawn up a new victualling contract requiring contractors to provide every seaman with a daily allowance of 1 gallon, wine measure, of beer, brewed with good malt and very good hops, and of sufficient strength and 1 lb of good, clear, sound, sweet and well conditioned wheaten biscuit. 2 lbs of beef killed and made up with salt in England for Sundays, Mondays, Tuesdays and Thursdays, or instead of beef for 2 of those days 1 lb of bacon or salted English pork and a pint of pease. On Wednesdays, Fridays and Saturdays 1/8th part of a full-sized north Sea cod or 1/6th part of a haberdine' [salt or dried cod] or 1 lb of well-savoured 'Poor John' [salt or dried hake] and 2 oz of butter and 4 oz of Suffolk cheese, or 2/3 of that weight of Cheddar. There was an alternative 'south of Lisbon' diet.

of Fairborne' in getting the ship out of Gothenburg where, had she been frozen in, 'most part of the sailors would have perished'. This was not an imaginary danger for this was the so-called 'Little Ice Age' when Scandinavian winter temperatures were significantly lower than they are today and Norwegian glaciers and the Arctic ice cap were far more extensive: in the winter of 1695 Iceland had been completely surrounded by ice. On a number of occasions between 1690 and 1728 Eskimos in kayaks had appeared on the coasts of the Orkneys.

By 3 January the *Association* was able to set sail, avoiding the coastal ice and convoying twelve merchantmen. Even now the voyage across the North Sea was slow but on the evening of the 15th, after repelling an attack by four French privateers, she once again anchored off the Long Sand Head. There was still another very severe gale and 'very great risks among the sands' to be overcome before the *Association* finally, on 23 January, almost two months after the Great Storm, arrived at the Buoy of the Nore, at the mouth of the Medway. In that time she had lost twenty-eight men 'by sickness contracted by the Hardships which they endured in the bad weather'.

The captains of the other great ships which had left the Downs with Shovell had also undergone taxing trials of their seamanship. On the Tuesday after the Storm, there being no news of them at the Admiralty, Sir David Mitchell ordered HMS *Greyhound* with a couple of ketches to take anchors, cables and some sails for second- and third-rates to the Gunfleet. If Sir Cloudesley's ships were not found there the stores were to be taken to Harwich and the *Greyhound* was to search for them. It was at this time that orders were also sent to the *Lyn* and *Margate* at Yarmouth to join the search, off the Galloper and Aldeburgh Knapps, Mitchell being unaware that these ships were themselves disabled. On the following day Mitchell gave further orders that a month's provisions be sent down to Harwich 'with all expedition'. In fact the dispersed ships were by this time on the other side of the North Sea.

On the *Russell*, Captain Isaac Townsend, having logged 'a mere Hurricane' at midnight, lost her best bower anchor in the early hours of the Saturday morning. The sheet and small bower anchors had been let go but they 'could not sustain the violence of the wind'. At four they were obliged to cut away the long boat and at six the rudder was lost, springing a leak which flooded the bread and fish rooms. The poop and quarter-deck guns were then thrown overboard 'the better to draw the water to her pumps' at the stern. Having already lost her anchors and cables from the bow of the ship, this appears to have had the desired effect.

By the Sunday the *Russell* was judged to be approaching the Dutch island of Goeree and was still being driven into progressively shallower water. Townsend ordered two guns to be flung overboard made fast to the sheet cables to slow down the drift landwards. All manner of desperate measures were taken to keep the ship afloat in the shoals off the coast of Zeeland; but at three o'clock in the morning of the 29th she struck on the Sand Hender. Suddenly, in Burchett's words:

> a great Breach was seen right to Leeward; whereupon they cast away the cables and set her foresail and fore-top sail with all possible diligence, by which time they were in 4 fathoms and a half and immediately the ship struck, but swimming still by the stern, the blow put her right before the wind, and so she miraculously got over the shoal, after she had touched several times.

The water deepened to 12 fathoms but then, once again became shallower as they approached the shore, running aground about 2 miles from Hellevoetsluis. Henry Barclay, apparently a friend of Defoe, who was on board wrote from there a letter dated 16 December, reporting that, on the previous night, 'it had pleased Almighty God, far beyond our expectation, to save our ship and bring us safe off again'. The *Russell* was taken into port for re-fitting and for a new rudder before eventually returning to England. The notion that the ship and its crew had been the beneficiaries of some kind of miracle seems to have been generally held. Barclay certainly thought so:

> Our Deliverance is most remarkable, that in the middle of a dark Night we should drive over a Sand where a ship that was

not half our Bigness durst not venture to come in the Day; and then without knowing where we were, drive into a narrow place where we have saved both lives and ship. I pray God give us all Grace to be thankful and never forget so great a mercy.

By 4 December Mitchell had extended the area of search for Shovell's great ships to the east side of the Galloper and 'so over near the coast of Holland or where else they can get intelligence of them'.

Like the *Association*, the *Revenge*, Captain William Kerr, had also been driven over the tail of the Galloper in less than four fathoms of water but, like the *Russell*, had been carried towards Hellevoetsluis. Lacking anchors and cables she had not been able to reach harbour but, after drifting helplessly for a number of days, had met with the *Nottingham*, one of the ships sent out with anchors and cables, so that she was eventually brought back into the Medway.

The *Dorsetshire*, Captain Edward Whitaker, had quickly lost her bower anchors and was driven north-eastwards with her head to the southward. At six on the Saturday morning she had struck three times on the Galloper 'there goeing a great sea which washed her over the sand'. She continued to drive in this manner until noon when the crew managed to wear her, bringing the head to the northward. At about this time, according to Lieutenant Thomas Russell, 'we saw 3 sail of our Company, the *Revenge*, *Association* and *Russell*'. On the Sunday morning several vessels driven out of Yarmouth Roads were seen and at nine Russell 'saw the Revenge bare away for Gowry [Goeree]'. For several days the *Dorsetshire* was blown about between the Galloper and Orford Ness but Whitaker did manage to take up a small bower anchor and cable 'belonging to another ship' which were of great service to him and by 15 December, according to Burchett, he was able to drop anchor at the Nore.

But what of Cloudesley Shovell himself and why the particular concern for his safety? As Admiral of the White he was the second most senior officer (after Rooke) on the active list. His actual achievements in battle had not been as distinguished as those of Blake or half a dozen later eighteenth-century sailors, although it was he who had broken the French line at Barfleur in 1692. He was, however, a man who commanded enormous respect and he does appear, both personally and by example, to have raised standards of skill and discipline among the officer class. He was the kind of man about whom legends grow: there was a tradition that, as a cabin boy, he had swum under fire with dispatches in his mouth!

On 3 December the *Triumph* was near the Gunfleet, off the Essex coast and Shovell was able to communicate a letter to the Admiralty where it was read on the following day, a copy being forwarded to Sir John Leake who was instructed to send the *Assistance* and *Chatham* to look carefully between England and Holland for the *Association*, *Dorsetshire*, *Revenge* and *Russell*. The letter reads as follows:

> Triumph near the Gunfleete
> Dec 3rd 1703
> Genm
> The 24th ultimo the day we sayled out of the Downes with the ships in the margine about the Long Sands head, we anchored in the evening in twelve fathome water, the North Foreland South West, distant about six leagues, On Saturday last soone in the morning wee had a most miserable Storme of Wind, which drove us to some streights, for after wee had veered out more than three cables of our best bower that Anchor Broke, soon after out Tillar broke from our sterne, and has shaken our Stern Post that we prove very leakey, and had our four Chaine Pumps and a hand pump going to keep us free, Wee let go our Sheete Anchor and Veered out all the Cables to it, butt that did not ride us, butt wee drove near a sand called the Galloper of which we saw the breach, I directed the Maine mast to be Cutt by the Board, after which we ridd fast of eight ships that came out of the Downes four are missing, the *Association*, *Russell*, *Revenge* and *Dorsetshire*, pray God they drove clear of the Sands, Wee have now fitted a Jury Maine Mast & Rudder, and the Ship works very well with them, and the Carpenter has stopt some of our Leakes, we are gott in neare the Gunfleete,

and if the Weather proves faire I hope we shall gett neare in, the *Cambridge* is now with us and I have ordered her to stay by us until we gett up, I am
Gen:m
Yr & C
Clo Shovell
PS I doubt it has fared worse with the four ships that have drove away than it has done with us. I have some hopes that some of them have drove to Sea, but if so they are without Masts, I judge it will be of service if some Friggts were sent out to look for them.
C:S:

Mitchell had, as we have seen, already taken this precaution. Clearly, Shovell was not concerned about the *St George* and *Royal Oak*, the other great men-of-war which he does not mention as missing.

Sir Cloudesley will, of course, be ever linked not with the *Triumph* but with another ship that had been in his company on the eve of the Storm, the *Association*. Returning to England from the Mediterranean four years later, the *Association*, Shovell's flagship, together with three other ships, was wrecked on the Western Rocks of the Scillies. Nearly 2,000 men were lost among them Shovell himself. Apparently thrown ashore alive but unconscious, he was murdered for the sake of an emerald ring. The body was retrieved and taken to London. Of the flag officers summoned to the Admiral's London home in Soho Square to accompany the hearse to Westminster Abbey on 22 December 1707 were Fairborne, Leake and Byng, all Great Storm survivors, and Matthew Aylmer, whose own son had been lost with the *Association*.

12

As Dismal as Death

But O ye Mighty Ships of War
What in Winter did you there?
Wild November should our Ships restore
To Chatham, Portsmouth *and the* Nore.
(*Essay on the Late Storm*, 1704, D. Defoe)

The nature of the historical record is such that we know far more of the small number of admirals caught up in the Storm at sea than of the many thousands of ordinary seamen. Although some of Defoe's correspondents appear not to have been members of the officer class, he never tells us their rate or rank. A notable exception to the general rule is supplied by the journal of Edward Barlow. This remarkable document, amounting to some 225,000 words, begins in the year 1656 and ends with Barlow's account of the Great Storm, forty-seven years later. The full title of the published transcript, *Barlow's Journal of his life at sea in King's Ships, East and West Indiamen and other Merchantmen from 1659 to 1703*, gives some idea of the scope of the writer's long and varied career.

Edward Barlow was born at Prestwich, near Manchester, on 6 March 1642, the son of a poor husbandman. The first part of his book is, strictly speaking, a memoir rather than a journal, written while he was imprisoned in Batavia. He relates how, at the age of thirteen, he was sent 'a-liking to a whitester' (on trial to a bleacher) and, the trial proving unsatisfactory he went off to London where an uncle apprenticed him to the Chief Master's Mate of one of the largest ships in the Navy, the *Naseby* ('but at His Majesty's return the *Royal Charles*'). His career at sea was to embrace all kinds of vessels from first-rate men-of-war to fishing pinks. He sailed to the Barbary Coast, Brazil, India and China, fought in the Second Dutch War, was imprisoned, press-ganged, shipwrecked on the Goodwin Sands and much more.

Basil Lubbock, who owned, transcribed and, in 1934, published *Barlow's Journal* describes the manuscript as 'closely and beautifully written on thick, hand-made, watermarked foolscap paper'. The text is illustrated with over 180 drawings, many in colour, some decorated with gold leaf. It was the convention in the seventeenth and eighteenth centuries for sailors writing a personal journal to include drawings of the coastline. In the absence of accurately drawn charts these could be an invaluable aid to the navigator: Barlow's are especially fine, as also are his illustrations of the ships in which he sailed.

It is understandable that the journal of a great sailor such as Edward Mountagu, the Earl of Sandwich, should be so well preserved; that the writing and drawing of an ordinary sailor such as Barlow should have survived at all is astonishing, that it should be in such good condition, the ink hardly faded, is a near miracle. So, too, is the beauty of the manuscript for, as Lubbock remarked, it is hard to comprehend how he managed to write and draw so well in the crowded confines of the foc's'le where he would have had no more than the lid of his sea chest to write on and a purser's tallow dip to see by.

The *Journal* ends in the most dramatic way possible with Barlow's description of the Great Storm. He was sixty-one years old and, presumably – for we know virtually nothing of him other than is contained in the *Journal* – it came at the end of his last voyage. On 13 'October' [in error for November] 1703, Barlow had sailed from Cork in Ireland, apparently as a passenger aboard HMS *Kingfisher*, part of a convoy of 15 men-of-war commanded by Rear Admiral Thomas Dilkes. The *Kingfisher*, Captain Tolbett [Talbot?], had convoyed the East India fleet from St Helena aboard one of the ships on which was another diarist Francis Rogers, a London merchant, who describes the departure from Cork:

> Now having lain near a fortnight windbound and alarmed in that time by the Irish of a French squadron looking for us, at

> length the wind favours us, coming Westerly. . . . The Admiral fires a gun, and looseth his fore topsail, the signal to the fleet for unmooring; after that another, and hauls home his topsail's sheet for weighing and gets out of the harbour lying up till the fleet got out.

The 'fleet' apparently consisting of the combined East and West India fleets and seventeen men-of-war. Next day they made the Scillies and, again according to Rogers, did 'see the Wolph [the Wolf Rock] breaking a league or two leeward of us'.

Dilkes, with eight of the men-of-war, left the fleet at Plymouth and a number of other warships fell out at Portsmouth, leaving only the *Kingfisher* and *York* to proceed with the merchantmen to the Downs. By the time they arrived, Shovell's Mediterranean ships, 'the Grand Fleet from the Straits', as Rogers has it, were already there. 'In their voyage and expedition they had met with little or no matter worthy of observation', wrote Barlow, dismissively. The *York* and *Kingfisher* were then ordered to escort the East Indiamen and other merchant ships safely into the Thames. On the day on which they sailed, Barlow records, two yachts and a frigate sailed to Holland, 'to fetch the King of Spain who our ships were to transport to Portugal'. Rooke had been at Hellevoetsluis for some weeks but the yachts were at last being sent to convey the royal party to Portsmouth. On the eve of the Storm this delicate diplomatic, naval and logistic operation was the government's chief preoccupation.

The warships saw the merchantmen into Westgate Bay and over the Kentish Flats, a zone of shallow water only navigable at high tide, and they arrived at East Tilbury on 20 November. Rogers left his ship there and:

> went to Gravesend that night, as the ship did next day, having been just two years from thence on our voyage. I went next day for London the ship coming after me.

Rogers's journal entry for 22 November was clearly written up some time later for it reads:

> This Monday morn (thanks be to God) I returned well to London, and the Friday night Nov: 27th following happened that memorable and terrible storm known by the name of the November storm which destroyed so many hundred sailors and many stout ships . . .

The *Kingfisher* anchored at the Buoy of the Nore on the 24th, at some stage having separated from the *York* because, as Barlow has it:

> The next day we had news of the loss of the *York* which came into the Downs when we did and, coming up the King's Channel, the pilot bringing her up, had run on ground on a sand not far from Harwich and in blowing weather the 23rd day of November was broken all to pieces, but most of her men were saved.

Unsurprisingly, given the length of time he had spent at sea, Edward Barlow had plenty of experience of stormy weather. One of his drawings shows 'The . . . Shipp *Experiment* . . . having stress of wether . . . in Lattitude 30 degreis South [off Mauritius] . . . in the year 1671'. The picture shows the ship, broadside on to the sea, the mizen mast has been cut by the board, the rudder is out of the water and waves are crashing over the weather bow. On several occasions he had to endure severe North Sea storms, sometimes riding out the weather for days on end. The Great Storm, 'which all England hath great cause to remember', nevertheless clearly alarmed him. In his estimation the *Kingfisher* escaped 'very narrowly', the best bower cable having broken and the ship being driven across the estuary towards the Blacktail Sands, 'all things appearing as dismal as death'. In a desperate attempt to prevent her running on to the Sands, all of the masts were cut and that seems to have slowed her down so that an anchor could be dropped which held, 'had we drove half a mile further, we had certainly been all lost and not one man saved'. As it was, two unsuccessful boats attempted to reach the shore and with them were lost twenty-four men, 'some of the best men we had on the ship'.

There the *Kingfisher* lay at anchor for two days, nobody coming near but the masts, yards, sails and wrecks of ships 'swimming by us'. Small jury masts were eventually set up and, in more moderate weather, they were able to regain the Buoy of the Nore. There Barlow learnt that, of the ships at anchor there when the Storm broke, a bomb ketch – in fact the *Portsmouth* with forty-four men – and several small merchantmen had been lost. In the Medway itself some of the moorings in the harbour at Chatham had given way and the *Vanguard*, a 90-gun man-of-war of 1,357 tons, fortunately not in commission and therefore without a crew, sank. It was the largest naval vessel lost in the Storm. At Deptford the log of the fireship *Strombolo* records a strong gale until midnight and then 'a perfect storm with showers until 3 a.m.' The frigate *Weymouth* was driven out of Sheerness, her captain obliged to cut all her masts by the board. At Gravesend, according to an account in the *Daily Courant*, the outward-bound East Indiaman the *Donegall* had '. . . her Tafferel, all her Round House and her Larboard Gallery broken down by the Martha shearing upon her . . .'. The stress placed upon the great merchantman when the smaller ship was pulled away 'strained her Head, Bowsprit and Cutwater' to such an extent that the captain feared she would need to be substantially rebuilt. More fortunate were the five West Indiamen driven ashore below Tilbury Fort where, as Defoe pointed out, 'the shore is ouzy and soft' and:

> . . . the vessels sat upright and easy, and here high tides which followed and which were the ruin of so many in other places, were the deliverance of all these ships whose lading and value was very great, for the tide rising to an unusual height, floated them all off and the damage was not so great as was expected.

Further east, two hospital ships, the *Swan* and *Princess Anne*, were anchored in Westgate Bay, 'Margett Towne bearing SE by E'. They rode out 'a most dreadful Storme of wind' although Captain Gye of the *Princess Anne* lost one of his anchors and part of a cable which, according to another of Defoe's correspondents, 'was weighed and carry'd after him to the River by one of our hookers*'. Two other ships, a small pink and the *Latchford* of Sandwich, however, were driven out of the Road by the wind. Neither was seen again. Where the pink came from was not known but the *Latchford* was bound home from London 'with divers men and women passengers all totally lost'.

Barlow's explanation of the Storm was conventional but given a personal twist which reflected his age and humble status:

> I pray God we may all repent, for doubtless this was a warning of God's anger against us, for a worse generation can scarce be in all wickedness: for no man values his word or promise, or matters what he doth or saith: so that he can but gain and defraud his neighbour. All commanders and masters are grown up with pride and oppression and tyranny. I want words to lay out the business and unworthy dealings of many men I have met not acting like Christians.

After the Storm the *Kingfisher* was taken up to Woolwich to be repaired – by an Admiralty Office order dated as early as 30 November. The following year she was once more to sail for St Helena to convoy home the East India fleet. Barlow left her, stepping ashore probably for the last time, at Gravesend before going up to London to see his wife and children. His *Journal* ends with thanks to God 'in preserving me from such imminent danger in the late storm . . . and in all my voyages through many and great dangers having used the sea employment so many years'. As the reader of *Barlow's Journal* sees him, grey-haired but still vigorous, his sea chest on his shoulders, disappearing among the sailors, fishermen, chandlers and other denizens of the Gravesend quayside there is a palpable sense of loss. Yet although Edward Barlow passes out of history at this point so that his death is, to the best of our knowledge, unrecorded, he left behind a remarkable memorial, almost a quarter of a million fascinating words, enchantingly illustrated, on a seafaring life that ended with the Great Storm.

* The hooker was developed from the ketch, a short, squat vessel with main and mizen masts. They were mainly employed for fishing but in this case was clearly involved in the important local industry of salvaging ground tackle.

When, on 24 November, Sir Cloudesley had sailed out of the Downs, he left behind Sir John Leake whose ship, the *Prince George* was to be taken to Portsmouth to be laid up for the winter, Graydon returned from the West Indies, Beaumont and his squadron guarding the Straits of Dover and a great number, possibly 160 sail or so, of merchantmen sheltering from the storms and waiting either to be piloted into the Thames or for a favourable wind to take them down Channel.

On the 25 November with a storm blowing in advance of the Great Storm, a number of warships put to sea to avoid the risk of being blown on to the Goodwin Sands, but that night, with the wind howling in from WSW, a Dutch ship was blown on to the Sands and lost with all hands. The following morning the warships returned, probably anchoring in the deeper water in the southern part of the anchorage off Kingsdown, smaller ships being further to the north, off Deal.

This disposition was probably critical in determining which ships were lost in the Great Storm. So too was the state of the tide. The flood tide runs up through the Downs from SSW to NNE for six hours; two hours before and four hours after high tide. There being, as we have seen, a new moon, high water in the Downs would have occurred a little before midnight. When, in the early hours of the Saturday morning, the Storm was at its height it would thus have been blowing from WSW greatly increasing the velocity of the tidal stream which would set strongly towards the Goodwin Sands.

The presence of the Goodwins certainly affected the precautions taken in advance of the Storm in a way which, in some cases, may actually have placed ships in greater danger. Because of the proximity of the Sands and the need, in the event of anchors being lost, to head for the narrow passage through them, the Gull Stream, captains would have wanted to make sail with all speed. Consequently, some at least – including Captain Martin of the *Prince George* who boasted of 'prudent foresight . . . by providing against the worst' – do not appear to have lowered topmasts and yards. This may actually have placed some ships in jeopardy although it should be said that the *Prince George*, a second-rate, three-decker, the largest and therefore the most vulnerable ship in the Downs, did successfully ride out the Storm.

The kind of dilemma in which captains and masters were placed is illustrated by the case of the merchantman in which an eyewitness, James Adams, was a passenger, bound, or so he hoped, for Lisbon. In an attempt to reduce wind resistance, as the threat of the Storm continued to increase, the master had cut down the masts but then, as it became obvious that her cables would not hold, he was obliged to improvise a sail or risk being blown on to the Sands. With a tarpaulin flying from the remains of the mizen mast, he slipped anchors and ran for the relative security of the open sea.

However adequate the measures taken, ships in such a crowded anchorage, (just as in Yarmouth Roads) were in great danger from others driving into them. In this way the *Prince George* may very well have shared the fate of the third-rate *Restoration*. At about three o'clock on the Saturday morning her anchors were still holding when through the dark, crashing waves and scudding spray the crew became aware of another ship bearing down on them. Some quick-thinking and skilful manoeuvring prevented a collision, but one of the *Restoration*'s dragged anchors caught in the hawse of the *Prince George* so that the two ships were riding at the anchors of one. An attempt was made to cut the *Restoration* away but without success. Then the *Prince George*'s best bower began to drag and the small bower was brought a-head and in that way the two ships rode together for a further half hour, 'the longest half hour ever they knew'. Then what Leake's biographer refers to as 'the invisible hand of Providence' relieved them, at the same time condemning Captain Fleetwood Emes and 385 others of the *Restoration*'s crew. Either the cable of Emes's ship parted or the fouled anchor may have slipped but all of a sudden she broke free of the *Prince George* and was driven away.

Another of the larger warships in the Downs that night was the third-rate, the *Shrewsbury*. On board was Miles Norcliffe who wrote to Defoe describing his experiences and, although the letter is not strictly accurate as to all of the details, it is included in *The Storm* because 'it seems to describe the Horror and Consternation the poor sailors were in at that time'.

At the beginning of the Storm the *Shrewsbury* was anchored alongside Beaumont's flagship the *Mary*. They would have been riding head to the wind and the incoming tide. At the height of the Storm the *Shrewsbury* lost both anchors and 'did run mighty fierce backwards, within 60 or 80 yards of the sands' but then 'As God almighty would have it, we flung our sheet anchor down, which is the biggest, and so we stopt'. At that point, according to Norcliffe, 'we all prayed to God to forgive us our sins, and so save us or else to receive us into his heavenly kingdom'. The sheet anchor held, 'but I humbly thank God, it was his gracious mercy that saved us'.

Others were not blessed with God's gracious mercy. As the day broke, with the wind still blowing alarmingly but the tide beginning to ebb, the *Prince George* observed 12 sail stranded on the Goodwin, Bunt Head and Brake Sands. Among those on the Goodwins were the third-rates the *Northumberland* (with 253 men), the *Restoration* (with 386 men) having drawn away from the *Prince George*, and the *Stirling Castle* (349 men) and the fourth-rate the *Mary* (273 men).

Less immediately under threat but nevertheless in a bad way were the *Nassau*, forced to cut away her masts, the *Garland* and *Dunwich* which had also lost their masts, the *Lichfield* which had lost her foremast and the *Postillion* with no mainmast. Several merchant ships were also mastless, most of the rest having foundered or been driven out of the Downs. Some of the smaller merchantmen drawing only 8–10 feet of water were probably driven right across the Sands at high tide thereby escaping to the open sea.

The actual sequence of events on that Saturday morning is not easily pieced together, the already confused waters having been muddied by Defoe's insistence on the culpability of the townsfolk of Deal in failing to mount a more effective rescue effort. A report from the town, dated the day of the Storm, appeared in the *Daily Courant* two days later and describes the position as it appeared from the land:

> Deale Nov. 27
> We had so violent a Storm at SW that the like has not been known in these parts in the memory of Man . . . it made all the

> houses in the town shake, uncovered several roofs, threw down chimneys, brick walls etc.
> P.S. at 1 in the Afternoon. It blows hard still but being cleared up to the NE we perceive 2 hulls of ships riding at anchor near the Breake which are suppos'd to be the *Sterling Castle* and *Restoration* or the *Northumberland*; 2 other great ships were seen on the Goodwin Sands one of them being the *Mary* who had her flag flying, but the Flood coming on we can see no more of them.

This does not appear to be consistent with the account in the biography of Sir John Leake which states that the *Mary*, *Northumberland*, *Stirling Castle* and *Restoration* were 'all to pieces by 10 o'clock' in the morning.

Those who have written about the loss of these four ships have had to rely on the accounts of two eyewitnesses in particular. According to James Adams, the merchantman in which he was a passenger was newly launched and her anchors and cables were able to keep her in position for a considerable time before she eventually drove out to sea. By 1 a.m., however, other ships were already beginning to drag their anchors and by 2 a.m. some were firing guns to alert others to their distress and Adams saw the *Mary* and the *Northumberland* disappear as they were driven on to the Goodwins. Shortly afterwards Adams's ship only narrowly missed a collision with the *Stirling Castle*, Captain John Johnson, which was also being driven towards the Sands. At about the same time he witnessed two other merchantmen breaking adrift; one rode into a pink and both ships sank, the other appears to have run out to sea.

Another eyewitness and surely the most fortunate man in the Downs that night was a seaman on the *Mary* who rejoiced in the decidedly un-naval name of Thomas Atkins. Atkins was the only man aboard the *Mary* to survive and that in the most remarkable way. He was washed off the stranded fourth-rate as she broke up but another wave threw him on to the quarter-deck of the *Stirling Castle*. Of that ship's crew of 349, seventy were saved together with the twice-fortunate Atkins. One story has it that Atkins saw Admiral Beaumont washed from the quarter-deck of the *Mary* and drown, another has it that he and two other officers lashed themselves to a piece of the wreck which was then washed away. What is certain is that Beaumont died that night in the Straits of Dover which he had patrolled for so much of his young life. Two of his younger brothers, also sailors had pre-deceased him. William had died of a fever in the West Indies in 1697 and Charles had been lost, together with 124 others, when his ship the *Carlisle* had inexplicably blown up in the Downs in 1700. Basil and Charles probably died within three miles of one another.

Beaumont's *DNB* biographer, the naval historian Sir John Knox Laughton, described Beaumont's portrait by Michael Dahl as that of 'a comely young man who might have become very stout if he had lived'. 'The circumstances', wrote Laughton, 'of his death have given to Admiral Beaumont's name a wider repute than his career as an officer would otherwise have entitled it to; his service throughout was creditable without being distinguished.' In a service in which, to a greater extent than in other areas of British public life, merit received recognition, the rapidity with which Beaumont gained his flag does suggest real potential. Burchett, who would have known him, probably went beyond the conventionally polite in writing of him that he was:

> A Gentleman who was very much lamented, and that deservedly too; for he was not only in every way qualified to serve his country, but was thus unhappily snatch'd away in the Prime of his Years.

Although Atkins was the only man on board the *Mary* to have survived, a number of other crew members did too, including Captain Edward Hopson and the purser and, presumably, a boat crew, who were ashore. The Great Storm was a more democratic disaster than, say, the Great Plague but of the thousands of seamen who perished, comely young men and grizzled old tars alike, Beaumont, arguably the least typical, because we know something of him, must be the representative.

By daybreak on the Saturday the Downs which the day before looked like 'a goodly forest' had, in Martin-Leake's not entirely apt phrase, been 'reduced to a desert'. Although by no means all of the ships that had been at anchor had been lost, many had been driven out to sea from whence they would gradually return over the days or even weeks ahead. The *London Gazette* contained a report from Deal, dated 4 December, that 'we have several of the merchant ships driven out of the Downs in the late Storm safe into Ramsgate Peer'. The ship in which James Adams was a passenger was driven so far north that when she at length made port it was in Norway where she remained, being repaired, for some weeks before returning to the Downs and resuming her voyage to Portugal.

As the tide went out on the morning after the Storm and the Sands were revealed, a number of hulls, in various stages of destruction, were revealed. Improving visibility meant men could be made out walking on the sandbanks and waving to attract attention. Some were fortunate but for the great majority help never came and soon, as the tide came in again, they were not waving but drowning.

Could these men – or more of them – have been saved? It is not a question asked by Daniel Defoe, whose assumption is that they could and should have been:

> And here I cannot omit that great notice has been taken of the townspeople of Deal, who are blamed, and I doubt not with too much reason for their great barbarity in neglecting to save the lives of abundance of poor wretches; who having hung upon the masts and rigging of the ships, or floated upon the broken pieces of wrecks, had gotten ashore upon the Goodwin Sands when the tide was out.

The 'barbarity' was, he implies, more than a simple refusal to launch boats in order to rescue the shipwrecked men, rather it was a callous indifference to those men's plight on the part of scavengers already at sea:

> Some boats are said to have come very near them [the stranded men] in quest of booty, and in search of plunder, and to carry off what they could get, but nobody concerned themselves for the lives of these miserable creatures.

It was a topic he also took up in his poem 'An Essay on the late Storm':

> These Sons of Plunder are below my Pen,
> Because they are below the Names of Men;
> Who from the Shores presenting to their Eyes
> The Fatal Goodwin, where the Wreck of Navies lyes,
> A Thousand dying Sailors talking to the Skies.
> From the Sad Shores they saw the Wretches walk
> By signals of Distress they talk;
> Then with one Tide of life they're vext,
> For all were sure to die the next.
> The Barbarous Shores with Men and Boats abound,
> The Men more Barbarous than the Shores are found:
> Off to the shatter'd Ships they go,
> And to the Floating Purchase row,
> They spare no hazard or no pain,
> But 'tis to save the Goods and not the Men.

In *The Storm*, however, Defoe does draw attention to an honourable exception, the town's mayor, Thomas Powell:

> He found himself moved with compassion at the distresses of the poor creatures, whom he saw as aforesaid upon the Sands, and the first thing he did he made application to the Custom House Officers for the assistance of their boats and men to save the lives of as many as they could come at, the Custom House men rudely refused either to send their men or part with their boats. Provoked with the unnatural carriage of the Custom House officers he called the people about him, and finding some of the common people began to be more than ordinarily affected with the distresses of their countrymen and as he thought a little inclined to venture, he made a general offer to all that would venture out, that he would pay them out of his own pocket five shillings per head for all the men whose lives they could save; upon this proposal several offered themselves to go, if he would furnish them with boats.

Finding the main point clear, and that he had brought the men to be willing, he, with their assistance, took away the custom-house boats by force; and though he knew he could not justify it, and might be brought into trouble for it, and particularly if they were lost, might be obliged to pay for them, yet he resolved to venture that, rather than hazard the loss of his design for the saving of so many poor men's lives, and having manned their boat with a crew of stout honest fellows, he with them took away several other boats from other persons, who made use of them only to plunder and rob, not regarding the distresses of the poor men.

Being thus provided both with men and boats, he sent them off, and by this means brought on shore above 200 men, whose lives a few minutes after must infallibly have been lost.

Nor was this the end of his care, for when the tide came in and it was too late to go off again, for all that were left were swallowed up with the raging of the sea, his care was then to relieve the poor creatures, whom he had saved, and who were almost dead with hunger and cold, were naked and starving.

And first he applied himself to the Queen's agent for sick and wounded seamen, but he would not relieve them with one penny, whereupon, at his own charge, he furnished them with meat, drink and lodging.

The next day several of them died, the extremities they had suffered having too much mastered their spirits. These he was forced to bury at his own charge, the agent still refusing to disburse one penny. After their refreshment the poor men, assisted by the mayor, made a fresh application to the agent for conduct money to help them up to London, but he answered he had no order and would disburse nothing; whereupon the mayor gave them all money in their pockets, and passes to Gravesend.

I wish I could say with the same freedom that he received the thanks of the Government and reimbursement of this money as he deserved, but in this I have been informed he met with great obstructions and delays, though at last, after long attendance, upon a right application I am informed, he obtained the repayment of his money, and some small allowance for his time in soliciting for it.

A year after *The Storm* was published some of Deal's leading townspeople threatened a libel action:

> Whereas, there has been this day produced to us a book called *The Storm*, printed in London in the year 1704, for G. Sawbridge in Little Britain, and sold by J. Nutt, near Stationers' Hall, pretending to give an account of some particular incidents that happened thereby, We find, amongst other things, several scandalous and false reflections unjustly cast upon the inhabitants of the Town and Borough of Deal, with malicious intent to bring a disreputation upon the people thereof, and to create a misunderstanding between Her Majesty's subjects, which, if not timely confuted, may produce consequences detrimental to the town, and tend to a breach of the peace. To the end thereof that the person who caused the publication thereof may be made known, in order to be brought to condign punishment for such his infamous libel, we have thought fit, therefore to appoint our Town Clerk to proceed against him in a Court of law, unless he shall within the space of ten days from the date thereof, make known unto us the person or persons and where he or they may be found, who furnished the libellous article in the book, commencing page 199 to the end of page 202, to whom we expect a truthful answer within the time specified. Communication to be made to the Mayor, Jurats and Corporation of Deal.
>
> Witness our signatures this 21st day of June, 1705.
>
> Thomas Horne, mayor, Joshua Coppin, Tobias Bowles, Samuel Fasham, Thomas Warren, Thomas Brothers, William Conning, John Pye, Thomas Powell, late mayor, and Benjamin Hulke.

It is interesting to see that among the signatories of this letter was Thomas Powell, the hero of Defoe's version of the rescue story. Nothing, however, seems to have come of this threat to go to law possibly because its authors knew that there was more than an element of truth in Defoe's allegations. Deal certainly had a less than envious reputation. In 1675 the ship in which Edward Barlow was then sailing, the *Florentine*, ran aground on the Goodwins. Before taking to a boat, he took his journal and some money from his chest but 'without taking a rag of clothes more than I had on my back'. In the two hours which followed between the ship being abandoned and her sinking, the wreck was plundered by some Deal boatmen and:

> to add grief to our misery, these heathens of Deal . . . did deny us the half of our clothes or what things they had removed from on board; but after they had stole and taken out what they pleased, we must be content with the third of what was left or none, for they are so base that they reckon all their own at such a time, though they take it before the owners' faces, not considering their loss and desolate condition, and the Turks could do no more.

Defoe, never a man to leave an axe unground, returned to the theme in his paper the *Review* in December 1708. Having excoriated the 'country cannibals' about the coasts of England and their barbarous treatment of sailors in distress, he focussed on the particular villainies of Deal men:

> Let the town of Deal tell the world how in the great storm their boats went off with the utmost hazard to save the wreck and get plunder, and how they let the poor, perishing wretches that were standing on Goodwin Sands stretch out their hands to them for help in vain, deluding their dying hopes, letting them see these monsters pursue a piece of a wreck and leave the tide to flow over these miserable creatures without compassion. It is true this was their negative behaviour only, and only shews their humanity, that when the men-of-war were driven by the violence of that horrible tempest on the Goodwin Sands, and lay beating there to pieces with the waves, the poor distressed mariners got upon the sands, which at low water ebbed dry. And from the shore several hundred of them were perceived walking dry on the sands in the utmost despair, running about like people out of their wits, wringing their hands, and making all the signals of distressed wretches just launching into eternity, for they were all sure to be overwhelmed by the return of the tide – a sight that would have moved the heart of a Mahometan . . .

This last expression is strikingly reminiscent of that of Barlow – 'the Turks could do more'.

Defoe recognised that such scavenging was by no means confined to the Downs – he also singled out 'Isle of Wight thieves' and 'Portland cannibals' – but it was certainly Deal that attracted the brunt of his ire. It was a cut-throat business that was not for the faint-hearted, competing boats often resorting to all manner of villainy to steal one another's water and put their man on a wreck first. The rewards could be considerable and great risks were taken in life-threatening seas. For such men the Storm was doubtless seen not as a disaster but as the opportunity of a lifetime.

The population of a town such as Deal would probably have been split between those, perhaps represented by the signatories to the libel letter, who were involved in legitimate activities that serviced the shipping in the Downs, and those poorer men who supplemented a meagre income from fishing by scavenging and even wrecking. It would hardly have been in the interest of such a man as Thomas Powell, a slop-dealer, selling ready-made sailors' clothes to ships' pursers, or the chandlers, victuallers, shipping company agents, postal workers and the many others who depended on the ships coming into the Downs, if the town's reputation should suffer.

It is by no means clear when Powell's men undertook their life-saving missions. If Defoe's account is to be believed, the mayor had much negotiating, encouraging and cajoling to do before any boats put to sea. The *London Gazette*'s Deal correspondent concluded his account of 27 November with the words 'Five sail, two of which are pretty big ones, are lost upon the Goodwin Sands. No boat can yet be sent off so we know not the particulars'. The *Daily Courant*'s writer suggests that, with the return of the flood tide, which would have been at about ten in the morning, the great ships were lost for good. Furthermore, Captain Martin of the *Prince George*, in the account which appears in Leake's biography, claimed that 'as soon as the storm was somewhat abated' the Vice-Admiral ordered the *Anne* and all of the ship's remaining boats to the *Stirling Castle* to save the men gathered on the poop, the only part of the ship still in tact. They succeeded in rescuing a lieutenant, the chaplain, the cook and seventy others 'about dead with cold', together with the coxswain of the yawl of the *Mary* (Atkins). Miles Norcliffe who was on board the *Shrewsbury* adds a postscript to his letter to Defoe saying that he sends it 'having opportunity by our Botes, that went Ashoar to carry some poor men off, that were almost dead, and were taken up swimming'.

It is possible that the men rescued by Powell were from merchantmen of which we know virtually nothing. We do know that over a thousand Royal Naval seamen died in the Downs as a result of the Storm. Given the fact that there were many more merchantmen at anchor it is reasonable to suggest that the losses among the merchant fleet were at least as great. Although the smaller merchant ships were less vulnerable to being stranded on the Sands and were fortunate that the worst of the Storm coincided with high water, they were probably more likely to be sunk as a consequence of collision and many may have foundered out at sea.

Uncertainty exists as to the fate of the bomb vessel *Mortar*. It may be that this was the fifth ship reported to be stranded on the Goodwins on the morning of 27 November in the *London Gazette*. In the list of ships cast away in Defoe's book, however, it is described as lost on the coast of Holland, together with the *Vigo Prize* lost at Hellevoetsluis. The naval historian Sir William Laird Clowes, writing at the end of the nineteenth century, refers to the *Mortar* as having been lost on the Goodwins. Defoe gave it a complement of fifty-nine, Clowes of sixty-five. Quite possibly it was driven out of the Downs and wrecked on the Dutch coast. This theory is to some degree supported by Clowes's remark that while she was stranded on the Goodwins she was not actually lost until 2 December. In view of the speed with which the larger ships broke up it seems unlikely that she would have survived there for so long. Some reports indicate that Captain Raymond died, but Clowes states that he continued to command vessels for several years and does not appear to have died until 1718. Defoe but not Clowes, who was of the opinion that the number of vessels destroyed is often overstated, lists the loss of the bomb vessel *Portsmouth* with its crew of forty-four officers and men.

As we have seen, the *Newcastle*, with 193 men, was lost at Spithead and the *Reserve*, with 175 men, at Yarmouth, while the store ship *Canterbury*, although later recovered, probably lost the majority of its crew of thirty-one near Bristol. Other losses included the out-of-commission *Vanguard* in the Medway, the advice boat *Eagle* at Selsey and the third-rate *Resolution* at Pevensey. In none of these ships were men lost.

This also appears to have been the case with the fire ship *Vesuvius* which ran aground near Southsea Castle. The Navy Board minutes of 3 December record that the captain and crew were to go on board the *Phoenix* because the *Vesuvius* 'cannot be saved'. In fact great efforts were made to recover her and she was not finally abandoned until the 19th.

It could very easily have been even worse: as Gilbert Burnet, Bishop of Salisbury, wrote in his *History of His Own Time*:

> If this great Hurricane had come at low water, or in a quarter tide, our Ships must have been driven out upon the Banks of Sand, that lie before the Coast and have struck and perished there as some of the men-of-War did; but the Sea being so full of water, all but some heavy ships got over these safe . . .

As it was things were bad enough. On 3 December a letter was read at the Admiralty from Captain Lyell of the *Resolution* describing the loss of his ship and he was directed to do what he could to save her stores 'and what else belongs to her'. Two days later an order went out that the wrecks and stores on the coast of Sussex and elsewhere be disposed of 'to Her Majesty's best advantage'. This was making the best of a very bad job: Saturday 27 November 1703 had been one of the blackest days in the history of the Royal Navy. During the eleven years of the War of the Spanish Succession the British Navy lost eighty-two ships from all causes. No fewer than twenty-four of them were lost in 1703, fourteen in the Great Storm.

13

Within the Bills of Mortality

Queen Anne's London was the greatest and, in many respects, the grandest city in the world. Had Christopher Wren's plans for the rebuilding of the city after the Great Fire of 1666 been practical (which they were not) and had they been adopted (they were not), London would have been more magnificent still. Even so, although St Paul's, the physical and aesthetic high point of the rebuilding programme, was still incomplete, the wider streets and new buildings, such as the Royal Exchange and the many new churches, were hugely impressive.

Arguably, the rebuilt city, although less prone than old, ramshackle, medieval London, with its narrow streets, countless alleyways and low timber buildings to the ravages of fire, was more susceptible to wind damage. Taller buildings produced a rougher surface, more likely to produce destructive turbulence and the widening of the major thoroughfares, such as Fleet Street, Cheapside and Cornhill is likely to have channelled the wind and concentrated the violence. Although wind speed over urban areas is generally rather less than over the countryside, there are important diurnal and seasonal differences which may have exaggerated the effect of the Storm over London. Increased turbulence over a city at night can transfer the greater high-level wind speeds to lower levels, a factor which tends to be of greater significance when wind speeds are high and in winter. As the Storm struck London on a winter's night, this may have marginally increased its impact. It must, however, be borne in mind that although London had a population of more than half a million and had expanded considerably in area since the Great Fire, the population was more concentrated and the built-up area much more limited than is the case with most modern cities that have been the subject of microclimatological study.

Daniel Defoe himself, whose powers of observation and whose speculative spirit are difficult to fault, recognised that turbulence played a part in the distribution of urban destruction. While 'the wind blew during the whole Storm between the points of SW and NW', he noted that where buildings had a north-south alignment, the east side of the roof would be stripped of its tiles and the west side 'which lay open to the wind be sound and untouched'. He offered two explanations: either the wind enters the buildings by the windows and doors and lifts off the tiling from the lee-side roof, or 'near some higher buildings [the] wind being repuls'd must be forced back again in Eddies . . . consequently taking the Tiles from the lower side of the Roof, rip them up with the more ease'. Furthermore, he also observed that:

> . . . in other places, a high Building next to the Wind had been not much hurt and a lower building on the Leeward side of the high one clear ript and hardly a Tile left upon it; this is plain in the Building of Christ's Church Hospital in London, where the Building on the West and South side of the Cloyster was 25 feet higher than the East side and yet the roof of the lower side on the East was quite untiled by the Storm and remains at the writing of this covered with Deal Boards above an Hundred Feet in Length.

The wind had certainly whistled about Charles I's statue at Charing Cross and up the Strand, the major thoroughfare between Westminster and the City, so that, according to the author of *An Exact Relation*, 'much of the houses as you move from Charing Cross to the Temple have (more or less) felt the effects of the Storm'. The Queen's Bench Walk in the Temple, between Fleet Street and the Thames, was 'wonderfully shattered, particularly that Row of buildings next White Fryers were all untiled, so that it seems as if it had been done by Hands'. Nor had the newly rebuilt churches escaped. The exception proved the rule. When Christopher Wren was told that every church steeple in London had been damaged – and there were more than 120 parish churches – he is said to have replied, 'Not St Dunstan's, I'm sure'. He meant St Dunstan's-in-the-East, Idol Lane – and he was right.

In terms of the dangers which a storm presented to the population, tall buildings of stone, brick and tile certainly had considerable life-threatening potential. Brick-built stacks of chimneys were high and so had far to fall and wind-borne tiles could inflict more injury than the thatch with which humbler houses had been covered.

It should not be thought that London was entirely new or that it was universally well built. Following the Fire, about one-fifth of the city was left standing and the speed with which rebuilding took place almost certainly meant that corners were cut. A hundred years after the Fire the *London Chronicle* complained that:

> the encrease of building has encreased the demand and consequently the price of bricks. The demand for bricks has raised the price of brickearth so greatly that the makers are tempted to mix the slop of the streets, scavenger's dirt and everything that will make the brickearth or clay go further.

After the Fire the price of building materials had been fixed but huge quantities of bricks were made – 5½ million in four years at the brick kiln at Moorfields alone and brickyards sprang up all around the capital. In such a sellers' market it is difficult to imagine that high quality was always maintained. Defective bricks may well have contributed to the collapse of chimneys and even whole houses in the Storm. Dorothy George, in *London Life in the Eighteenth Century*, says of the London of that time that one of its conspicuous features was:

> the number of old ruinous houses which frequently collapsed. In different stages of decay they were patched together and let as tenement houses, common lodging houses or brothels, or were left empty and derelict, inhabited 'only by such as paid no rent', vagrants, beggars, runaway apprentices . . . To Samuel Johnson in 1738 London was a place where 'falling houses

thunder on your head.' When a messenger ran into a City tavern with an urgent piece of news, the instant supposition (in 1718) was that he had come to warn the inmates that the house was falling.

The prevailing system of leasehold also tempted the builder to build for no longer than the lease would last. The Swiss visitor César de Saussure, writing some thirty years after the Storm, explained:

> The contractor builds according to the term of years. Should the ground be leased for sixty years, he will not build so thoroughly as for ninety-nine, and he knows so exactly what is required, that houses are often on the point of tumbling down a short time before or after the time has expired. The proprietor of the house then regains possession of the property and of the house, good or bad.

And the Storm itself may have helped to weaken houses which did not collapse for some time after the event.

From Southwark at the southern end of London Bridge, still the only crossing of the Thames at London, the view of the city's skyline on the morning after the Storm must have been astonishing. While on the Friday morning it had possessed all of the elegance and grace which, fifty years later, would so reinvigorate the imagination of Canaletto, twenty-four hours afterwards all was wreckage and devastation. According to the newspaper the *Post Man*, the effect of the 'violent storm of wind' was that:

> there is hardly any house but has had a share in the Calamity. The churches have also suffered very much, several Pinnacles blown down, a vast quantity of Lead roll'd up in heaps and carried an incredible distance. The Inns of Court, particularly the Temple at Lincoln's Inn, have had their share in the disaster, 5200 weight of lead were blown down from the Old Mathematical School in Christ's Hospital and 4000 from the new which is wrapped

around a stack of chimneys; and near a 100 tall trees torn up by the roots in St James's Park and Moor Fields.

By the time he came to write *The Storm*, Defoe was able to be more particular about the damage to the churches:

> Two of the new built Turrets at the Top of St Mary Aldermary Church were blown off, whereof one fell upon the Roof of the Church; of eight Pinnacles on the Top of St Alban's, Wood Street 5 of them were blown down; Part of one of the Spires of St Mary Overies blown off; four Pinnacles of St Michael, Crooked Lane blown quite off; the Vanes and spindles of the weather cocks in many places bent quite down; as at St Michael Cornhill, St Sepulchre's, the Tower and divers other Places.

The most remarkable sight was in the view of the unknown author of a broadsheet entitled *The Amazing Tempest: Being a surprising Account of the great Damage done in and about the City of London, Southwark &c. By the Late Terrible and Astounding Tempest of Wind and Rain that happened on Friday night last*:

> . . . the large sheets of lead on Bow Church which by the wonderful strength of the Wind was rould up in folds, just as if it had been a piece of limber [i.e. flexible] cloth, as may be seen by any person who takes the pain to go as far as Cheapside to view it.

The same author was of the opinion that:

> There is scarcely an Alley, Lane or Street all over the City of London but what has two or three stacks of Chimnies, more or less, blown down: besides incredible Damage to their Glass, Windows &c. so that consequently the whole Damage of this great and populous City must be very considerable as regards some single tenements have suffered more than 20 pounds Damage, and very few but which have suffered by the sad violence of that amazing tempest, in one degree or another.

Of course the authors of anonymous broadsheets, like Johnson's writers of lapidary inscriptions, were not on oath but there is plenty of evidence to suggest that this assessment did not greatly exaggerate the true situation, a similar view being expressed by a writer such as Narcissus Luttrell, not writing commercially. The *Daily Courant* for Monday 29 November was obliged to admit that the Storm, 'did so much damage in and about the City that we cannot undertake to give a full account of it . . . The number of Chimneys blown down and roofs until'd and otherwise damaged not easy to be reckoned'. Of the damage done to windows some was done, in part at least, according to Defoe, even in very broad streets, by 'the flying of tile sherds from the other side'.

At the height of the Storm many Londoners do appear to have been presented with a genuine dilemma; whether to stay in their shaking homes or run outdoors and risk being bombarded with flying debris. 'Most people expected the fall of their houses', wrote Defoe:

> And yet in this general apprehension, nobody durst quit their tottering habitations: for whatever the danger was within doors, 'twas worse without: the bricks, tiles and stones, from the tops of the houses, flew with such force and so thick in the streets, that no one thought fit to venture out, though their houses were near demolished within.

Some verses on the Storm published a few weeks later expressed the problem as follows:

> Stay we within? Dangers hang o'er our Head,
> Our houses are our Refuge and our Dread.
> But step we forth? The boist'rous Tempest brings
> A thousand Deaths upon her rapid Wings.

Most people certainly seem to have opted for the cover provided, however treacherously, by a roof. A 90-year-old woman who moved out of her house in Jewin Street was promptly killed by a brickbat.

The terraces of houses which were built by speculative builders in accordance with the Rebuilding Act of 1667 were of four storeys on the principal streets and two or three storeys in the alleys and side streets. Most also possessed a basement and garrets so that even the smaller houses tended to make up in height for what they lacked in width and depth, and would have three flights or 'pairs' of stairs. Typically, the basement, which was below street level, was surrounded by an excavated 'area' and would contain the kitchen and, perhaps a back kitchen which would be the servants' quarters. The ground floor would be occupied by the parlour in larger houses or by the shops and counting houses of tradesmen and the first floor would include the dining room and drawing room. The upper floors would house the bedrooms, those of the servants being in the garret. Many houses, however, were subdivided and might contain several households, especially in the poorer districts. Chimneys collapsing in such houses had a long way to fall.

A further factor that must have had a bearing upon the number of injuries and fatalities was the sheer density of population even in relatively respectable parts of the town. Dr Gideon Harvey and his neighbours wrote the following account of their experience of the Storm:

> About three o'clock in the morning, the violence of the wind blew down a stack of chimneys belonging to the dwelling house of Dr Gideon Harvey (in St Martin's Lane, opposite New Street) on the back part of the next house wherein dwelt Mr Robert Richards an apothecary; Captain Theodore Collier and his family dwelt in the same. The chimney fell with that force as pierced through the roofs, carrying them quite down to the ground. The two families, consisting of 14 men, women and children, besides 3 that were in from the next house were at that instance disposed as follows: a footman that usually lay in the back garret, had not a quarter hour before, removed himself into the fore garret, by which means he escaped the danger: in the room under that lay Captain Collier's child, of two years old, in bed with the nurse, and a servant maid lay in the bed by her; the nurse's child lying in a crib by the bedside, which was found, with the child safe in it, in the kitchen, where the nurse and maid likewise found themselves: their bed being shattered to

pieces, and they a little bruised by falling down three stories; Captain Collier's child was, in about 2 hours, found unhurt in some pieces of the bed and curtains which had fallen through two floors only, and hung on some broken rafters in that place which had been the parlour: in the room under this, being one pair of stairs from the street, and two from the kitchen, was Captain Collier in bed, his wife just by the bedside, and her maid a little behind her, who likewise found herself in the kitchen, a little bruised and ran out to cry for help for her master and mistress, who lay buried under the ruins. Mrs Collier was, by the timely aid of neighbours who removed the rubbish from her, taken out in about half an hour having received no hurt but the fright, and an arm a little bruised: Captain Collier in about half an hour more was likewise taken out unhurt. In the parlour were sitting Mr Richards, with his wife, the three neighbours, and the rest of his family, a little boy about a year old lying in the cradle: they all ran out at the first noise and escaped. Mrs Richards stayed a little longer than the rest, to pull the cradle with her child in it along with her, but the house fell too suddenly on it, and buried the child under the ruins; a rafter fell on her foot and bruised it a little, but she likewise made her escape and brought in the neighbours who soon uncovered the head of the cradle, and, cutting it off, took the child out alive and well.

This wonderful preservation being worthy to be transmitted to posterity, we do attest to be true in every particular.
Gideon Harvey
Theo. Collier
Robert Richards

A not dissimilar tale was told to Mr King, lecturer at St Martin's-in-the-Fields by a Mr Woodgate Giffer who lived in St Martin's Street (on the other side of the Royal Mews, where Trafalgar Square now stands, from St Martin's Lane). Between two and three o'clock a neighbour's stack of chimneys broke through Giffer's garret roof into the stairwell upon which he 'thought it convenient to retire into the Kitchen' with his family. They had not been there for more than fifteen minutes before 'my Neighbour's stack of Chimneys on the other side fell upon my stack . . . beat in the roof, drove down the several floors through the Parlour into the Kitchen' burying the maid who was just coming through the door. There she lay for five hours 'in the Rubbish' but protected by some joists that 'lay athwart each other which prevented her perishing'.

Good fortune also seems to have attended John Hanson, the Registrar at Eton College, who, according to Defoe:

> . . . being at London about his Affairs, and lying that dreadful night, Nov. 26th at the Bell-Savage Inn on Ludgate Hill, was, by the Fall of a Stack of Chimneys (which broke through the Roof and beat down two Floors above him, and also that in which he lay) carried him in his Bed down to the Ground, without the least hurt, his Cloaths and everything besides in the Room being buried in the Rubbish; it having pleased God so to make it, that just so much of the Floor and Ceiling of the Room (from which he fell) as covered his Bed, was not broken down. Of this great Mercy he prays he may live for ever mindful, and be for ever thankful to Almighty God.

The task of digging out those trapped beneath the rubble of fallen houses must itself have been fraught with danger while hearing their cries above the roar of the wind, the thunder of falling masonry and shattering of glass must have been next to impossible. Such difficulties would have faced the rescuers of Frances Phelps whose story was told by her husband William:

> William Phelps and Frances his wife lived at the corner of Southampton buildings, over against Gray's Inn gate in Holborn; up three pairs of stairs in the back room that was only lathed and plaistered; he being then very ill, she was forced to lie in a little bed in the same room. About one o'clock in the morning, November 27th, the wind blew down a stack of chimneys of seven funnels that stood very high, which broke through the roof, and fell into the room upon her bed; so that she was buried alive as she lay. She cried out Mr Phelps, Mr Phelps, the house is fallen in on me; there being so much upon her, that one could but just hear her speak. A coachman and a footman lying on the same floor, were soon called to her assistance. They all fell to work,

though in the greatest danger themselves; and took her out without the least hurt; neither were any of them hurt; though there was much fell after they took her out. And when the bricks were taken off the bed the next morning, the frame of the bed on which she lay was broken all to pieces.

William Phelps

Falling chimneys accounted for a substantial proportion of the casualties. A huge number were blown down. Defoe provided the example of Cambray House, 'commonly so called' [Canonbury House] in Islington, belonging to the Earl of Northampton but divided up into tenements, where he counted 'eleven or thirteen' stacks of chimneys 'wholly thrown in or the greatest part of them at least'. As Henry Chamberlain, the eighteenth-century historian of London had it, they fell 'with such impetuosity that many people were killed, and others dreadfully mangled in the ruins'. Citizens of all ages and conditions suffered and the author of *An Exact Relation of the Late dreadful Tempest* . . . (1704) spared few of the details:

A watchman in Penitent [Pennington] Street, Ratcliff Highway as he was going his Rounds was unfortunately killed by the fall of a stack of chimneys, being found dead in the middle of the street the next morning by some of his Neighbours.

Mr Mias [Myers?], an eminent Distiller in Duke Street, Piccadilly and his Maid servant were killed by the fall of a stack of Chimneys; at the same time his Wife was bruised and knocked down but being let blood there appears great hopes of her recovery. A child in Lamb's Alley, without Bishopsgate, being asleep in a Cradle next it's Parents' bedside was unhappily killed by the fall of a Chimney; beating out the Infant's Brains, and mashing the whole body in the Father's and mother's Sight; who were kept alive by the pre-ordained Will of God, though the Cradle where the child lay was not half a yard distant from their bedside. From whence we may observe, That even Innocency in a General Calamity, suffers with the Guilty: and the poor Babe is destroyed with the Stroke of Divine Vengeance, while the sinful Parents are permitted to stretch out their lives to a longer date.

Nor did the Queen's residence, the royal palace of St James's, escape:

> Part of the palace of St James's was blown down and a woman killed by the Fall of a Chimney. Her Majesty was allarmed, and got up with his Highness the Prince and all the maids of Honour, who escaped the signal Danger; for in the Room where they were a Stack of Chimneys fell, within a few minutes after they had left the same.

The Queen herself is said to have stood at a window in the Palace watching as the acacias, limes and elms in St James's Park were torn up by the savagery of the wind and a great length of garden wall crashed to the ground.

Falling chimneys also accounted for the death of two children in Whitechapel, two women in their beds near Hermitage Bridge and Mr Bull, an eminent merchant of Hackney, his maidservant being 'desperately hurt'.

The opportunity to moralise was rarely missed in contemporary accounts. The author of *The Amazing Tempest* drew attention to the fate of Mr Atkins, a carpenter of White Cross Street:

> being desired by his Wife to read a Chapter [of the Bible], when the Tempest was at its greatest fury but he refusing to perform that Christian Office in such a time of Distress, he was unfortunately killed by the fall of a Chimney, but his Wife (tho' then close by him) was miraculously preserved, having not received the least damage.

Defoe was shocked by the behaviour of a man and woman of Aldersgate Street who, having been forced into a cellar by the fall of a chimney were eventually dug out at eight the following morning. Without pausing to express gratitude 'to either God or man for their timely deliverance', the man 'immediately asked for his clothes having left 50*s* in the pocket' while she enquired of 'a trunk in which there were some pieces of gold'.

Still more remarkable to the God-fearing Daniel were those

who took advantage of the chaos created by the Storm to indulge in criminal activities:

> I cannot but observe here how fearless such People as are addicted to Wickedness are both of God's Judgement and Uncommon Prodigies; which is visible in this Particular, That a Gang of hardened Rogues assaulted a Family at Poplar, in the very Height of the Storm, broke into the house, and robb'd them: it is observable that the People cryed Thieves, and after that cryed Fire, in hopes of raising the Neighbourhood, and to get some Assistance; but such is the power of Self-Preservation, and such was the Fear the Minds of the People were possess'd with, that no Body would venture out to the Assistance of the distressed Family.

In addition to the havoc caused by the Storm in the streets and alleys of the City and suburbs, vast devastation and considerable loss of life occurred on the River Thames which was, while not the sole explanation for London's prosperity, a major cause of it. There was only one bridge – London Bridge, often simply known as Bridge – which divided the river into two quite distinct stretches, both the scene of much noisy, colourful and economically vital activity. The Bridge itself, dating from the twelfth century, although much repaired, was lined with buildings so that, in the words of Zacharias Conrad von Uffenbach, 'one does not take it for a bridge because it has on both sides large and handsome houses, the lower storeys of which are shops. Well over halfway across the bridge towards Southwark is a single place about eight feet long where there is not a house and the Thames can be seen through the iron palings'.*

* There seem to have been more gaps prior to the Fire of 1666. On 24 January of that year there was another 'Great Storme' when, according to Pepys, 'It was dangerous to walk the streets, the bricks and tiles falling from the houses that the whole streets were covered with them – and whole Chimneys, nay whole houses in two or three places, blown down. But above all the pales on London-bridge on both sides were blown away, so that we were fain to stoop very low for fear of blowing off the bridge'.

The bridge itself had twenty narrow arches, separated by stone piers, through which the water rushed so that 'shooting the bridge' was often uncomfortable and sometimes perilous. The bridge was thus the head of navigation for ocean-going traffic. Below it the riverbank was lined with quays, wharfs and warehouses, shipyards and wet- and dry-docks. The river itself, from the Pool of London downstream to Limehouse, a distance of two miles, was full of shipping, from coastal vessels, such as Newcastle colliers, to the great East Indiamen laden with tea and silks. Upstream were to be found barges and wherries which would negotiate the passage of the bridge in order to take goods to and from the port, and the boats of hundreds of watermen, oarsmen and scullers, who plied a flourishing passenger trade up, down and across the river. Larger parties were carried by galleys, rowed by several oarsmen. Those that could afford it chose river rather than road whenever convenient, preferring to face the abrasive wit of the watermen rather than the push and shove of the Sedan chairmen, un-sprung hackney carriages and universal dirt. 'You cannot see anything more charming and delightful than the river,' wrote de Saussure.

Whether it was more or less delightful than the streets on the night of the Storm is debatable. Like them it could be a fatal place to be.

Given the extent to which the bridge and the houses, which 'stand high upon it and are not sheltered', were exposed, Defoe was surprised that it received 'but little Damage' which he explained in terms of the 'in draft of the Arches underneath the Houses giving vent to the Air'. Another account, however, suggests that 'a great number of vessels, barges and boats were sunk in the River Thames and the arches of London Bridge were stopp'd with them'. Above sixty barges and lighters were said to have driven foul of the bridge. The author of *A Wonderful History of all the Storms, Hurricanes, Earthquakes* etc., published like Defoe's book in 1704, states that:

> The Storm raged furiously on the Thames, breaking a great number of Lighters and Boats to pieces above bridge . . . it broke the Iron Chains of some that moored in the open river, shoaled Lighters and Boats upon the Starlings [the piling

> protecting the piers of the bridge] and staved many of them in pieces so that the surface of the water, the Day appearing, was seen to be strewn with all their wrecks . . .

It appears as though the wind, blowing downstream at this point piled the wrecks up against the upstream side of the bridge and, on the downstream side swept the Pool of London almost clear of shipping. Defoe describes this downstream destruction in one of the finest passages in *The Storm*. He explains how, because of the orientation of the reaches of the river as it meanders about Rotherhithe, the vessels, driven from their moorings, tended to converge upon Limehouse Hole, an area which already had the characteristics described by Dickens in *Our Mutual Friend* as the place where Rogue Riderhood 'dwelt deep and dark . . . among the riggers, and the mast, oar and block makers, and the boat builders and the sail-lofts, as in a kind of ship's hold stored full of waterside characters'. They were characters whose factual forebears venturing down to the waterfront that Saturday morning had been met by an amazing scene. Further up river the view must have been equally surprising if less dramatic:

> It was a strange sight to see all the ships in the river blown away, the Pool was so clear that, as I remember, not above four ships were left between the upper part of Wapping and Ratcliff Cross, for the tide being up at the time when the storm blew with the greatest violence. No anchors or landfast, no cables or moorings would hold them, the chains which lay across the river for the moorings of ships, all gave way.
>
> The ships breaking loose thus, it must be a strange sight to see the hurry and confusion of it, and as some ships had nobody at all on board, and a great many had none but a man or boy left on board to look after the vessel, there was nothing to be done, but to let every vessel drive whither and how she would.
>
> Those who know the reaches of the river, and how they lie, know well enough, that the wind being at south-westerly, would naturally drive into the bite or bay from Ratcliff Cross to

Limehouse Hole, for that the river winding about again from thence towards the new dock at Deptford, runs almost due south west so that the wind blew down one reach and up another, and the ships must of necessity drive into the bottom of the angle between both.

This was the case, and as the place is not large and the number of ships very great, the force of the wind had driven them so into one another, and laid them so upon one another as it were in heaps, that I think a man may safely deny all the world to do the like.

The author of this collection had the curiosity the next day to view the place, and to observe the posture they lay in, which nevertheless 'tis impossible to describe; there lay, by the best account he could take, few less than 700 sail of ships, some very great ones between Shadwell and Limehouse inclusive, the position is not to be imagined, but by them that saw it, some vessels lay heeling off with the bow of another ship over her waste, and the stern of another upon her forecastle, the bowsprits of some drove into the cabin windows of others; some lay with their sterns tossed up so high, that the tide flowed into their forecastles before they could come to rights; some lay so leaning upon others, that the undermost vessel would sink before the other could float; the number of masts, bowsprits and yards split and broke, the staving the heads, and sterns and carved work, the tearing and destruction of rigging, and the squeezing of boats to pieces between the ships is not to be reckoned; but there was hardly a vessel to be seen that had not suffered some damage or another in one or all of these articles.

The amount of damage done to shipping in the river was so considerable because at that time the great dock-building era had scarcely begun: there were no docks further upstream than Blackwall, most ships being anchored in the exposed and crowded fairway. When their moorings broke under the immense strain exerted by the wind they were driven, as Defoe explains, until they were either blown ashore or ran foul of one another. Between the Bridge and Limehouse, he says, only four ships remained at anchor and these, according to Chamberlain, were 'so damaged by beating against each other as to be entirely unfit for further use'. Downstream of Limehouse the greatest individual loss appears to have been of the East Indiaman galley *Sarah*, 'lading for Leghorn', at Blackwall. She seems to have sunk at anchor and although eventually re-floated, 'yet her back was broke or so otherwise disabled, as she was never fit for the sea'.

The passing of the Storm, at about eight on the Saturday morning, did not bring to an end the difficulties facing the sailors and watermen on the Thames. As the Storm system moved away over Scandinavia ideal conditions were created for a North Sea surge, the phenomenon which in the 1970s persuaded the authorities of the necessity of building the Greenwich Flood Barrier. A sudden drop in atmospheric pressure, such as occurred with the passage of the deep depression which produced the Storm, causes a rise in sea level in the North Sea; a drop of 30 mb producing a rise of 30 cm. To this must be added the effect of the gale-force northerly winds in the rear of the depression pushing the elevated seas southwards, the effect being amplified by the fact that the southern part of the North Sea is narrower and shallower, an effect which is further exaggerated within the Thames estuary. Interestingly, this mechanism was, in part at least, understood at the time. Defoe, who seems to have read of it in William Derham's letter to the Royal Society, describes the surge in the following terms:

> Another unhappy circumstance with which this Disaster was join'd, was a prodigious Tide, which happen'd the next day but one and was occasion'd by the Fury of the winds; which is also a Demonstration, that the Winds veer'd for part of the time to the northward and it is observable, and known by all that understand our Sea Affairs that a North West Wind makes the Highest Tide, so that this blowing to the northward [sic] and that with such unusual Violence, brought up the Sea raging in such a manner, that in some parts of England 'twas incredible, the water rising Six or Eight Feet higher than it was ever known in the Memory of man; by which ships were fleeted up upon the firm Land several Rods off from the Banks . . .

The combined effect of the surge and the spring tide, occurring shortly after the new moon, was greatest on Sunday, 28 November. Between two and three o'clock in the morning the tide rose so high that it overflowed the high wharf near Billingsgate and caused 'more Damage in Cellars and Warehouses than any tide whatsoever did before' and to cause the flooding of the lower lying parts of the City and Westminster, including Westminster Hall. The high tide during the Storm had driven vessels further ashore than many could believe, whereas the still higher tide which followed was in some cases beneficial. Defoe, writing of the vessels driven on to the mudbanks near Tilbury, five of them bound for the West Indies, explained that the high tide enabled them to be easily re-floated:

Not all the reports are consistent. Luttrell, writing on the day of the Storm (27th) is broadly in agreement with Defoe, claiming that most of the boats and barges in the river were forced ashore, that the East Indiaman was lost at Blackwall, 'besides several merchant ships and colliers'. A report in the *Post Man*, dated 2 December, however, states that 'The Merchant Ships in the river that were run aground in the late Storm, are for the most part got off again without any considerable damage in their rigging and we do not hear of any that were lost this side of Blackwall'. These different reports may simply reflect the combined effects of re-floating vessels thought to be lost and the desire, in the immediate aftermath of the Storm, not to give encouragement to the enemy.

We cannot be sure of the number of fatalities in and about the capital although the Bills of Mortality provide a guide. These were records of baptisms and burials kept by the Company of Parish Clerks, originally with the intention of monitoring the spread of the plague and other infectious diseases. For a number of reasons they are not entirely reliable, although exactly how dependable they are has been a question of debate since the eighteenth century. The Bills of Mortality – the expression came also to refer to the district covered by the returns – consisted of more than 100 parishes, which meant that how comprehensive they were depended upon the efficiency of a large number of parish clerks. The bills also excluded the very considerable numbers of

Dissenters and foreigners who had their own burial grounds. So far as the Storm was concerned, it has also been suggested that in compiling the bills a deliberate endeavour was made to lessen public consternation 'by keeping out of sight as many fatal accidents as possible'. A case, perhaps, of the victims being spun in their graves?

Defoe claims that the Bills of Mortality list twenty-one deaths as a result of the Storm. The author of *A Wonderful History of All the Storms* . . . (1704) lists twenty, namely:

Two by the fall of a Chimney in St Andrew's Holborn
Two by the fall of a House in St Botolph by Aldersgate
One by the fall of a Chimney in St Botolph by Aldgate
Two by the fall of a Chimney in St Dunstan by Stepney
Three by the fall of a Chimney in St James Westminster
One by the fall of a Chimney in St Martin-in-the-Fields
One by the fall of a Chimney in St Bennet Finch [Fink]
One by the fall of a House in St Giles-without-Cripplegate
One by the fall of the Eves of Houses in the Temple
One by the fall of a Chimney in St Mary Magdalene Bermondsey
One by the fall of a roof of a house in St Andrew's Holborn
One by the fall of a House in St Katharine's Coleman Street
One by the fall of a Chimney in St Botolph by Bishopsgate
One by the fall of a House in St Giles-without-Cripplegate
One by the fall of a Chimney in St Paul's Shadwell

Although the Borough of Southwark was included within the Bills there is no reference here to the burial of the man and two children said to have been killed by the fall of a house in Queen Street, Southwark. It is also noticeable that there are no recorded deaths by drowning, yet all the contemporary accounts refer to several people being drowned in the river. Three men, a woman and a boy were said to have been cast away between Chiswick and Fulham and two men at Blackfriars apparently died endeavouring to save their wherry. Defoe specifies that 'about 22 people were drowned in the River upon this sad occasion . . . which considering all circumstances is not a great many'. This confirms him in the belief, more in accordance with his prejudice than his reason, that 'the River of Thames is the best harbour in Europe'.

The author of *An Exact Relation* is of the opinion that:

> . . . it must be acknowledged that the Fire of London, whose uncontrolled and flaming Rage laid in Ashes our Metropolis, was not so considerable a Misfortune, as this never to be forgotten Disaster.

Writers on natural catastrophes are, perhaps, inherently inclined to exaggerate their effects. This anonymous author is certainly no exception but in two, not unimportant, respects he was correct. Compared with the Fire, the Storm caused far more deaths and injuries – Defoe reckoned 200 injured and maimed – in and about the capital to which it was, of course, by no means confined.

14

Carpenters, Caulkers and Seamen

The rescued members of the crew of the *Stirling Castle* made their way to London, probably under directions from the muster-master at Deal. On 1 December, the Wednesday following the Storm, the Navy Board minutes record that a 'memorial' was to be sent to the Queen 'to know what should be done with the men saved out of the ships that are cast away, whether they should be paid off or put into other ships'. The answer that came back must have been the latter because the minute for 7 December records the attendance of the *Stirling Castle*'s men who all agreed to transfer to the *Norfolk*, tickets of leave being given them 'for a month from yesterday'. Those who returned to and remained with the 80-gun *Norfolk* during the following summer would have seen action at the siege of Gibraltar and the bloody Battle of Malaga.

Within a week of the Storm the search for Shovell had been organised, ketches had been sent to Harwich and the Downs with anchors, cables and stores for the stricken ships and the least damaged ships were being rapidly patched up to persuade the French that England's wooden walls had not, in fact, collapsed and to enable the everyday task of protecting merchant shipping to resume. Portsmouth and the Thames ports were already preparing for the more extensive repair work designed to ensure that the Navy was ready for the year ahead.

Some things had necessarily been put in abeyance. On the eve of the Storm an exchange of prisoners had been about to take place. This had been delayed but on 30 November Nottingham,

Secretary of State for the Southern Department, appears to have sanctioned the exchange. Two days later the Commissioners of Sick and Wounded Seamen and for Exchanging Prisoners of War wrote to Nottingham advising him that although the transports were ready to sail from Dover and Guernsey:

> we have stopped them: for the seas are full of ships disabled by the late storm, to which the said prisoners may give intelligence.

There was certainly a real fear that the French might take advantage of the weakness of the Navy. The exchange of prisoners, many of whom were in a wretched condition, did take place shortly afterwards.

In fact, of course, France had suffered too, but in the absence of post from the continent, itself delayed by the bad weather, this was not recognised for some time. It was not until 14 December, for example, that Narcissus Luttrell, whose finger was always close to the pulse of affairs, confided to his diary that:

> Our merchants have advice from Holland, that in the late storm the peer head of Dunkirk, with the risebank, were broken down by the strength of the wind, and some pieces of cannon dismounted, so that now it might be bombarded from the sea.

Those who realised that the greatest threat to English shipping came not from the French navy but from the prosecution by privateers of a *guerre de course*, must have been encouraged to read of the loss in the Storm of sixteen privateers from St Malo alone.

Admiral Rooke's squadron on the coast of Holland, waiting to bring 'Charles III' of Spain on the next leg of his journey to Portugal, had also suffered in the Storm. Initial reports of the destruction of two English men-of-war and a transport ship were exaggerated: the 50-gun *Vigo Prize* had been lost at Hellevoetsluis but all but four of a crew of over 200 had been saved. The safe delivery of Charles to the Peninsula was the Government's first priority and by 10 December another minister, Sir Charles Hedges, was writing to Rooke urging him to make all speed:

> considering how well disposed (as we know) the Spaniards are to receive the King of Spain we should make all possible haste with the Portuguese expedition. You are therefore to proceed to England with the King of Spain as soon as the wind serves with such ships as are ready to sail with you. Transport at Spithead is ready . . . Notwithstanding the late storm everything is ready here for his passage.

Rooke was to be accompanied by a Dutch squadron under Admiral Callenburgh but several of his ships had been driven from their anchors, some apparently as far as Norway. If Callenburgh was in need of any 'tackle' lost in the Storm, Hedges instructed, he should be supplied out of Her Majesty's stores, 'paying for the same'. At this stage Rooke was still seeing to his damaged ships and, according to Luttrell, was hoping to sail in a fortnight's time. The Admiral's estimated time table was about right: Charles landed at Portsmouth on 26 December but he did not reach Lisbon until the end of February.

The loss of shipping and of sailors was of great concern. Ironically, the question of manning the Navy had been debated in the House of Commons on the day the Storm struck. Practical politics as well as humanity dictated that further losses be avoided. News of the destruction of the Eddystone lighthouse and the subsequent loss of the *Winchelsea* reached London on 3 December and the next day Sir David Mitchell sent orders to Sir Edward Harrison, the Commissioner at Plymouth, that as soon as any frigates were in readiness and could be spared from other necessary duties, they should be sent to cruise 'to give the Trade notice of the Lighthouse being down'. HMS *Lyme* was to be sent to the Scillies to ascertain whether the light there (the coal-burning lighthouse on St Agnes) was still operating. If she found that it had been blown down she was to cruise between 7 leagues to the south and 12 leagues to the west of it to give notice of the loss of both lights. If it should be found to be in good order, which it was, then the *Lyme* was to cruise 7 leagues south of the Eddystone to give notice of the loss of that light, returning to Plymouth every fourteen days.

The scale of the losses at sea evoked a great wave of sympathy in the country and within a fortnight of the event plans for making payments to the widows of drowned sailors were well advanced – a quite exceptional display of civic generosity for the age. Nor was there any tradition of charity towards shipwrecked sailors. When the fifth-rate *Satisfaccion* sank off the Dutch coast in 1662, the King granted the survivors half-pay, 'which', writes Pepys, 'is more then is used in such cases for they never used to have anything'. The crew were not impressed and to the apparent surprise of the diarist, who was involved in paying them off, 'were most outrageously discontented and did rail and curse us'. However distinguished the service of their loved ones, dependents could not rely on a tight-fisted Treasury paying up. In 1689 Micaiah Browning's ship, the *Mountjoy*, had broken the boom across the Foyle to relieve the besieged protestants of Londonderry. In England Browning, who was killed in the action, became a national hero but in the year of the Great Storm his widow was petitioning for the payment of nine years' arrears of the pension that had been granted to her. Shamefully, she was only paid 'as much as is due in the queen's time' (that is, one of the nine years).

On the Wednesday after the Storm, however, the Commons had petitioned the Queen not only to make good the navy's losses but also to grant relief to dependents from the public purse. Anne, who frequently exercised the royal prerogative of mercy in the case of those condemned to death, was not the woman to refuse. On Friday 3 December the Speaker read out her reply to the House:

> Gentlemen,
> I return you many thanks for the Assurances you give me, of your dispatching the necessary Supplies for carrying on the War, and of making good the Expense of the Damage happened to the Navy by the late Storm; for the repairing of which I shall use all possible Diligence and Application, and with great hopes of seeing it speedily effected, by the blessing of God, and your kind Assistance. I shall carefully comply with what you desire, for relieving the Families of such poor Seamen as have perished in the Storm; and always concur with you in promoting the publick Welfare.

The consequence was that the families of sailors lost in the Storm received the same compensation as did those of men killed in the Queen's service. Payment began on 13 January 1704: the total sum distributed amounted to £15,158 11*d.* At the time of the Queen's reply to the Commons Shovell's ships had still not been heard of so that the cost of this unique act of generosity on Parliament's part might have been far greater than proved to be necessary.

Like his Queen, the Lord High Admiral's instinct was to behave humanely, as is revealed in a letter from him addressed to the Navy Board and dated 30 March 1704:

> Gentlemen:
> A Petition having been sent to me in the name of Elizabeth Mann, widow of Richard Mann (sen.) late belonging to her Majesty's ship *Resolution* which was cast away in the late dreadful storm, setting forth that she not only lost her husband but had two sons in the said ship, viz. Richard Mann (jun.) and John Mann, and praying that she may be allowed the bounty money, that she should be paid as a widow and as a mother too. I do therefore . . . direct you to govern yourselves accordingly . . . pursuant to the Queen's order in Council of 17th December last . . . and for the future, all others be paid bounty money in the like manner.
>
> I am etc.

Another mother, Lady Beaumont, also memorialised the Queen, claiming the family's dependence upon Basil and asking for a pension. The petition was successful and £50 a year was granted to each of his six sisters.

Following the loss of the *Association* in 1707, Lady Elizabeth Shovell and other widows petitioned the Queen for similar consideration. By that time Prince George had himself died and had been replaced as Lord High Admiral by the Earl of Pembroke who informed the Queen that, unless an officer died in action, his dependents were not entitled to a bounty. The Secretary to the Admiralty, Josiah Burchett, however, pointed out that an exception had been made in the case of the Great Storm. In fact, as Simon Harris, Shovell's biographer, has shown there were other precedents.

Admiral Sir Francis Wheler had perished in the terrible storm off Gibraltar in 1694 and his wife was granted a pension of £200 a year, as was the widow of Admiral Sir Thomas Dilkes when he had died at Leghorn earlier in 1707. The granting of a bounty to ordinary seamen was, of course, a very different matter and an innovative feature of government policy following the Great Storm.

The loss of so many men presented considerable problems for a service which even in the best of times tended to rely upon the press gangs to man its ships. During the war there was an average of about 40,000 men in the navy and the Storm appears to have accounted for about 4 per cent of that total, not an inconsiderable proportion to replace when competition from the army and the better-paid merchant navy are taken into consideration. It would have been surprising if the *Stirling Castle* survivors had been paid off.

A notice in the *London Gazette* for 6–9 December suggests that some enterprising individual saw scope for a form of privatised recruiting. It is unlikely to be a coincidence that the proposal was made so soon after the Storm:

> Whereas a Paper signed M. was lately sent to the Council of his Royal Highness, for the officers of the Admiralty, offering to bring into the service some hundreds of seamen, these are to give notice to the person who sent the said paper that he may any day of this week have the opportunity of attending them at the Admiralty Office between the hours of ten in the morning and one in the afternoon in order to his being discussed with concerning his offer.

It was a widely held view that the loss of seamen was, from the point of view of national defence, a greater blow than that of the warships. In his paper the *Observator*, Defoe's Whig rival John Tutchin employed the device of a dialogue between 'Countryman' and 'Observator'. The edition for 1–4 December 1703 contained the following exchange:

> COUNTRYMAN: Master Observator, this is a Terrible Token of the Displeasure of the Almighty; never was such a Storm of Wind, such a Hurricane and Tempest known in the Memory of

> Man, nor like to be in the Histories of England; I am told at London the Damage done in the Kingdom, by the Storm, amounts to more than a Year's Taxes.
> OBSERVATOR: I am of the same Opinion; But our Sea Loss is the greatest because Irreparable; we can build more Ships, we can make good the loss of our Navy in a few Months but Seamen are not built in Years . . .

As we have seen, the Commons were discussing the manning of the navy on the Saturday of the Storm and, on the following Saturday, a Committee of the Whole House was again debating the topic. It was not at that time known how many of Shovell's ships had weathered the Storm and there was an understandable tendency to exaggerate the scope of the disaster as the following contribution to the debate shows:

> MR SMITH: By computation there are about 65,000 seamen. 10,000 to 12,000 have been lost this year by the late catastrophe and by sickness in the West Indies and in Sir Cloudesley Shovell's squadron.

Deaths from disease certainly greatly exceeded those in action and could have done little to encourage new recruits. Mr Smith – probably John Smith, MP for Andover and future Speaker and Chancellor of the Exchequer – suggested that the Act of Navigation, which excluded foreigners from naval service, should be amended to permit their entry. In Marlborough's armies after all the majority was non-British. Another speaker, Mr How, was in favour of the naturalisation of foreigners to allow them to enter the navy, advocated the pressing into employment of 'idle fellows such as gamesters etc.' and, ungrammatically, asked 'Why should a gentleman have six footmen hanging behind their coaches when two may do?'

The House of Commons, in which the mercantile interest was well represented, wished to reinforce the recruiting power of the Royal Navy without damaging that of the merchant marine. On 16 December they resolved that greater efforts should be made to recruit apprentices for the merchant service from the parish poor and on 7 January it was resolved by a Committee of the whole House:

> That in all Cases where the Law requires the Master and Three-fourths of the Mariners in navigating any ship to be English, it shall be sufficient, if the Master, and one half of the Mariners be English.

Pay was never used as a recruiting aid in the Royal Navy, the pay rates of ratings throughout the eighteenth century being those established in 1653!

Those for whom the Storm proved a particularly fair wind were those condemned men who were reprieved on condition they entered the Navy. Byng, as we have seen, intervened on the part of two Portsmouth deserters, and on 8 March 1704 thirteen Newgate prisoners were 'listed into the Queen's service'. Prisoners of war, especially if they were nationals of neutral countries, were encouraged to change allegiance. In December 1703 the Navy's numbers were swelled by the entry of four Danish seamen, taken aboard a captured French privateer. Huguenots could also occasionally be persuaded to join the alliance against their Catholic monarch.

The immediate concern, however, was not so much manning the fleet as providing the dockyards with a labour force capable of doing the necessary repair and building work needed if there were to be sufficient ships – men-of-war and auxiliaries – to meet the demands of the following summer. By early December the Navy Board was expressing concern about 'the want of Carpenters, Saylemakers and Caulkers to carry on the work of re-fitting the fleet for next summer's service'. Orders were given that, as the great ships came into harbour, their captains should discharge their carpenter's crew to work in the yards until such time as the ship was again ready to go to sea. The same regulations were to apply to caulkers* and sailmakers.

* Caulking was the process of rendering the sides and decks of ships impervious to water. Oakum, consisting of tarred hemp fibres from old, unpicked ropes, was driven into the seams with the aid of a caulking iron.

The pressure of work and the shortage in particular of joiners saw a switch away from the kind of ornamental carved work, which was such a feature of seventeenth-century warships, to more practical tasks. On 16 January the Lord High Admiral gave his approval to a Navy Board suggestion that 'the charge of carvers and joiners and other ornamental work . . . be lessened aboard her Majesty's ships for the future'. The amount of ornamentation, although by no means eliminated altogether, was strictly controlled: 'carved work . . . reduced only to a lion and tailboard for the head, with mouldings instead of brackets between the lights of the stern galleries . . . ' etc.

Even in peacetime the royal dockyards were the largest industrial units in the country and the numbers employed swelled considerably during wartime. They were the responsibility of the Navy Board which, in the case of the larger yards, was represented by resident commissioners. When the nation was at war winter was the busiest time in the dockyards, ships being laid up and refitted in preparation for the summer sea campaign. In the winter of 1703/4, storm damage added significantly to the amount of work to be done and concern was expressed about the capacity of the yards, especially Portsmouth.

The large dockyard workforce was poorly paid and their pay was often in arrears so that, unsurprisingly, the workers had a reputation for unruliness, even militancy. During this critical period, in which the fleet was being rebuilt, it was clearly of great importance to avoid poor labour relations so the Board must have been dismayed to receive a petition, dated 16 February 1704, from the Chatham riggers and labourers:

> Rt. Hons: Your suppliants are riggers and labourers belonging to Chatham Yard . . . we your suppliants did duly attend our labour daily from seven in the morning to four in the afternoon which is the usual and ancient custom limited. And yesterday, coming by Commissioner St Lo's order at six in the morning, we told him we were ready to obey his commands, provided the usual allowance for labour from six to six might be allowed us which he would not comply with, but told us we should have no more wages than we had from seven to four . . . and

> thereupon drew his sword and drove us from the dock gate and told us he would send us all to the West Indies, not withstanding we, your Hon's suppliants, are masters and owners and have several servants under us.

Commissioner St Lo was the same George St Lo who had been in charge at Plymouth when the Eddystone lighthouse was being built. Here, under pressure no doubt to speed up the re-fitting of damaged ships, he does appear to have mishandled a situation which, very probably, became threatening. Normally, overtime at Chatham was reckoned in 'nights' and 'tides'. A 'night' being a period of five hours and was paid as for a full day while a 'tide' was an hour and a half of overtime for which shipwrights received 18*d* and labourers 4*d*. The men's petition was successful. The Commissioner was increasing the working day by three hours and was instructed by the Board to give two 'tides' per day extra pay. A prolonged interruption of work was not to be countenanced.

A further question which arose concerned the priority that should be given as between the building and rebuilding programmes. Initially, it was resolved to repair the smaller warships, of fourth-rate and downwards, that only required minor work, first; followed by the third-rates of 70 guns, then the third-rates of 80 guns and, lastly, the second- and first-rates. It was, however, also decided that because it was quicker to build new ships than rebuild old ones, priority should be given to new construction.

Despite the threat of industrial action, the shipyard workers appear to have laboured mightily to restore the fleet in time for the coming summer. Daniel Defoe was greatly impressed by the speed and efficiency of work on the Medway, in which the shipyard workers themselves appear to have taken great pride. In the *Tour* he wrote that:

> The expedition that has been sometimes used here in fitting out men of war, is very great, and as the workmen relate it, 'tis indeed incredible; particularly they told us, that the *Royal Sovereign*, a first-rate of 106 guns, was riding at her moorings, entirely unrigged, and nothing but her three masts standing, as is usual when a ship is laid up, and that she was completely

> rigged, all her masts up, her yards put to, her sails bent, anchors and cables on board and the ship sailed down the Black-Stakes in three days . . . I do not vouch the thing but when I consider, first, that everything lay ready in her store houses, and wanted nothing but to be fetched out and carried on board; a thousand or fifteen hundred men to be employed in it and more if they were wanted; and every man knowing his business perfectly well, boats, carriages, pullies, tacklers, cranes and hulk all ready, I do not know but it might be done in one day if it was tried; certain it is, the dexterity of the English sailors in these things is not to be matched in the world.

Evidence of the speed with which work was undertaken in the shipyards is provided by the *Hampton Court* which had arrived in Plymouth Sound in such a grievous state following the Storm. On 4 February she left the Hamoaze to join the fleet escorting 'Charles III' to Portugal and by the 28th of that month was in the Tagus. By the beginning of March the Navy Board were able to report that the fitting of ships intended for the next summer's service was in 'very great forwardness' and the fleet was, in fact, able to face the forthcoming campaigning season at virtually full strength. If there had to be such a devastating Storm it could hardly have come at a better time, allowing as it did the entire winter period for reconstruction.

Seven new warships were completed in 1704 – one first-rate (the *Royal Anne*), two third-rates, three fourth-rates and a fifth-rate. Three of the new vessels, the 64-gun *Mary* and the *Reserve* and *Newcastle*, both of 54 guns, were given the names of ships lost in the Storm. Among ships launched in the following year were a new *Stirling Castle* and a new *Northumberland*. A year after the event the Navy Board estimated that the cost of replacing the ships lost in the Great Storm, cannons and ordnance excepted, would be £134,232. It was a considerable sum, exceeding the total receipts in 1704 from the postal service.

15

FAST, FACT AND FICTION

The parish register of Cheltenham in Gloucestershire draws attention not only to the immediate effects of the Storm but also to one of the inevitable consequences. At a time when insurance was beyond the experience of all but a tiny proportion of the population, which in any case only covered fire, the consequences of natural disaster could be dire, even for the survivors:

> A terrible tempestuous Wind on 27 day of November about ye hours of one to seven in ye morning, which did very great damage both at sea and also on land, to the ruine of very many families.

It certainly seems likely that there were many, already living close to the margin of poverty, for whom the Storm, through physical injury or by damage to property, meant permanent impoverishment, in many cases extending down the generations. Of such indigent and illiterate people notice was rarely taken, so that their misfortunes have gone unrecorded. We tend to know of a more prosperous class of victim. Edward Shortall was perhaps lucky in that his plight excited the pity of well-to-do fellow citizens who recognised that they might themselves have gone 'There but for the Grace of God'.

Four years before the Storm, Shortall, of Wild Street in the parish of St Giles-in-the-Fields, London, a cook and 'honest substantial housekeeper for 24 years' had been robbed of all his gold, money and plate 'to above the value of 570 and odd pounds' and the magistrates provided him with a testimonial recommending him as a fit object of Christian charity. Shortall, it appears, never made use of the testimonial but, by his own efforts 'resettled himself in his trade'. Having once more accumulated some capital, he then, in the words of a supplement to the original testimonial:

> went to Dublin and laid out above Eighty Pounds there upon Linen Cloth, and other Goods and on 21st November last, 1703 the said Edward Shortall imbarqued the said goods on board a ship bound for London, whereof Captain Nelson was Commander. And the said Ship, Commander, Crew, Passengers and Goods were all cast away in the late great storm; whereby the said Edward Shortall, with his Wife and Children, are driven to the last Extremity, as having nothing left 'em for their sustenance, but are in a starving languishing condition and now necessitated to beg the Charity of good Christians: and to prove this latter loss, the said Shortall has Affidavits ready by him to produce, made by himself and others now in London who had seen the said goods imbarked on board the said ship: and that the said ship was lost in the said Storm is generally well known both in Dublin and London.

Although there is much evidence of charitable giving following the Storm, human nature being what it is, rumours of ruin, doubtless spiced with a sprinkling of *Schadenfreude*, seem to have been widespread. In Bristol, for example, a chronicler asserted that that one of the city's leading merchants, Sir John Duddleston was reduced to penury having lost £30,000. That Duddleston had sustained losses seems very likely, probably most Bristol merchants did, but their extent was almost certainly exaggerated, for little more than a year after the Storm he himself was donating to the relief of the poor and by 1715 he had recovered sufficiently to be elected Master of the Merchant Venturers' Society, an office which he still held when he died in the following year. It is to the credit of Daniel Defoe that, although himself a ruined man, his book contains not the slightest suggestion of gloating over the misfortunes of others – quite otherwise.

Religious disputes had continued irrespective of the emergency and on Saturday 27 November, only hours after the passage of the Storm and with strong winds still sweeping across the country, Mr Bromley rose in the House of Commons to introduce a bill for the prevention of Occasional Conformity. The Storm itself triggered a fresh skirmish in one of the other ongoing causes of division, the debate over the decadence of the stage. The attack was led by Jeremy Collier, minister of a non-juring congregation in London and the author, in 1698, of a *Short View of the Immorality and Profaneness of the English Stage*. On this occasion the sights of Collier and his supporters were set not upon the *risqué* comedies of Wycherley and Congreve but on two works of William Shakespeare himself. The initial attack took the form of *Mr Collier's Disuasive from the Playhouse* addressed to a 'person of quality' [the critic and playwright, John Dennis], in which he argued that putting on such plays as *Macbeth* and *The Tempest* in the days immediately after the Storm was not only distasteful but positively blasphemous, mocking the seriousness of the warning from God which that event represented. *Macbeth*, beginning as it does in a storm and containing such lines as 'Shipwrecking storms and direful thunders break' brought out the worst in an ungodly audience. When Lennox delivered the lines:

> The night has been unruly. Where we lay
> Our chimneys were blown down, and as they say,
> Lamentings heard; i' th' air, strange screams of death,
> And prophesying with accents terrible –

they went into an irreverent rapture and, according to Collier, 'were pleased to Clap to an unusual length of Pleasure and Approbation'. On 16 December another non-juror, Robert Nelson, was discussing with the Society Promoting Christian Knowledge 'whether acting *The Tempest* upon the next Wednesday after the late dreadful storm, at the new play-house in Little Lincoln's Inn Fields, was proper or seasonable'.

Despite the frivolity of sophisticated theatre-goers, the great majority of the population seem to have regarded the Storm with the utmost gravity. The following 19 January was appointed a fast day 'for the Imploring of a Blessing from Almighty God upon Her Majesty, and her Allies, engaged in the present War as also for the Humbling of ourselves before Him in a deep Sense of His heavy Displeasure shewed forth in the Late Dreadful Storm and Tempest'. Services were held across the country, using a form of worship especially devised for the occasion by Archbishop Thomas Tenison of Canterbury. In London, as Narcissus Luttrell, noted:

> the fast was strictly observed . . . the archbishop of York preached before the Queen, the bishop of Oxford before the Lords, Dr Gastrill before the Commons, and Dr Blackall before the Lord Mayor.

John Evelyn's diary entry for 19 January referred to 'the publique fast after the dreadfull storm, the Churches so crowded few could get into them'.

During the services collections were taken for what William Talbot, Bishop of Oxford, described as 'two kinds of Objects both certainly deserving of our Charity', namely, the widows and orphans of the seamen lost in the Storm and 'the persecuted, banished Protestants of Aurange [Orange]'.

It is impossible to assess the total amount of money raised by charitable donations of various kinds towards the relief of victims of the Storm and their families but the national nature of the appeal and the popularity of the cause suggest that it was very probably a record at the time. Fragmentary evidence does survive. Thus in the Vestry Minutes of St Stephen's, Coleman Street in the City of London, are to be found the names of the 117 parishioners 'that gave towards the Relief of poor seamen's widows and orphans, who perished in the violent storm'. The total sum collected in this, probably one of the wealthier parishes in the capital, close to the Guildhall, was £20 3*d*. Individual contributions varied from the rich Mr Thorall's £2 3*s* to sixpence, the equivalent, presumably, of the widow's mite.

During the reign of Queen Anne the printed sermon reached its height of popularity and the message of many of the sermons delivered on the fast day was immortalised by being committed to print. Even today Talbot's words delivered before the House of

Peers in Westminster Abbey are impressive. He begins by saying that he will not 'take up your time in describing that Amazing Tempest . . . which has left such Marks behind it, that we can hardly pass the Street, or travel the Roads but we see some remains of it'. Much less will he search for natural causes for 'the Lord was in the Wind . . . it was Appointed by Him . . . whose Word the Storms and Tempest fulfil, to awaken and chastise . . . a sinful people'. Then, in a powerful passage, he reminded his congregation, possibly the most sophisticated being preached to that day, of the terror of the event:

> I shall only beg of you to remember, what Thoughts you then had, when your hearts, if I may use Our Saviour's Words in another case, were failing you for fear, and for looking to those things which you then apprehended, were coming upon you. They were such Thoughts, as I shall venture to say, neither the most Graphical Description of the Astonishing Storm, nor Rhetorical Amplification of the hurt done by it, can now raise in you.

In addition to such sermons preached on 19 January, the British Library possesses one by Dr John Cockburn, the Anglican chaplain in Amsterdam delivered in that city on 5 December, 'appointed . . . a day of publick prayer and thanksgiving' and another, preached in London on 7 January before the Worshipful Society of Merchants trading to Spain. The impact of the Storm had not, of course, been confined to the British Isles.

Storm sermons did not cease to be delivered on 19 January, however. A Mr Taylor left an endowment to fund a memorial sermon to be delivered every year at the Congregational Church in Little Wild Street, Drury Lane. In 1734 the preacher, Mr A. Giffard focussed upon 'some of those extraordinary instances of mercy the Lord was pleased to show during that dreadful calamity' and in 1737 Mr Aaron Ward gave 'an account of the damage that was done by it', both men relying heavily on Defoe's *The Storm*. Furthermore, according to Dean Plumptre, the biographer of Bishop Ken, writing as late as 1888, the Wild Street sermon still survived as 'a memorial of the impression the storm made on mens' minds'.

Although Defoe's writing had a particular appeal to Dissenters, such as those of Wild Street, *The Storm* also seems to have impressed devout Anglicans such as the Yorkshire diarist Ralph Thoresby who on 1 January 1711 outlined a plan of devotional reading:

> I design for the future to read a chapter in the Bible, morning and evening, and in secret, besides the said other treatises; accordingly I begin at the first of Genesis. Lord give a blessing! Evening, son Ralph read us the conclusion of the dreadful storm, anno 1703 . . .

Another diarist also recalled the Storm some years after the event. He was Dr Claver Morris, a Somerset physician who, prior to her father's intervention, had at one time been engaged to the daughter of Bishop Kidder of Bath and Wells.

> JULY 6 1709
> I din'd with Mrs Strode at Downside; Mrs Langton, Mr Brown & his Wife and Mr Henry Strode being there too. We play'd 6 Hand Cribbage. Mr Brown (when I was setting them right in what I had predicted about Dr Kidder's Death) asked whether I could think (were I injur'd) that God would take notice & even work a miracle to punish him, because he injur'd me. I told him that I hop'd and did believe I was as much under the Protection of god as himself: And that it was as great an offence to my Creator for any one to Murther me as it was another etc.

Ironically, in 1718 Morris's own daughter, Betty made a clandestine marriage with a Mr Newman of North Cadbury, a match the doctor admitted to his diary, 'I . . . had taken all the Pains I possibly could to prevent'.

In addition to Defoe's *The Storm*, the catastrophe inspired all manner of literary outpourings in both prose and verse. Among them a long *Poem Upon the Late Storm and Hurricane* by one John Crabb, Fellow of Exeter College, Oxford, launched upon the world by an astute publisher on 18 January, the eve of the fast. Crabb's particular poetic speciality would appear to have been hyperbole. Nelson himself scarcely deserved the laurels which Crabb heaped on Admiral Beaumont's brow:

> Beaumont, who made France tremble when he spoke
> And could such wonders do; In Clouds of Smoke
> Could at noon-day create a Dismal Night,
> And make the Sun himself withdraw his Light;
> Who from his thundering surly roaring Gun,
> Could make fierce Aetna and Vesuvius run:
> That great, that Mighty Man is now no more,
> But a dead Carcass spew'd upon the Shore.

In the years ahead more distinguished writers than Crabb continued to refer back to the Storm. After Marlborough's victory at Blenheim in the following year, Joseph Addison was recruited to write *The Campaign*, in which he compared the Duke's direction of the battle to that of the avenging angel guiding the Storm, 'Such as of late o'er pale Britannia passed'. The immense popularity of the poem throughout the eighteenth century did much to help keep the memory of both Blenheim and the Storm alive. It has even been suggested that *The Campaign* and this line in particular were the making of Addison and that, consequently, had there been no Storm there would have been no *Spectator*. In a very different tone, Addison's partner Richard Steele in issue number 220 of The *Spectator* (12 November 1711) wittily imagined a student of astrology who used mathematically devised tables to write Latin verse:

> he shew'd his Verses to the next of his Acquaintance, who happened to understand Latin; and being informed that they described a Tempest of Winds, very luckily prefix'd them, together with a Translation, to an Almanack he was just then printing, and was supposed to have foretold the last great storm.

It was, however, in the works of Daniel Defoe that the Storm rumbled on longest. In 1708 he was still, as we have seen, complaining, in a *Review* piece published on 18 December, of the behaviour of the townsfolk of Deal during the Storm. Likewise there are several references to the Storm in the *Tour*, published in 1724–6. One modern editor, Pat Rogers, describes the Great Storm as 'a topic of inexhaustible fascination for Defoe'.

Storms and shipwrecks certainly play a significant part in Defoe's fiction. Even before Crusoe is cast ashore on the desert island, the young runaway's first ship goes aground, having been caught in a storm in Yarmouth Roads. A key scene in *Captain Singleton* also occurs when, in a terrible storm of thunder and lightning, the hero 'thought myself doomed by Heaven to sink that Moment into eternal Destruction'. The question of divine retribution was one on which the Storm must have concentrated Defoe's mind ; his own opinion probably being reflected in a relatively obscure work, *Dickory Cronke:*

> Wicked men may sometimes go unpunished in this world but wicked nations never do; because this world is the only place of punishment of wicked nations, though not for private and particular persons.

A person widely believed to have been the object of God's wrath was Oliver Cromwell. One of the more bizarre stories associated with the Storm concerns Cromwell's head. The Lord Protector had died on 3 September 1658, three days after a storm in which the devil was said to have 'taken bond' for him. He had been buried in Westminster Abbey, following what Evelyn describes as a 'superb funeral', on 23 November. With the Restoration, new, less dignified arrangements were made for the disposal of the Protector's body. On 4 December 1660 Parliament voted that the bodies of the leading regicides Cromwell, Ireton and Bradshaw be exhumed, drawn to the gallows at Tyburn and there be buried. The date chosen for this grisly ceremony was 30 January 1661, the anniversary of the execution of Charles I. John Evelyn witnessed the event and describes it with the relish of a true Royalist:

> The first solemn fast and day of humiliation to deplore the sins which had so long provoked God against this afflicted church and people, was ordered by Parliament to be annually celebrated in order to expiate the guilt of the execrable murder

> of the late King Charles I. This day – O the stupendous and inscrutable judgements of God – were the carcasses of that arch-rebel Cromwell, of Bradshaw, the judge who condemned His Majesty, and of Ireton, son-in-law to the usurper, taken out of their superb tombs among the kings at Westminster, dragged to Tyburn, hanged on the gallows there from nine in the morning until six at night, and there buried under that fatal and ignominious monument in a deep pit.

This, however, was not before their heads had been severed from their bodies: the next week Sam Pepys, who, unlike Evelyn, was troubled 'that a man of so great courage as he [Cromwell] was should have that dishonour', went to Westminster Hall and there saw the three heads, impaled upon poles, set up at the southern end of the Hall, Bradshaw's in the middle directly over the place where he had presided over the court which had condemned the King.

According to one account Cromwell's head remained in that location until it was blown down, the pole itself snapping just below the head, in the Great Storm. The story goes that it was found by a sentry who, at least in the imagination of the Victorian antiquarian William Chaffers, 'having a natural respect for an heroic soldier, no matter of what party, took up the head and placed it under his cloak until he went off duty'. One version of the tale then has it that the sentry kept it hidden in a chimney only telling his wife of its whereabouts on his deathbed. She then sold the head to one Du Puy whose collection of curios, including the head, was seen in London by the traveller Zacharias Conrad von Uffenbach in 1710. Another account has it that the sentry took the head to the house of a female relative of Cromwell by the name of Russell who, not wanting to keep it in the house, may have loaned it to Du Puy.

By the 1780s the head had been passed down through the Russell family to Samuel Russell, a showman, who exhibited it in Covent Garden before selling it on for the not inconsiderable sum of £118 in 1787. It then passed through several more hands before coming into the possession, in the second decade of the nineteenth century, of Dr Josiah Wilkinson. It remained with the Wilkinson family until as recently as 1960 when, having been bequeathed to Cromwell's old college, Sidney Sussex, Cambridge, it was once more reburied, a plaque near the entrance to the college chapel bearing the words, 'Near to this spot was buried on 25th March 1966 the head of OLIVER CROMWELL, Lord Protector of the Commonwealth of England, Scotland and Ireland. Fellow Commoner of this College 1616–17'.

There seems to be little doubt that this head was indeed Cromwell's. Detailed forensic examinations showed that the embalmed head, having the appearance of hard, dry leather but still in a reasonable state of preservation, was a good match of the portraits and death masks of the Lord Protector. The head has been trepanned, consistent with embalming, and the flattened nose may be a consequence of the fall from Westminster Hall. Part of a seventeenth century pike is still lodged inside the skull.

Whether or not the head did fall to the ground on the night of the Great Storm, there can be little doubt that it made a good story, especially in the absence of a reliable, or more dramatic, provenance. In the late eighteenth century when the Storm was still a lively and terrifying presence in the folk memory of southern England – comparable, perhaps, with the fear of Napoleon in the following century – it would have provided an added element of melodrama to excite the minds of visitors to Mr Russell's Covent Garden exhibition.

The Great Storm certainly did provide a suitable backdrop to a blood-curdling tale. The story of the notorious robber and escapee Jack Sheppard, who was eventually caught and hanged at Tyburn in 1724, inspired a remarkable outpouring of plays, ballads and tracts well into the nineteenth century. In 1839 Harrison Ainsworth published his novel *Jack Sheppard* and the following year there appeared the anonymously written *The Life of Jack Sheppard the Housebreaker* containing the following description of the Great Storm, a splendid example of the Victorian spine-chilling genre:

> The darkness was almost palpable and the wind which had been blowing in gusts was the next minute suddenly lulled. Anon a roar like a volley of ordnance was heard and the wind again burst its bondage – the gale becomes a hurricane. That

hurricane was the most terrible that ever laid waste a city. Destruction everywhere marked its course, steeples toppled and towers reeled beneath its fury. Trees were torn up by the roots and houses were levelled with the ground – others were unroofed; the leads on the churches were stripped off, and shrivelled up like rolls of parchment. All only darkness, horror, confusion, rain! Men fled from their tottering habitations and returned to them scared by greater dangers. The end of the world seemed at hand.

The hurricane had now reached its climax. The blast shrieked as if exalting in its wrathful mission, stunning and continuous, the din seemed almost to take away the power of hearing. He who had faced the gale would have been instantly stifled. Piercing through every crevice in the clothes, it in some cases, tore them from the wearer's limbs, as from his grasp. It penetrated the skin; benumbed the flesh; paralysed the faculties, the intense darkness added to the terror of the storm. The destroying angel hurried by, shrouded in his gloomiest apparel. None saw, though all felt his presence, and heard the thunder of his voice. Imagination, coloured by the obscurity, peopled the air with phantoms. Ten thousand steeds appeared to be trampling aloft, charged with the work of devastation. Awful shapes seemed to flit by, borne on the wings of the tempest, animating and directing its fury. The actual danger was lost sight of in these wild apprehensions; and many timorous beings were scared beyond reason's verge by the excess of their fears.

The point of this masterpiece of what might be called the Meteorological Melodramatic was that, so it was claimed, Sheppard, appropriately enough for so serious a hellraiser, had been born at the height of the Storm. In fact, John Sheppard, the son of Thomas an 'honest carpenter' of Spitalfields was born in December of the previous year. Alas for Jack, his father died in the year after the Storm and he was brought up in the London Workhouse in Bishopsgate.

The night of the Storm was, of course, a precarious time to come into the world, not only because of the obvious hazards but also because women in labour more often than not lacked the assistance of midwives, reluctant to take the risk of leaving their homes. As Richard West had pointed out, Defoe may have been particularly conscious of this problem as his own wife, Mary, had quite recently given birth. 'Several women in the city of London,' he wrote, 'who were in travail, or who fell into travail by the fright of the storm were obliged to run the risk with such help as they had; and midwives found their own lives in such danger that few of them thought themselves obliged to show any concern for the lives of others.'

Someone who did survive the double trauma of birth during the Great Storm was Theophilus, the son of the actor, playwright and future poet laureate Colley Cibber. Theophilus was educated at Winchester and followed his father on to the stage, a career move which was to ensure that his life was to have a tragic symmetry. On 27 October 1758 he embarked on the *Dublin Trader* at Chester bound for a season on the boards of the Irish capital. The ship ran into a storm in the Irish Sea and a fortnight later a trunk was washed up on the coast of Galloway 'directed to Mr Cibber in Dublin'. Theophilus had died as he had been born.

16

IN MEMORIAM

The Great Storm formed a benchmark in people's lives, an occasion of common, yet infinitely varied, experience – dramatic, terrifying, memorable. For a time it formed a kind of temporal datum, much as did the Second World War. A memorial in the church at Limington, near Yeovilton, in Somerset, provides a poignant example. It is dedicated to the memory of:

> Elizabeth younger daughter of Mr Edward Beaton, Gent. who departed this Life in the 16th year of her age, about 14 days before the great hurricane, in the year of Our Lord 1703.

The new post-Storm era had begun with the massive job of clearing up. In London according to Defoe, 'the streets lay so covered with tiles and slates, from the tops of the houses, especially in the out-parts, that the quantity was incredible'. Every year each ward appointed a number of scavengers, eight in the case of Aldersgate in 1703, who were responsible for street cleaning and were chosen at the end of December. To them fell the task of removing the vast amount of debris left by the Storm. In the countryside the responsibility for removing the fallen trees and keeping the highway clear would have been that of the vestry-elected surveyor of the highways. In many parishes it must have been a daunting task. Even when obstacles to movement had been removed the landscape bore the signs of devastation for weeks, if not months. A description of the impact of the Storm in and around St Ives in Huntingdonshire gives a picture of the transformation wrought by the event:

> The steeple of the church at St Ives [was] blown down, many houses stript of their Tiles and thatched houses in the country were mostly layed bare, and the roads and fields strowed with their coverings, as if Mats had been spread over them.

It would be facetious but not entirely inaccurate to say that following the Storm the price of tiles went through the roof. As we have seen, plain tiles, which had cost 21*s* per thousand, reached a price of £6 in London and pantiles rose from 50*s* per thousand to £10. In other parts of the country local roofing materials also shot up in price. For a time London bricklayers were able to charge 5*s* per day for their labour.

Fortunately, for Londoners at least, after the Storm had passed there was 'no rain in any considerable Quantity . . . for near Three Weeks'. This enabled people to patch up their properties as best they could, although such was the shortage of substitutes for conventional materials that many buildings seem to have remained open to the sky. Unsurprisingly, the repair of some was afforded a greater priority than others. Gresham's College, the nearest institution London had to a university and the place where the first meeting of the nascent Royal Society had taken place in 1660, survived the Great Fire, after which it was for a time used to house the Royal Exchange. This would not have been possible after the Storm in which it was itself badly damaged. A fortnight afterwards the House of Lords read a bill to enable the Lord Mayor and aldermen of the City to begin rebuilding. On the same day, and in the light of the flooding of Westminster, they also considered how best to preserve the nation's records.

By contrast with the speed with which action was taken in some places, according to Daniel Defoe 'an incredible number of houses remained all the winter uncovered and exposed to all the inconveniences of wet and cold, but:

> Those people who found it absolutely necessary to cover their houses, but were unwilling to go to the extravagant price of tiles, changed their covering to that of wood as a present expedient, till the season of working of tiles should come on, and, the first hurry being over, the prices abate. And 'tis to this

> score that we see, to this day, whole ranks of buildings, as in Christ Church Hospital, the Temple, Ask(e)'s Hospital, Old Street, Hogsden [Hoxton] Square and infinite other places, covered entirely with deal boards; and are like to continue so, perhaps a year or two longer, for want of tiles.

There was, Defoe predicted, likely to be an absolute shortage of tiles; he doubted if all the tiles that could be made that summer (of 1704) 'would meet the need of a 10 mile radius from the City'. Whether or not buildings were repaired might depend upon factors other than the availability of building materials. In London, where many properties were leased out to tenants who would themselves frequently sub-let, those coming to the end of a lease would have little incentive to carry out extensive repairs to a house which they might have no interest in within a relatively short period of time. It was, however, in the landlord's interest to carry out repairs and prevent the deterioration of the property. The Assembly Order Books of the Charterhouse, the charity school and hospital, provide an example of this kind of concern:

> 10 April 1704 – John Searanck and his wife Elizabeth are tenants of some houses and grounds behind the Wilderness [just to the north of the Charterhouse], which houses were damaged by the late storm. They to surrender the c. 7 years of the lease yet to come and are granted a new one at the same rent and covenants to make good the damage.

Nevertheless, lack of building materials seems to have been the recurring problem. Brick- and tile-making were very much seasonal activities, often delayed until April when the weather was warmer and drier and the stacks of unbaked bricks and tiles were no longer susceptible to the damaging effects of excessive wetness or frost. Evidence that this was the case in 1704 is to be found in the Berkshire Churchwardens' Presentments. On 24 April the Long Wittenham churchwardens reported that 'Our church is out of Repaire occasioned by the late dreadfull Storme but now aboute repairing' while on the following day, from West Woodhay came a report that the Church and Chancel were out of repair 'by reason of the late violent storm That did our church so much damage that we have not been able (by reason of the Badness of the weather wch hinder'd 'em from makeing tiles till now) to procure materials to repair it'. Henry Stanton wrote to Defoe from Fareham in Hampshire pointing out that 'the damage sustained by us is such that we are obliged to make up of Slit Deals to supply the want of Slats and Tyles until summer come to make same. And so much Thatching wanting that it cannot be repaired until after another Harvest'.

It seems likely that the price of materials in the provinces never reached the exorbitant levels demanded in the capital. The bursary records of St John's College, Cambridge, reveal, in the aftermath of the Storm, two payments for 4,000 tiles, one at 26*s* per thousand and one of 23*s* and a payment for 30 'roof tiles' of 7*s* 6*d*. This, however, appears to be more than the college was accustomed to pay and when tiles were next purchased, in 1711, the cost per thousand was 17*s* while a hundred 'roof tiles' cost 11*s* 6*d*. Sometimes there were expenses that might strike the modern reader as odd; thus, in the churchwardens' accounts for the repair of the roof and spire of the church at Tetbury in Gloucestershire we find:

> 'Paid John Graham for Beer to mix with and strengthen the Torrass [cement] – 1. 4. 6*d*.

Once materials became available repair work must have been going on across the country. At Leamington Hastings in Warwickshire, from where Edward Kingsburgh, the curate, had written to Defoe to report 'the middle of the Isle [of the church] clearly stript of the Lead from one end to the other', a considerable amount of rebuilding work took place. An entry in the Church Register, dated 1705, summarises the activity:

> This Register Book was provided for the Parish of Leamington Hastings. Anno Domini 1704. Dr William Binckes, Dean of Lichfield, being Vicar. In which year the South side of the Church including the Arches was finished. A great part whereof had been taken down and rebuilt from the foundations

the year before. In the same year also, viz. 1704, a good part of the lead of the body of the Church was new laid and made good, having in a wonderful manner been blown off and carried over the North side of the Churchyard by a most violent storm, which happened in November 1703, viz. November 27th.

The Churchwardens' Accounts for 1703 specify some of the expenditure:

6 loads of lead	£1	1*s*	0*d*
repairing churchyard wall & gate		7*s*	9*d*
2 loads of sand for glazier		5*s*	0*d*
Common Prayer Books		12*s*	0*d*

It seems likely that the decision to take down the South Aisle and rebuild it, utilising the old stone, was taken as a consequence of the damage caused by the Storm. The date 1703 is to be seen over the South Porch.

It is not always easy to specify the costs of Storm damage repair either because the Storm occurred during a period of ongoing repairs or because the need to rectify Storm damage was used as an opportunity to carry out more general repair work. Thus at Ely the cathedral, although it 'suffer'd very much and in every part of it . . . the loss which the church and college sustained being by computation £2000', nothing like that figure appears in the Treasurer's Accounts. The damage took place at a time when the cathedral was completing a major rebuilding programme following the collapse of part of the North Transept in 1699. The accounts do, however, reveal that while £132 7*s* 6*d* had been spent in 1702–3 and £39 2*s* 0*d* in the year 1704–5, £248 18*s* 0*d* was expended in the year of the Storm.

Some records, frustratingly, refuse to mention the Storm. The Vestry Minutes of St Giles Cripplegate in London refer to the setting up of a committee on 16 December 1703 'to view the Church and Steeple as to what repairs are wanting'. Further minutes tell us that the pews in the body of the church and under the galleries are 'extremely out of repairs' but we cannot be sure that any of this was Storm damage.

Much less doubt surrounds the case of St Michael's, East Peckham. Like many churches with that dedication, it stands on high ground, a beech-covered hill, looking southwards towards the broad valley of the Medway in mid-Kent. In the Great Storm the steeple of St Michael's was toppled and the decision was thereafter taken, as at nearby Brenchley, where the church of All Saint's suffered a similar indignity, to replace the spire with something rather less ambitious. In the case of St Michael's this was a shingled spirelet topped with a weather-vane, dated 1704. Such a weather-vane is still to be seen although it is not the original. In 1928 it was decided that a new vane was needed but the Annual Parochial Meeting wisely voted to perpetuate the date in which the spirelet was erected rather than the year in which the new vane was set up, thus helping to preserve one of the most significant dates in the church's architectural history.

The locality of St Michael's also contains another, albeit specious, memorial to the Great Storm. Immediately to the south-east of the churchyard is to be found Steeple Field. Local tradition had it that it was so named because, on its collapse, this is where the spire fell. In fact, not only is it very unlikely that it could have fallen so far but the field had been so called since at least the early seventeenth century.*

All manner of memorials, from tombstones to weather-vanes and avenues of replacement trees were soon to be found scattered across the country. Those remembering Dame Elinor Drury and Lady Penelope Nicholas have already been mentioned. Some recall the event rather more obliquely. From Slimbridge in Gloucestershire, where an elm tree was blown down in the churchyard, William Frith, a churchwarden, wrote to say that the minister 'hath given it for a Singer's Seat in our said Church with this inscription thereon: Nov. 27 A.D. 1703, Miserere &c' [i.e. the words of the 51st Psalm – 'Have mercy upon me O God'].

Some creations of the aftermath of the Storm were longer-lasting than others. In St Peter's churchyard in Exeter several elm

* I am grateful to the historian of St Michael's, Mrs Margaret Lawrence, for this information. She points out that 'Steeple' may, quite aptly, be a corruption of 'steep hill'.

trees were blown down and 'for the sake of uniformity' the rest were felled and 'a porch of lime trees planted in their room'. By 1731 it was said that this avenue of limes 'adorns that place and admits a pleasant prospect' but, by the early nineteenth century, 'these were not thriving; most of them were grubbed up and standing elms were planted'.

In the parish church at Stoughton, near Leicester, there is a memorial erected by his sister Anne, to Basil Beaumont – 'Never was found in any one Person more Virtues and Perfections than he was blest with'. Of the memorials to the dead of the Storm the grandest is that to Bishop Kidder and his wife, Elizabeth, now to be found in the North Transept of Wells Cathedral. The couple were survived by two daughters, Susan, the wife of Sir Richard Everard, Bart, of Great Waltham in Essex and Anne, who was unmarried. No doubt because of the animosity that had existed between Kidder and the Dean and Chapter, the daughters were sued for dilapidations, including the damage which had killed their parents! Fortunately, George Hooper, who succeeded Kidder, decided to meet the costs of repairs from his own pocket, relieving the daughters of what must have been an especially unwelcome debt.

Had it not been for Hooper's generosity Anne, who outlived her sister, may not have been able to leave £300 for the erection of a monument to her mother and father in the cathedral. The memorial in black, white and coloured marble is described in Britton's *History of Wells Cathedral* of 1824:

> This is erected by their daughter . . . who is represented by an elaborate figure, reclining on a slab and looking at two urns, supposed to contain the ashes of her ill-fated parents, at the side are two Corinthian columns, supporting an entablature and open pediment, crowned with flaming lamps and a lozenge shield of the family arms. Beneath the entablature is expanded drapery with cherubim in basso-relievo.

The epitaph, some fifty-two lines of Latin, diplomatically praises Bishop Ken ('Decessaris optimi') but says nothing of Elizabeth other than that she was a faithful wife ('conjugem fidissimum'). While Kidder was seventy when he died even

Elizabeth's age was unknown ('Septuagenarius ille illa incerto Anno obiit').

Fine as is the Kidder memorial and glorious as its setting, it is less splendid and its location less distinguished than that to another who has appeared in this story, albeit a survivor. Captain Charles Wager of the *Hampton Court* had safely brought his shattered ship into Torbay after battling with the ferocity of the Storm in the Channel. In 1703 he was thirty-seven, having joined the Navy in 1690. In 1707 he was made Rear Admiral of the Blue and took up command in Jamaica. In the following year, off Cartagena, flying his flag in the 70-gun *Expedition* and deserted by other ships of the squadron, he destroyed the Spanish treasure fleet in a night action of great gallantry that impoverished the French war effort and, thanks to the prize money, made Wager rich as well as famous. In 1709 he was knighted and from 1732 to 1742, the year before he died, was First Lord of the Admiralty. G. M. Trevelyan graphically described his memorial:

> As the visitor enters Westminster Abbey by the north door, he will see hard on his right, overlooked by Chatham from his monument, the tomb of Admiral Wager, whereon a bas-relief records in marble the forms of those old ships, battling for the treasure in the tropic midnight, at the moment when the great galleon bursts asunder in flame and smoke, and disappears from before the startled eyes of its English enemies.

Captain Wager and his crew of the *Hampton Court* were fortunate: many sailors fared much less well. Of the 1190 lives that were lost on the Goodwin Sands a remarkable amount has been discovered following the snagging of a fisherman's net in 1979. A shift in one of the sandbanks had exposed three men-of-war, the *Stirling Castle*, *Northumberland* and *Restoration*, all victims of the Storm. Some preliminary survey work was carried out on the wrecks and a number of objects of immense historical significance recovered before the sites were reburied by a further shifting of the sand in 1980. In 1998, however, more movement once again exposed what were now Designated Protected Wreck Sites, especially that of the *Stirling Castle*.

Exposure is a mixed blessing. Damage is caused by the scouring action of the tides and as a consequence of fishing nets becoming snagged on a revealed area of the *Stirling Castle*'s hull 17 metres long and 3.3 metres wide. Knowledge of the exposure of the wreck also creates the threat of illegal treasure hunting. The positive side of the exposures is to be seen in the Goodwin Gallery of the Ramsgate Maritime Museum. In addition to items belonging to the ships themselves, including cannon, the ships' bells of both the *Stirling Castle* and the *Northumberland*, great wooden pullies and an amazingly well-preserved copper cooking kettle, there are all manner of objects personal to the sailors themselves. Among this remarkable and, in view of the circumstances of their owners' deaths, poignant collection are to be seen thimbles, a pounce pot, inkwells, tankards, keys and leather objects including a hat, a shoe and book covers, possibly of a Bible. A pewter plate and spoon with the initials 'JJ' probably belonged to John Johnson, the captain of the *Stirling Castle*, while a wooden platter with the scratched initial 'R' is likely to have been that of an ordinary sailor. Of a different kind of significance, found in the hold of the *Stirling Castle* are some 300-year-old pre-Phylloxera grapes. There are onion-style wine bottles with glass seals, one bearing the initials and all-important date 'CB 1703'. A recent and outstanding find is one of the *Stirling Castle*'s 70 guns; a 12-ft long cannon, together with its wheeled wooden carriage and gun-manoeuvring block-and-tackle, a sad reminder of the guns forlornly fired to summon help as the doomed men-of-war were driven onto the Sands. It is of vital importance that every effort be made to survey and, as far as possible conserve, these vulnerable archaeological sites while affording every respect to the graves of so many victims of the Storm.

Last but certainly not least of the memorials to the Great Storm is the Great West Window in Edward Shipman's 'large and noble structure', St Mary's, Fairford. The damaged windows were repaired thanks to the will of Elizabeth Farmor, proved in 1706, under which £200 was left for repairs and protective wire frames. Ten years later John Wheeler, glazier of Fairford, was contracted to re-lead all the windows and when John Macky wrote his *Journey through England* in 1722 he voiced the opinion that, 'It is worth a Traveller's while to go a little out of his way to see the

Painted Glass Windows in the Church at Fairford'. The West Window he described as 'a bold Piece of Christ's sitting in Judgement . . . not inferior to that of Michael Angelo at St Peter's in Rome'. It is impossible to say how good the restoration had been although John Byng [Lord Torrington], often a harsh critic,* visiting Fairford in 1787, although he believed the West Window to be 'a ludicrous representation of the day of Judgement', thought the windows, 'charmingly colour'd' and noted that they were 'well preserv'd by wire lattices'. By 1860, however, the part of the West Window above the transom was in a poor state of repair: the glass was said to have bellied like sails before the wind, there had been a great deal of fragmentary patching up and the 200-year-old Civil War whitewash was still traceable. Restoration work was carried out by Chance Brothers of Smethwick who used entirely new glass. During 1999–2000 the whole of the Great West Window was taken out, cleaned and repaired by Keith Barley of York. It has now been replaced and, for the first time since the Great Storm, has been restored to the magnificence which Edward Shipman had known before looking with dismay upon its devastation on that terrible Saturday morning three centuries ago.

* Byng had a rather singular taste in stained glass, describing the Virtues in the Reynolds Window in New College Chapel, Oxford as 'half-dressed, languishing harlots'.

BIBLIOGRAPHY

Of the contemporary published accounts of the Storm by far the most important (and used extensively here), is Daniel Defoe's *The Storm: or a Collection of the most Remarkable Casualties and Disasters which Happened in the late dreadful Tempest both by Sea and Land* (1704). Two other anonymously produced accounts were *An Exact Relation of the Late Dreadful Tempest; or a Faithful Account of the Most Remarkable Disasters which hap'ned on that occasion . . . Faithfully collected by an Ingenious Hand to Preserve the memory of so Terrible a Judgement* (1704) and *A wonderful history of all the storms, hurricanes, earthquakes &c. which have happn'd in England for about 500 years past . . . with a particular and large account of the dreadful storm, that happen'd on the 26th and 27th November, 1703 etc.* (1704).

For the historical background G.M. Trevelyan's *England under Queen Anne*, especially vol. 1 (1932), remains eminently readable and valuable. An excellent modern treatment is provided by Julian Hoppit, *A Land of Liberty? England, 1689–1727* (2000).

For the meteorology of the Storm the most important account is to be found in H.H. Lamb (with K. Fryendahl), *Historic Storms of the North Sea, British Isles and North-West Europe* (1991). Lamb comes to much the same conclusions, but by a better signposted route, as C.E.P. Brooks, *The English Climate* (1954). An earlier work, published a hundred years ago, which used ships' logs to make up for the paucity of land-based data was H. Harries, *The Great Storm of 1703: an anniversary study*, Cornhill Magazine, N.S. 3.

Although Samuel Pepys died a few months before the Storm, his *Diary*, ended 34 years earlier, is an indispensable source of information on the late Stuart navy, especially in the definitive edition of R.C. Latham and W. Matthews (1971). Three other works are frequently referred to in this book: Narcissus Lutrell's *A Brief Historical Relation of State Affairs from September 1678 to April 1714*, 6 vols. (1857); E.S. de Beer (ed.) *The Diary of John Evelyn*, 6 vols.

(1955); and Daniel Defoe's *A Tour through the Whole Island of Great Britain* (Pat Rogers' Penguin edition of 1971). Unspecified references to 'Defoe' are to *The Storm*. Contemporary newspapers used include the *London Gazette*, *Post Man*, *Daily Courant* and *The Observator*.

Preface

Durschmied, E., *The Weather Factor*, 2000.
Lamb, H.H., *Climate History and the Modern World*, 1997.
Michaels, A., *Fugitive Pieces*, Toronto 1996.

One: Dies Irae

Carbonell, F.R., *A Handbook to Fairford Church and Windows*, 1893.
Chapman, R., *The Necessity of Repentence asserted . . . to threaten this Nation with*, 1703.
Joyce, J.G.A., *The Fairford Windows*, 1872.
Latimer, J., *Annals of Bristol in the Eighteenth Century*, 1887.
Pearson, M.G., 'The Hurricane of 1739', *Weather*, vol. 24, 1969.
Plumptre, E.H., *The Life of Thomas Ken, D.D.* 1890.
Robinson, A.E., (ed.) *The Life of Richard Kidder D.D., Bishop of Bath & Wells, written by himself*, 1924.
Simpson, R.H., Riehl, H., *The Hurricane and its Impact*, 1981.

Two: The Birth of the Storm

Cox, J.C., *The Parish Registers of England*, Totowa N.J. 1974.
Curtis, L.A., *The Versatile Defoe: An Anthology of Uncollected Writings of Daniel Defoe*, 1979.
Fitzgerald, B., *Daniel Defoe: a Study in Conflict*, 1954.
Healey, G.H.H., *The Letters of Daniel Defoe*, 1955.
Moore, J.R., *Daniel Defoe: Citizen of the Modern World*, Chicago, 1958.
Victoria County History, *Essex*, vol. 2.
West, R., *The Life and Strange Surprising Adventures of Daniel Defoe*, 1997.

Three: Dark is His Path

Barlow, E., *Meteorological Essay, concerning the origin of Springs, Generation of Rain and Production of Wind*, 1715.

Brazendale, D., *Lancashire's Historic Halls*, Preston, 1994.

Britton, C.E., 'Windy Tuesday, 18th February 1661/2', *Meteorological Magazine*, 1939

Callender, G., (ed.) *The Life of Sir John Leake, Rear-Admiral of Great Britain by Sir Stephen Martin-Leake*, 1920.

Defoe, D., *An Essay on the Late Storm*, 1704.

Fauvel, J., Flood, R., Shortland, M., Wilson, R., (eds). *Let Newton be!* 1988.

Manley, G., *Climate and the British Scene*, 1952.

Moore, J.R., 'Defoe, Thoresby and "The Storm"', *Notes and Queries*, clxxv, 1938.

Porter, R., *Enlightenment: Britain and the Creation of the Modern World*, 2000.

Four: On the Wings of the Storm

Bagley, J.J. (ed.), *The Great Diurnall of Nicholas Blundell of Little Crosby, Lancashire*, vol.1, 1968.

Beresford, J., (ed.) *The Diary of a Country Parson*, 1927.

Calendar of State Papers, Colonial Series, America and West Indies, 1704–5.

Rowe, M., 'The Storm of the 16th October 1987 a brief comparison with three other historic gales in southern England (1362, 1662, 1703)', *Journal of Meteorology*, vol.13, 129, 1988.

Schomberg, I. *Naval Chronology or a Historical Survey of Naval and maritime Events*, vol.1, 1815.

Tinniswood, A. *His Invention so Fertile: a Life of Sir Christopher Wren*, 2001.

Five: Hurry-Durry Weather

Browning, A. (ed.), *English Historical Documents*, vol. viii, (1660–1714), 1966.

Carr Laughton, L.G., 'Maritime History', *Victoria County History, Hampshire*, vol. 5.
Davis, H. (ed.), *Jonathan Swift, Political Tracts, 1711–1713*, 1978.
Fisher, H.A.L., A *History of Europe*, 1936.
Harris, S., *Sir Cloudesley Shovell: Stuart Admiral*, 2001.
Izacke, R., *Remarkable Antiquities of the City of Exeter*, 1731.
Laughton, J.K., *Memoirs Relating to Lord Torrington*, 1889.
Le Fevre, P., 'Re-creating a Seventeenth Century Sea Officer', *Journal of Maritime Research*, May, 2001.
Morris, C. (ed.), *The Journeys of Celia Fiennes*, 1947.
National Maritime Museum Library, ADH/L/H/26, H.M.S. Hampton Court – lieutenants' logs.
Park, C.C., 'The Great Storm of 26/27 November 1703 South West England', *Journal of Meteorology*, vol. 4, 37, 1979.
Public Record Office, ADM51/4213, H.M.S. *Hampton Court* – captains' logs.
Thompson, E.M., (ed.), *Correspondence of the Family of Hilton, being Chiefly Letters Addressed to Christopher First Viscount Hilton, 1601–1704*, vol. 2, 1978.
Underwood, E., *Brighton*, 1978.
Williamson, J.A., *The English Channel*, 1959.
Wilson, W.E., *The Pilot's Guide to the English Channel*, 1948.

Six: This Fatal Piece

Hardy, W.J., *Lighthouses: their History and Romance*, 1895.
Majdelaney, F., *The Red Rocks of Eddystone*, 1957.
Semmons, J., *Eddystone – 300 years*, Fowey, 1998.
Stanhope, P.H., *(Earl) History of England: comprising the reign of Queen Anne until the Treaty of Utrecht*, 1870.

Seven: This Far the Waters Came

Clark, C., *The Weather and Climate around Bruton and Castle Cary*, 1995.
Gregory, K., 'The Impact of the October '87 Storm', *Geography Review*, vol. 2, 4, 1989.

Holmes, T.S., *The Parish and Manor of Wookey*, no date.
Horton, B., *The West Country Weather Book*, 1995.
Latimer, J., *The Annals of Bristol in the Eighteenth Century*, 1887.
Perry, A.H., *Environmental Hazards in the British Isles*, 1981.
Phillips, O., *Monmouthshire*, 1951.
Seyer, S., *Memoirs Historical and Topographical of Bristol and its Neighbourhood*, 1823.
Tindal, N., *Continuation of Rapin's History of England*, 1743–47.

Eight: About Three Hundred Sail of Colliers

Burchett, J., *Complete History of the most Remarkable Transactions at Sea*, 1720.
Merriman, R.D., *Queen Anne's Navy*, 1961.
Public Record Office, ADM 3/19, Navy Board Minutes.

Nine: Damage Most Tragicall

Albion, R.G., 'Forests and Sea Power', *Economic History Review*, 1930.
Baker, T.H., *Records of the Seasons: Prices of Agricultural Produce and Phenomena Observed in the British Isles*, 1883.
Guildhall Library, MS 12834, vol. 2, Christ's Hospital View Book.
Hoskins, W.G., *Devon*, 1954.
Jones, E.L., *Seasons and Prices: the Role of Weather in England's Agricultural History*, 1964.
Moon, N., *The Windmills of Leicestershire and Rutland*, 1981.
Overton, M., 'Weather and Agricultural Change in England, 1660–1739', *Agricultural History*, 63, 1989.
Rackham, O., *The Last Forest: the Story of Hatfield Forest*, 1989.
Shillingford, A.E.P., *England's Vanishing Windmills*, 1979.
Smith, A., *The Weather: the truth about the health of our planet*, 2000.

Ten: Her True and Faithful Lover

Blomefield, F., *History of Norfolk*, 1739.
Bowley, P., *The Story of West Horsley Manor and its Church*, 1993.

Hoskins, W.G., *Essays in Leicestershire History*, 1950.
Le Neve, J., *Monumenta Anglicana: being transcriptions on the monuments of several eminent persons deceased on or since 1615–1718*, 1719.
Norfolk Record Office, Riddlesworth, N, 106 Pidock, will of Lady Elinor Drury.
Prior, M., 'Wives and Wills, 1558–1700' in Chartres, J. and Hey, D, *English Rural Society: Essays in Honour of Joan Thirsk*, 1990.
Russell, R., *Letters of Lady Rachel Russell*, vol. 2, 1853.

Eleven: Sir Cloudesley is Expected

Anderson, R.C., 'English Flag Officers, 1688–1713', Mariner's Mirror, vol. 35, 4, 1949.
British Library, ADD MSS 5440 f. 3, Sir Cloudesley Shovell's letter to Navy Board, 3/12/1703.
Burchett, J., *Complete History*.
Callender, G., *Sir John Leake*.
Harris, S., *Sir Cloudesley Shovell*.
Larn, R. and Larn, B., *Shipwrecks on the Goodwin Sands*, 1977.
Laughton, C. and Heddon, V., *Great Storms*, 1927.
National Maritime Museum Library, ADM/L/A/213, H.M.S. Association, lieutenants' log books.
Public Record Office, ADM 3/14, Navy Board Minutes.

Twelve: As Dismal as Death

Burnet, G., *History of His Own Time*, 1734.
Callender, G., *Sir John Leake*.
Clowes, W.L., *History of the Royal Navy*, 1898.
Ingram. B.S. (ed.), *Three Sea Journals of Stuart Times*, 1936.
Laker, J., *History of Deal*, 1921.
Lewis, J., *History and Antiquities as well Ecclesiastical as Civil of the Isle of Tenet*, 1723.
Lubbock, B. (ed.), *Barlow's Journal, 1678–1703*, 2 vols., 1934.
Secord, A.W., *Defoe's Review*, facsimile edition, New York, 1938.

Thirteen: Within the Bills of Mortality

Anon., *The Amazing Tempest: being a surprising account of the great damage done in and about the city of London, Southwark etc. by the late terrible . . . tempest of wind and rain etc.* 1703.
Brazell, J.H., *London's Weather*, 1968.
Chamberlain, H., *A New and Complete History of the Cities of London and Westminster etc.* 1770.
George, M.D., *London Life in the Eighteenth Century*, 1930.
Harvey, G., *The City Remembrancer*, 1769.
Kington, J., 'The Great Storm of 1–2 October, 1697', *Weather*, vol. 53, 1998.
Quarrell, W.H. and Mare, M. (eds), *From the Travels of Zacharias Conrad von Uffenbach*, 1934.
Rasmussen, S.E., *London: the Unique City*, 1934.
Waller, M., *1700: Scenes from London Life*, 2000.
Von Muyden, Mme C. de Saussure, *A Foreign View of England in the Reigns of George I and George II*, 1902.

Fourteen: Carpenters, Caulkers and Seamen

Harris, S., *Sir Cloudesley Shovell.*
Journals of the House of Commons, vol. xv.
Mahaffy, R.P. (ed.), *Calendar of State Papers, Domestic Series*, vol. 11, 1703–4.
Merriman, R.D., *Anne's Navy.*
Public Record Office, ADM 3/14, Navy Board Minutes.

Fifteen: Fast, Fact and Fiction

Abbott, G., *The Who's Who of British Beheadings*, 2000.
Anon., *The Life of Jack Sheppard the housebreaker*, 1840.
Anon., *A testimonial upon the case of Edward Shortall, Cook, late of Wild Street in the parish of St Giles etc. in the late reign. With an account of his loss by sea in the late storm, November 1703*, 1704.
Collier, J., *Mr Collier's Dissuasive from the Play-house, with a letter to a person of quality occasioned by the late calamity of the tempest*, 1704.

Crabb, J., *A Poem Upon the Late Storm and Hurricane*, 1704.
Guildhall Library, MS 4458, Vestry Minutes, St Stephen Coleman Street.
Guildhall Library, MS 4992, vol. 1, W. Chaffers.
Guildhall Library, MS 6048, Vestry Minutes, St Giles Cripplegate.
Hobhouse, E., *The Diary of a West Country Physician, AD1689–1726*, 1934.
McIntyre, I., *Garrick*, 1999.
Moore, J.R., 'Defoe, Thoresby and "The Storm"', *Notes and Queries*, clxxv, 1938.
Plumptre, E.H., *Thomas Ken*.
Quarrell, W.H. and Mare, M., *Travels*, 1934.
Steele, R. in C. Gregory Smith (ed.), *The Spectator*, no. 220, 1907.
Talbot, W., Bishop of Oxford. *Sermon preached before the House of Peers in the Abbey Church of Westminster, 19 January 1703/4*, 1704.

Sixteen: In Memoriam

Berkshire Record Office, Archdeaconry Papers, c.143, fo. 351 (West Woodhay).
Berkshire Record Office, Archdeaconry Papers, c.143, fo. 143 (Long Wittenham).
Britton, J., *History of Wells Cathedral*, 1824.
Bruyn Andrews C., *The Torrington Diaries*, 4 vols, 1934–38.
Guildhall Library, Charterhouse Muniments, Assebly Order Book D. p. 46.
Guildhall Library, MS 6048, Vestry Minutes, St Giles Cripplegate.
Lawrence, M., *Through this Door: St Michael's Church, East Peckham*, 1998.
Macky J., *A Journey through England*, 2 vols. 1722.
Park, C.C., 'The Great Storm'.
Rogers, J.E.T., *History of Agriculture and Prices*, 6 vols. 1866–87.

Information on the archaeological operations on the Goodwin Sands can be obtained from the website of the Seadive Organisation: www.seadive.org.

INDEX